Praise for *The Corporate Whistleblower's Survival Guide*

"Blowing the whistle is a life-altering experience. Taking the first step is the hardest, knowing that you can never turn back. Harder yet is not taking the step and allowing the consequences of not blowing the whistle to continue, knowing you could have stopped them. Your life will be forever changed; friends and family will question your actions if not your sanity, your peers will shun you, every relationship you treasure will be strained to the breaking point. This handbook is required reading for anyone considering blowing the whistle."
—**Richard and Donna Parks, Three Mile Island cleanup whistleblower and wife**

"*The Corporate Whistleblower's Survival Guide* will be an immense help! For while there are no one-size-fits-all 'right answers,' the authors have effectively translated their decades of actual experience, insights, and resources in this field onto paper. A realistic framework will now exist to help people confronting such difficult situations."
—**Coleen Rowley, FBI 9/11 whistleblower and a 2002 *Time* Person of the Year**

"Lays out exactly what potential corporate whistleblowers must know to help improve their chances of both surviving whistleblowing and stopping the misconduct they set out to expose. My only hope is that we can help spread the word so that all potential corporate whistleblowers read this book *before* they take their first steps down that lonely road."
—**Danielle Brian, Executive Director, Project on Government Oversight**

"As commissioner, I relied on whistleblowers like Jeffrey Wigand to learn the inside story about the deceptive practices of the tobacco industry. Later, I became a whistleblower. I was fortunate to have the guidance of the Government Accountability Project and its legal director Tom Devine to traverse this rocky terrain. *The Corporate Whistleblower's Survival Guide* draws on GAP's vast experience to capture what happens when someone blows the whistle, and it distills it in plain English. I highly recommend it."
—**Dr. David Kessler, former Commissioner, Food and Drug Administration**

"A readable and reliable road map for navigating the rocky shoals of candor in a corporate setting. From construction site to cubicle to boardroom, this compendium is an indispensable resource—don't leave home without having read it."

—Jeff Ruch, Executive Director, Public Employees for Environmental Responsibility

"*The Corporate Whistleblower's Survival Guide* can be read as a history of corporate whistleblower protection, as a survey of law and regulations, as an assessment of varying approaches to whistleblower protection, and as a framework for evaluating current debates. In this regard the guide can be of value to corporate officials, to legislators, and to those interested in public policy."

—Robert G. Vaughn, A. Allen King Scholar, American University Washington College of Law

"The only fault I find with this book is that it was published too late to help my case. I encourage all truth tellers, sentinels, and honest and brave soldiers for truth to read this book before they start running the gauntlet of our legal system."

—David Welch, bank insider-trading whistleblower, Bank of Floyd, Floyd, Virginia

"When faced with wrongdoing on the job, making the decision to be a whistleblower is extraordinarily difficult. But 'committing the truth' will help many individuals take that step—responsibly and productively and with the support needed to really make a difference. Through guidance on making a decision, bringing the right information to the right people, and dealing with the media constructively, as well as explaining critical legal rights and limitations, Devine and Maassarani have created a guidebook that can make that difference—not just for whistleblowers but also for all of us who benefit from their actions."

—Susan Wood, former Director, Food and Drug Administration's Office of Women's Health, who resigned to protest politically motivated delays in approving the Plan B "morning-after" pill

The Corporate Whistleblower's Survival Guide

The Corporate Whistleblower's Survival Guide

A Handbook for Committing the Truth

Tom Devine

and

Tarek F. Maassarani

Published in Association with the
Government Accountability Project

BK

Berrett–Koehler Publishers, Inc.
San Francisco
a BK Currents book

Berrett-Koehler Publishers, Inc.
235 Montgomery Street, Suite 650, San Francisco, CA 94104-2916
Tel: (415) 288-0260   Fax: (415) 362-2512   www.bkconnection.com

Ordering Information

Quantity sales. Special discounts are available on quantity purchases by corporations, associations, and others. For details, contact the "Special Sales Department" at the Berrett-Koehler address above.

Individual sales. Berrett-Koehler publications are available through most bookstores. They can also be ordered directly from Berrett-Koehler: Tel: (800) 929-2929; Fax: (802) 864-7626; www.bkconnection.com.

Orders for college textbook/course adoption use. Please contact Berrett-Koehler: Tel: (800) 929-2929; Fax: (802) 864-7626.

Orders by U.S. trade bookstores and wholesalers. Please contact Ingram Publisher Services, Tel: (800) 509-4887; Fax: (800) 838-1149; E-mail: customer.service@ingrampublisherservices.com; or visit www.ingrampublisherservices.com/Ordering for details about electronic ordering.

Berrett-Koehler and the BK logo are registered trademarks of Berrett-Koehler Publishers, Inc.

Printed in the United States of America

Berrett-Koehler books are printed on long-lasting acid-free paper. When it is available, we choose paper that has been manufactured by environmentally responsible processes. These may include using trees grown in sustainable forests, incorporating recycled paper, minimizing chlorine in bleaching, or recycling the energy produced at the paper mill.

Library of Congress Cataloging-in-Publication Data
Devine, Tom, 1951–
   The corporate whistleblower's survival guide : a handbook for committing the truth / Tom Devine and Tarek F. Maassarani.
      p. cm.
   Includes bibliographical references and index.   6|2011
   ISBN 978-1-60509-985-9 (hardcover : alk. paper)
   ISBN 978-1-60509-986-6 (pbk. : alk. paper)
1. Whistle blowing—Law and legislation—United States. 2. Discrimination in employment—Law and legislation—United States. 3. Employees—Dismissal of—Law and legislation—United States. I. Maassarani, Tarek F. II. Title.
   KF3471.D48 2011
   344.7301—dc22
                                                                    2010053687

16   15   14   13   12   11   10   9   8   7   6   5   4   3   2   1

Cover design by Ian Shimkoviak, The Book Designers.
Interior design and composition by Gary Palmatier, Ideas to Images.
Elizabeth von Radics, copyeditor; Mike Mollett, proofreader; Medea Minnich, indexer.

*This book is dedicated to all the whistleblowers
who have been our teachers, inspiration, and calling.*

Contents

CHAPTER **3**

What to Know Before You Blow   41

Whistleblower Toolkit   211

Foreword

by Dr. Jeffrey Wigand

*All that is necessary for the triumph of evil
is that good men do nothing.*

— Edmund Burke

There are concepts and then there are the names we use to describe them. One concept that badly needs a new name is *person of conscience*. Currently, the name used to identify this person is *whistleblower*. But the name *whistleblower* needs to be replaced. Why? The term is laden with pejorative connotations, such as *rat, tattletale, fink,* and *turncoat*. Obviously, these words signify opprobrium rather than approbation. The word we use to describe a person of conscience should be free of negative connotations. Indeed the word should connote courage, strength, virtue, and an overriding concern for the good of humanity. The term *whistleblower* lacks these properties. The fact is, there is no single word that connotes the meaning of *person of conscience*. So, I propose that instead of using the term *whistleblower* to refer to a person of conscience, we call a spade a spade. A person of conscience should be referred to as a *Person of Conscience*. The capitalization signifies the important role that such Persons play in protecting and promoting the human good.

When I was first introduced to this book while it was still in draft form, it immediately rekindled many memories both pleasant and unpleasant of my experiences as a Person of Conscience. It is my strong belief and conviction that Persons of Conscience deliberately put themselves in harm's way for the betterment of others. Persons of Conscience perform selfless acts that merit accolades rather than disparagement.

In 1988 I accepted a job at the Brown & Williamson Tobacco Corporation (B&W) as vice president of research and development after six months of extensive interviews. B&W was part of the world's second-largest tobacco concern. Why did I join the company? My primary goal was to use the knowledge I had acquired during 20 years of healthcare experience to save lives by developing a "safer" cigarette and to ultimately see Food and Drug Administration (FDA) approval for tobacco products. I was also hired to modernize an organization steeped in empirical scientific methods. During my tenure I observed, witnessed, and learned about many actions that were clearly unethical. What made these actions unethical? The fact that they were performed for the sole purpose of maximizing profits regardless of the lost lives, lost productivity, and exorbitant healthcare costs.

In 1993 I was fired for protesting the company's continued efforts to conceal the addictive and toxic nature of cigarettes. Sadly, the company eliminated its program to develop a safer product. Why? The program posed a legal liability to the company. If it made a "safer" product, then all the current products were "unsafe." Lawyers sanitized scientific research and other documents that demonstrated that the company clearly knew that nicotine was addictive and that tobacco products when used as intended killed not only the user but also innocent bystanders and that it knowingly used an additive shown to be a potential human carcinogen. My firing from B&W was the beginning of a deliberate and systematic process of physical and legal intimidation and threats not uncommon to Persons of Conscience (witness the Nixon administration's notorious "Malek/May Manual").

In early 1994 I started working with CBS *60 Minutes* on what became a successful investigative report to expose just one piece of the fraud perpetrated by Big Tobacco.

I was motivated by determination and righteous indignation for corporate executives who had a total disregard for human life. I was motivated by righteous indignation for corporate lawyers who treated science as the enemy when it obstructed profits and who had the authority to rewrite research findings, falsify company records, remove evidence of public health hazards, and orchestrate a relentless campaign to increase addiction while exposing the user and innocent bystanders to some 5,000 toxic chemicals and 600 chemical additives used in formulating tobacco products to enhance the addiction process, ease initiation, and maintain the addiction, sometimes more carcinogenic than the nicotine itself.

Cooperating with *60 Minutes* led to my secretly working with the FDA on its investigation of cigarette design, addiction, and additives used in tobacco products to foster youth initiation and sustained use. This began an 18-year journey, which undoubtedly included dark moments. My children's lives were threatened. My marriage ended. I was followed. I was subjected to a multimillion-dollar retaliatory investigation and was sued. I had to live 24/7 with armed security forces to protect my family, start my car, or open my mail. I was threatened with criminal prosecution for revealing the truth. And this is all *after* I was fired! Despite being a high-level insider, I had no idea what I would be subjecting myself to when I exposed the lies concealing an industry's secret, indefensible culture. I knew it was going to be a tsunami of sorts and that the truth would win out in the end. My thoughts in the initial phases were of survival rather than a stellar victory.

What is most gratifying is knowing that my action made a difference. My being a Person of Conscience aided 39 state attorneys general in holding the tobacco industry accountable for its widespread and systematic harm. Our combined efforts stimulated a campaign for the regulation of tobacco products as an addictive drug. It led to congressional hearings, Department of Justice investigations resulting in a racketeering trial of the industry, and finally an Oscar-nominated movie, *The Insider*. The most important thing to me, however, was knowing that I helped mitigate the widespread and systematic harm perpetrated by my employer and its industry. I could not be a bystander, choosing to remain silent when I knew that the knowledge I possessed could make a difference. I am often asked if I would do it again and if it was worth it. My response is always an unequivocal *"Yes—and in a New York minute."*

My journey did not end in 1999 with *The Insider*, which served as a platform to further disseminate the inner workings of the tobacco industry and was an unexpected but welcome final vindication. Indeed my journey is not yet at its endpoint, as it continues today. The fact is, my decision to become a Person of Conscience has led me to true happiness and enabled me to recognize and fulfill my calling.

The Corporate Whistleblower's Survival Guide contains the Government Accountability Project's combined lessons learned over three decades of working with thousands of Persons of Conscience. Read it if you are an employee even thinking about becoming such a Person. At a minimum, you need to know what consequences to expect and the nature of your legal rights. Read it if you are an organizational leader wise enough to listen to messengers instead of silencing them. Anyone should read it to understand what it means to challenge abuses of power and what we risk when corporate secrecy and intimidation prevail. That is ample reason to read and digest the real-life experiences relayed in this book.

Four lessons in particular are worth highlighting and incorporating into your decision-making process:

1. Be prepared   Being a Person of Conscience will likely be the worst, best, highest-risk, highest-stakes, most inspiring, *and* most disillusioning experience of your life. Your life will never be the same. Do your homework carefully before exposing yourself and have a proactive strategy and plan rather than just being reactive. Share the choices and the decisions with those who will be most affected by them.

2. Don't quit midstream   If you are going to do that, don't even start. *You must fully commit to your decision, come what may.* If I had allowed the tobacco industry to silence or defeat me, it would have had greater abusive power. Making a difference requires a marathon commitment. It has taken me 18 years to make some difference, but the more I learn, the greater the challenge and the opportunity to make a continued difference in the world arena. Persons of Conscience have a crucial role in society, and their voices need to be heard. History is replete with lessons that illustrate that listening to a Person of Conscience could have prevented numerous tragedies.

3. Be certain that you have allies   No one can challenge an institution alone. I know. I would have been crushed without the committed support of kindred spirits in my family, my students, the public, the media, crusading lawyers, and government officials who actually were dedicated public servants.

4. Do not quit until the truth has been fully exposed   Armed with the truth as an individual, you can effectively challenge bureaucratic abuses that are able to continue only if the victims don't know what is being done to them. This does not contradict the point on alliances. In fact, the truth is the most effective means for building alliances.

If you are faced with the choice of becoming a Person of Conscience, this book will help you make a difference without paying an unnecessary price, as there are many pitfalls in the process that one can avoid. I can assure you that an individual *can* effectively challenge abuses that institutions would prefer remain hidden. Your commitment to the truth will be your most important ally. In the words of W. H. Murray, "The moment that one commits oneself, then Providence moves too."

—J. S. Wigand, MA, PhD, MAT, ScD

Introduction: Whistleblowing in Corporate America

The new millennium ushered in a wave of corporate scandals that cheated ordinary shareholders and employees out of billions of dollars in lifetime savings, investments, and pensions. More than two dozen major accounting scandals followed the October 2001 discovery of Enron's sham bookkeeping, bribery, and energy market manipulation. Brought to light by whistleblowers at Enron, WorldCom, and other companies, these revelations seriously strained public confidence in the stock market and set off sweeping congressional reforms.

Legislators moved quickly to pass the Public Company Accounting Reform and Investor Protection Act of 2002—commonly known as Sarbanes-Oxley (SOX). Enforcement actions and criminal convictions continued apace. In 2003 the Securities and Exchange Commission (SEC) entered into a $1.435 billion settlement with 10 of the United States' largest investment firms over charges that the firms' bankers had inappropriate influence over their own analysts. In 2005 American International Group (AIG), the fourth-largest company in the world, came under investigation for accounting fraud in a scandal that cost the company $1.64 billion to settle with federal and state authorities and a $2.7 billion decline in its net worth.[1]

Corporate Whistleblowers Who Paved the Way for Reforms in the Twenty-First Century

Although governmental whistleblowers long have made headlines, the events surrounding Enron, WorldCom, and other corporate collapses in the early 2000s increasingly brought corporate whistleblowers into the

1

limelight. The country became aware of corporate misdeeds occurring on an unprecedented level. Two women stood at the center of these realizations.

At Enron, Vice President of Corporate Development Sherron Watkins realized something was wrong with the company's finances. The numbers didn't add up. She wrote a memo to Enron Chief Executive Officer (CEO) and Chairman Ken Lay, trying to raise awareness of the problems before the company self-destructed. Enron's management chose to seek her removal rather than deal with the issues she raised. When Enron came under scrutiny, Watkins was the key witness in bringing the fraud to light.[2]

Cynthia Cooper was vice president of internal audits at WorldCom, now MCI. Her audit of the company's finances uncovered suspicious activities. After being told by her supervisor to delay her analysis for a financial quarter, she continued investigating with her team and took her findings directly to WorldCom's board of directors.[3] Her efforts exposed the corporate fraud that was occurring at the company, sparked serious corrective action that saved MCI from Enron's fate, and focused attention on the questionable independence of corporate audits—an "oversight" mechanism that had come to enable widespread deception in corporate America.

Both of these women made the difficult choice to jeopardize their professional lives to bring wrongdoings they witnessed to the attention of their supervisors. Like most whistleblowers, they experienced tremendous stress and had difficulty retaining their positions, finding new ones, and maintaining their everyday lives outside of the office.[4] Unlike many whistleblowers, however, they both made a difference and received the recognition they deserved. In 2002 they, along with Federal Bureau of Investigation (FBI) whistleblower Coleen Rowley, were named *Time* magazine's Persons of the Year.[5]

Post-Enron government action did little to stave off the reckless lending practices that arose from decades of government deregulation of the financial industry. Most notably, mortgage companies had been issuing shaky subprime loans and passing on the risk to investors in the gilded form of securitized mortgage credit. The inevitable financial losses in 2007 exposed other precarious loans and inflated assets and triggered a global financial crisis. On September 15, 2008, Lehman Brothers caved, filing the largest bankruptcy in US history. A panic in the financial markets accompanied sagging stock and housing prices, sending many large investment and commercial banks reeling. Congress and the Federal Reserve spent $700 billion and $1.2 trillion, respectively, on bailouts and emergency loans to large corporations, including the scandal-mired, government-sponsored Fannie Mae and Freddie Mac that owned or guaranteed about half of the country's $12 trillion mortgage market.

A Whistleblower at Lehman Brothers

As heavy losses pushed Lehman Brothers down the road toward eventual bankruptcy, Senior Vice President Matthew Lee, a 14-year company veteran, sent a letter to senior management in May 2008, warning of accounting irregularities. Lehman's board instructed its auditor, Ernst & Young, to look into the matter. Lee told Ernst & Young investigators that Lehman temporarily moved $50 billion in assets off its balance sheet to help hide the firm's risks from Wall Street investors and regulators. These concerns faced a dead end when Ernst & Young announced that Lee's allegations were unfounded. In late June, Lee was laid off as part of broader downsizing at the firm, according to Lehman. Lee's concerns were ultimately vindicated by a federal bankruptcy examiner's report released in March 2010.[6]

In March 2009 corporate America again broke records when Wall Street investment adviser Bernard Madoff pled guilty to running the largest Ponzi scheme in history. After nearly two decades, the house of cards finally collapsed—leaving thousands of investors defrauded of $65 billion and forcing businesses, charities, and foundations around the world to close shop. Sadly, a whistleblower had spent 10 years trying to alert the government, industry, and press about the fraud. Damaged by the 2008–2009 economic implosion, scandals, and bailouts, public trust in corporate America has yet to be regained.

Unfortunately, corporate wrongdoing is not limited to large accounting firms, financial lenders, and publicly traded corporations. Every year thousands of employees from the full range of business organizations witness wrongdoing on the job. These discoveries may jeopardize the physical or financial well-being of others and endanger our shared environment and economy. Whistleblowers may see managers at a nuclear facility violate safety codes, a chemical company dump hazardous waste unlawfully, or a food-processing plant attempt to sell contaminated meat to consumers.

Most employees remain silent, concluding that it is not their concern or that nothing they could do would stop the problem. Often they cannot afford to get themselves into trouble. Remaining an uninvolved bystander, however, risks serious consequences for all but the tiny circle that profits from the abuse and deceit. Others choose to bear witness and speak out, seeking to make a difference by "blowing the whistle" on unethical conduct in the workplace. This may sound like an elaborate undertaking, but even a simple note or a frank discussion with one's supervisors can sometimes suffice to bring about real change or spark retaliation.

At the Government Accountability Project (GAP), we define whistleblowers as individuals who use free-speech rights to challenge abuses of power that betray the public trust. Under the Whistleblower Protection Act (WPA), the legal definition of whistleblowing as applied to government workers is disclosing information that an employee reasonably believes is evidence of illegality, gross waste, gross mismanagement, abuse of power, or substantial and specific danger to public health or safety.[7] Corporate whistleblower rights, including SOX, are generally organized as witness protection clauses in enforcement provisions of selected parent statutes. Whatever the context, whistleblowers typically are insiders who learn of wrongdoing and decide to speak up about what they know—people of conscience who act for the good of the public at great personal risk.

Whistleblowers' actions have saved the lives of employees, consumers, and the general public, as well as billions of dollars in shareholder and taxpayer funds. Whistleblowers have averted nuclear accidents, exposed large-scale corporate fraud, and reversed the approval of unsafe prescription drugs. But rather than receive praise for their integrity, they are often targeted for retaliatory investigations, harassment, intimidation, demotion, or dismissal and blacklisting. Ernie Fitzgerald, a whistleblower who exposed billions of dollars of cost overruns at the Pentagon, described whistleblowing as "committing the truth," because employers often react as if speaking the truth about wrongdoing were tantamount to committing a crime.[8]

GAP was created to help employees "commit the truth" and thereby serve the public interest. Since 1977 we have provided legal and advocacy assistance to thousands of employees who have blown the whistle on lawlessness and threats to public health, safety, and the environment. This experience has given GAP attorneys and organizers valuable insights into the strategies and the hazards of whistleblowing.

The Need for This Handbook

In 1977 GAP produced its first whistleblower primer, titled *A Federal Employee's Guide to the Federal Bureaucracy*. Twenty years later GAP distilled the knowledge it had accumulated into a publication titled *The Whistleblower's Survival Guide: Courage without Martyrdom*. Then in 2002 GAP, the Project on Government Oversight (POGO), and Public Employees for Environmental Responsibility (PEER) collaborated to write *The Art of Anonymous Activism: Serving the Public while Surviving Public Service*. Now, with corporate scandals continuing and the development of new private-sector whistleblower protections, we believe it is time to write a handbook tailored to the corporate whistleblower.

The Corporate Whistleblower's Survival Guide draws from prior publications and GAP's experience assisting some 5,000 whistleblowers over the past 33 years. Our goal is to share lessons learned so that potential corporate whistleblowers know what they are getting into and can develop proactive strategies both to make a difference and to survive. We hope that a broad audience including concerned citizens, policymakers, journalists, and public interest groups will find its contents helpful in understanding the difficulties and the social significance of whistleblowing. Nevertheless, this handbook was written primarily with one set of readers in mind: private-sector employees of conscience.

Chapter 1 of this survival guide provides guidance for those who are making the weighty decision whether to blow the whistle. Chapter 2 discusses the dangers that whistleblowers face and should weigh into their decision making. Chapter 3 covers survival strategies for how best to blow the whistle and make a difference. It contains tips on how to go forward, often in the absence of adequate legal safeguards, without sacrificing your career. Chapter 4 discusses where to blow the whistle. Chapter 5 suggests possible allies along the way. Chapter 6 details the legal landscape in which the whistleblower stands. Chapter 7 makes recommendations for legislative and corporate reform, providing a blueprint for government and corporate leaders who recognize that it is bad business to silence or eliminate what is often their only warning signal of impending disaster.

The current patchwork of corporate laws fails to provide a coherent and functional system of legal rights. As a rule, instead of protection, whistleblowers who assert their "rights" attract retaliation. The good news is that corporate whistleblowers can and do survive while bringing about positive change. But survival seldom comes from lawsuits in isolation. The key to committing the truth and getting away with it is strategic legal campaigns grounded in public solidarity that effectively turn information into power. This handbook reviews lessons learned and tactics that have worked despite the law.

Fortunately, times are a-changin'. When GAP was founded in 1977, whistleblowers were considered traitors. It was a weathervane of change when Sherron Watkins and Cynthia Cooper joined FBI attorney Coleen Rowley as the 2002 Persons of the Year. After the 2006 congressional elections, a Democracy Corps survey of likely voters rated strengthening whistleblowers' rights as one of their highest priorities for the new Congress, only behind eliminating illegal government spending.[9]

Accompanying this sea change have been promising shifts in the legal landscape. In 2002 Sarbanes-Oxley pioneered jury access for whistleblowers, which has since been emulated in nine significant laws covering the nuclear, ground transportation, retail commerce, health, and financial industries as well as defense contractors. These more refined statutes have perfected the relatively crude SOX 2002 pioneer statute, which itself was updated in the financial Dodd-Frank law. The Obama administration has appointed the strongest, most experienced team in history to enforce corporate whistleblower laws through administrative adjudication.

And yet the promised land of comprehensive, consistent whistleblower rights is still on the other side of the rainbow. Until that goal is reached, whistleblowers will have to rely on their wits, not necessarily their rights. Hopefully, this book will provide critical guidance on whether and how to commit the truth and thus turn information into power.

A Message to Corporate Leaders

While this handbook is a corporate survival guide for whistleblowers, there is an overarching lesson to be learned by corporate leaders: it is bad business to kill or silence the messenger. Rarely do whistleblowers want to break ranks with their employer or risk being exiled from the workplace. The overwhelming majority are motivated by loyalty to the company and professional pride in its positive role in society. They first try to work within the corporate system. A 2010 Ethics Resource Center report, supplementing its 2009 National Business Ethics Survey, found that only 4 percent of whistleblowers made their disclosures outside the corporate system, and only 3 percent even to hotlines; 46 percent went to their supervisor.[10] If you respond constructively and in good faith, all the sections in this handbook about strategy, advocacy, and legal rights become irrelevant.

Whistleblowers fear personal and institutional liability. They are concerned with the consequences of nearsighted corporate bureaucrats whose internal misconduct creates long-term threats to the company or society. Instead of remaining silent due to fear of retaliation or cynicism, whistleblowers should be an invaluable asset to corporate leadership in exposing corruption that betrays the company's own interests and the public trust.

When whistleblowers who overwhelmingly are loyal to the company remain "silent observers," you lose. The 2010 Ethics Resource Center report also found that while some 50 percent of employees witness misconduct on the job, roughly 40 percent do not act on their knowledge.[11] Those 40 percent have tremendous potential to prevent or recoup losses. A 2007 PricewaterhouseCoopers global crime survey of more than 5,400 corporations in 40 countries found that over 40 percent had been victimized by one or more serious economic crimes and that 80 percent of that group reported damage or significant damage to their institutions.[12] The average loss from fraud per company was more than $3.2 million in 2007.[13] Furthermore, PricewaterhouseCoopers reported that whistleblower hotlines as well as internal and external sources were the initial means of detection in 43 percent of the cases, more than the combined results from corporate security, internal audits, fraud risk management, rotation of personnel, and law enforcement.[14] Similarly, a 2008 report of the Association of Certified Fraud Examiners (ACFE), reviewing 959 cases of fraud, credited exposure of 46.2 percent of that fraud to tipsters compared with only 3.2 percent detected by law enforcement; 57.7 percent of the tips came from employees. The ACFE advised that employees "should be encouraged to report illegal or suspicious behavior, and they should be reassured that reports may be made confidentially and that the organization prohibits retaliation against whistleblowers."[15] It pays to listen to the messenger.

Senator Charles Grassley (R-IA) calls whistleblowers the "canaries in the coalmine." Of course no one wants bad news that will disrupt short-term production schedules or profits. But the unwelcome news may be invaluable in preventing disasters that you may not know about until there are garish headlines of scandal or tragedy for which you may be held responsible, with damage control the only option left. At GAP we view a corporation's response to whistleblowers as a measure of organizational maturity—a test of willingness to defer short-term gratification for long-term benefit. We hope that through your leadership you will make this handbook irrelevant to your employees.

CHAPTER 1

Deciding to Blow the Whistle

The decision to blow the whistle may be among the most significant choices you will make in your life. We want to help you make the best decision possible.

This book seeks to provide full disclosure of the many risks you are considering. It will explain your rights under the law, outlining both the protections provided for private-sector employees under Sarbanes-Oxley as well as the patchwork of other statutes. We will explore the challenges you face when relying on your legal rights. We will also describe what we have learned about patterns of institutional response against employees who step forward to speak the truth about corporate misconduct.

If you decide to blow the whistle, fully informed of the risks, we want you to do it in a smart and strategic manner that will serve your own interests and lead to positive change. You may want to remain anonymous, or you may choose to go public. You may decide to take your story to the media, or you may prefer to talk to public officials with the power to correct the problem. Your decisions will affect your future, your family, and your career. A well-planned strategy offers you a chance of succeeding. Unplanned and uninformed dissent could be the path to professional suicide.

What Constitutes a Whistleblower Case?

Through our work with whistleblowers over the years, GAP has learned which strategies are most likely to be successful and which are recipes for frustration or failure. GAP has three primary criteria for evaluating potential whistleblower cases:

- Is the wrongdoing at issue substantial enough to warrant the risks of reprisal and the investment of human and financial resources to expose it?

- Are the allegations reasonable, and can they be sufficiently substantiated?

- Can the disclosure make a difference beyond the whistleblower's merely risking retaliation?

Facing Conflicting Values and Goals

Your decision about whether and how to blow the whistle is intensely personal. It means making a choice between deeply held and conflicting values. To illustrate, our society celebrates team players and snubs naysayers. Yet we also admire rugged individualists and have contempt for bureaucratic sheep who simply go along to get along.

Similarly, no one wants to be viewed as a squealer or tattletale. A common synonym for an informant is a "rat." But we have equal contempt for those who look the other way, do not want to get involved, or make a conscious choice to see nothing. "See no evil, hear no evil, speak no evil" means we have sacrificed our humanity. Consider the words of one nuclear whistleblower: "People have to stop seeing whistleblowers as tattletales . . . I don't know what you do, living in a culture that thinks if you have standards that you're a tattletale."

The conflict of values extends to other aspects of our identity as citizens. Many whistleblowers go public with their dissent in the name of transparency and openness. Another cornerstone of our cherished freedoms, however, is the right to privacy. You will have to choose.

Your decision also raises deeply personal issues of loyalty and livelihood. From many angles you must answer the question, *Loyalty to whom?*

Most people have at their core a fundamental loyalty to their family and, by extension, the company that allows them to support it. As the adage goes, you don't bite the hand that feeds you. We also feel loyalty to our colleagues with whom we may spend more time than our families. Whistleblowing can risk their livelihoods as well. At the same time, we share a duty of loyalty toward the public, whether our neighborhood, our country, or the global community. There is a basic duty to help enforce the law that goes hand in glove with the rights of citizenship. Whistle-blowers are often motivated by a patriotic duty to their country or a civic loyalty to the law and the bedrock principles that guide it.

Any decision about how to act on these conflicting values is not easy, yet it is one that only you can make. At this crossroads, and at many more if you go decide to go forward, the "right" choice means being centered and true to yourself while honoring your responsibilities to those affected by your decision. Whichever choice you make, your life will never be the same. As observed by Professor C. Fred Alford, who has worked closely with whistleblowers after their cases were over, "There is something about blowing the whistle, and suffering the consequences, that takes hold of a whistleblower's life and never lets go."[1] Whistleblowers who speak out instead of remain silent always have a common reason: whether right or wrong, for better or worse, they could not live with themselves if they did not get involved.

Doing the Right Thing

"I am honored that people think I am a hero . . . but I do not accept that moniker as others are much more deserving of it. I did what was right . . . have no regrets and would do it again. As you see, we were just ordinary people placed in some extraordinary situations and did the right thing as all should do."

—*Dr. Jeffrey Wigand, former high-ranking tobacco industry executive who disclosed the truth about the industry's disregard for public health and safety*

"I regret being so naive . . . I think the American public needs to realize that very few federal protection policies are actually really followed. It seems if you see no evil, hear no evil, no harm has really been done. But, if you are really ethical, it is hard to have an easy life. . . . The sad fact is that there are so many environmental crimes that will affect our families . . . everyone will suffer in the long run . . . in health, and also the expensive health bills will have to be paid; the environment will be damaged. People will not hold anyone responsible, partly because companies don't have the money to clean up this big mess that could have been prevented."

　　—Inez Austin, senior engineer who spoke out against hazardous practices
　　at the Hanford nuclear cleanup site

"If you think what you are doing is right, you should do it, though you have to understand the likely consequences. If you are prepared to accept those consequences, then go for it. I don't regret raising this at all, and I certainly would raise it again. I think you also can't raise these things in a halfhearted way. If you are going to blow the whistle, then you should do it as loudly and publicly as possible."

　　—Dr. Aubrey Blumsohn, scientist who blew the whistle on Procter &
　　Gamble's interference with a research study of its osteoporosis drug

---

A recent study by Dr. Aaron Kesselheim and colleagues showed that "compulsion to do the right thing and not money is the primary motivation when drug company employees report fraudulent activity to the government."[2] Interviewing 26 whistleblowers associated with 17 separate cases of pharmaceutical whistleblowing since 2001, the study concluded that the potential of a multimillion-dollar settlement played a minor role in their decision-making and, in retrospect, was not often worth the personal costs whistleblowers suffered. Instead, "they seemed to want to right a wrong, or bring to light something that was ethically compromised," said Dr. Kesselheim.[3]

One thing is for certain. With truth on their side, individuals *can* make a difference. Whistleblowers are the Achilles' heel of organizational misconduct, provided they bear witness when it counts. Used astutely, truth is still the most powerful political weapon in our society, capable of defeating money and entrenched political machines. Armed with the truth, whistleblowing Davids repeatedly have exposed and defeated Goliaths who put their goals of economic or political power above the public interest.

Whistleblowers at Their Best

At their best, whistleblowers embody the professional integrity of true public citizens. Through their actions they add conscience and integrity to our concept of citizenship. Within large organizations they are the human factor that counterbalances the tendency of bureaucracies to put organizational self-interest above all else, even when it means institutionalizing patterns of wrongdoing.

Consider the following handful of examples drawn from GAP's experience representing whistleblowers. Our clients have:

- sparked the removal of the painkiller Vioxx found to cause some 50,000 fatal heart attacks, as well as obtained stronger consumer safety enforcement for other prescription drugs,[4] including Crestor (for lowering cholesterol),[5] Meridia (for weight loss), Bextra (for pain relief), Accutane (for acne), Serevent (for asthma),[6] Ketek (for sinusitis, bronchitis, and pneumonia),[7] Actonel (an osteoporosis drug),[8] ProHeart 6 (a dog medication),[9] and Prevnar (an infant vaccine);[10]

- exposed and stopped both a former oil industry lobbyist appointed to head the White House Council on Environmental Quality censoring government reports on climate change, and agency gag orders restricting the communication of critical climate change research findings with the public;[11]

- helped convince the House of Representatives initially to vote against legal immunity for major telecommunications companies after disclosing that a major telecom's "Quantico Circuit" provided an unknown third party with unfettered access to every mobile communication over its network, including phone conversations, e-mails, and Internet use;[12]

- forced the cancellation of an already-approved and nearly complete nuclear power plant because its construction was compromised by falsification of X-rays on safety welds, uninspected safety systems, and shoddy materials such as automobile junkyard metal substituted for nuclear grade steel;[13]

- exposed systematic illegality and forced a new cleanup after the Three Mile Island nuclear incident by revealing utility company plans to remove a reactor vessel head using a crane whose brakes and electrical system were destroyed in the accident (the vessel head consisted of 170 tons of radioactive rubble that, if dropped, could have triggered another accident; whistleblowers went public with the evidence two days before the head lift was to take place and delayed its operation for 18 months until the crane was repaired and tested);[14]

- released data about possible public exposure to radiation around the Hanford, Washington, nuclear waste reservation, where Department of Energy (DOE) contractors failed to account for 440 billion gallons of radioactive waste;[15]

- shut down the manufacturing division of a multinational corporation that had cornered the market on devices that test the accuracy of precision calibration tools after exposing that test results were random (averting tragedies arising from defective goods such as heart valves, computer equipment, automobiles, and airplanes—any product where precise conformance to design specifications means the difference between success and failure);[16]

- provided evidence that led to the closure of two incinerators and the cancellation of three others after it was shown that the operating ones had dumped toxic substances such as dioxin, arsenic, chromium, mercury, and other heavy metals into the environment of five states and in some instances next to churches and schoolyards;[17]

- sparked public backlashes that three times forced the government to abandon its plans to replace its meat inspections with a corporate "honor system";[18]

- reduced from four days to two hours the amount of time racially profiled minority women going through US customs could be stopped on suspicion of drug smuggling, strip-searched, and held incommunicado for hospital laboratory tests without access to a lawyer or even permission to contact family and in the absence of any evidence that they had engaged in wrongdoing;[19]

- exposed Transportation Security Administration orders to cancel Federal Air Marshal coverage for the highest-risk, cross-country airplane flights during the middle of a subsequently confirmed post 9/11, larger scale terrorist hijacking alert, orders that were rescinded after congressional protests following the disclosure;[20]

■ sparked a top-down removal of upper management at the US Department of Justice (DOJ) after revealing systematic corruption in the DOJ's program to train police forces of other nations to investigate and prosecute government corruption;[21]

■ exposed failure by US Marine Corps procurement officials to deliver mine-resistant vehicles and nonlethal crowd dispersers that caused Iraqi civilian and one-third of American combat deaths and injuries, before the whistleblowing disclosure led to delivery of the lifesaving equipment.[22]

Reality Check for the Aspiring Whistleblower

Nothing is more powerful than the truth. But few paths are more treacherous than the one that challenges an abuse of power. Time and time again, GAP has seen whistleblowers pay an enormous professional and personal price for their actions. Because we want you to be prepared, we will not mince words in describing the risks of your decision.

One person against a corporation is not a fair fight. In terms of raw power, the corporation holds all the cards. It enjoys a presumption of legitimacy and legal authority vis-à-vis its employees. It boasts extraordinary resources and connections with politicians, the media, industry, and the larger community. It defines the workplace and its rules and regulations within the law. It bears primary responsibility for holding itself accountable. We will discuss how to even the odds by turning information into power and using the law; but in conventional terms, the deck will be stacked against you no matter how solid your evidence or astute your strategy.

When company employees go public with tales of malfeasance, the focus often turns quickly to whether there was a reprisal or justified corporate response. No matter how irrelevant, this often focuses attention on the whistleblower's personality and work record instead of the issues that prompted the whistleblowing. Rather than face the problems brought to light, managers often blame the "disgruntled employee," who is portrayed as vengeful, imbalanced, or self-serving.

Shooting the Messenger

You will surely suffer some level of harassment or retribution for blowing the whistle because bureaucracies instinctively tend to eliminate anything perceived as a threat. Academic studies confirm that more than 90 percent of whistleblowers report subsequent retaliation.[23] You may not believe that your employer is your adversary, but the record shows that employers often do not want to be told what is wrong with their operations. Frequently, the antidote to bad news is secrecy enforced by repression to cover up misconduct, avoid costly delays and litigation, and protect the short-term bottom line.

Not all of these repercussions are immediately obvious. For every outspoken critic who is immediately terminated, a number of others are simply transferred to a cubicle with no further job responsibilities. Some people face such direct harassment from their chain of command that they finally quit. Others are given lateral transfers to isolated or unpopular field offices. Still others face no immediate consequences but find over the years that they are repeatedly passed over for promotions in favor of less dedicated employees who have not been branded troublemakers.

Above all, being a whistleblower is lonely and stressful. You may not be a welcome member of your professional community anymore. Without acting directly, supervisors who once valued your contributions may transfer you to less interesting projects or slowly remove your responsibilities. Co-workers may shun you out of fear, while others are reduced to whispering their admiration in the bathroom. Professor Alford targets this isolation as more emotionally painful than tangible retaliation. "What bothers whistleblowers the most [is] not that the boss retaliated—this at least was understandable: he or she had interests to protect—but that colleagues they thought were friends, colleagues with whom some whistleblowers had spent more time than their families, refused to recognize the whistleblower."[24]

The Personal Price

Work pressure puts additional tension on personal relationships. You may be on a lot shorter fuse at home, while your family may have a difficult time understanding and sympathizing with what you are going through. It is not uncommon for marriages and other relationships to fall apart in the wake of whistleblowing. These dynamics can lead to stress-related health problems such as ulcers, headaches, anxiety, fatigue, and alcoholism.

In perhaps the most comprehensive survey of whistleblowers in the academic literature, authors Joyce Rothschild and Terance D. Miethe reported the following:

> As a consequence of their whistleblowing experience, the majority of the whistle-blowers in our sample suffered intensely. The most common fallout from their whistleblowing involved: (a) severe depression or anxiety (84 percent), (b) feelings of isolation or powerlessness (84 percent), (c) distrust of others (78 percent), (d) declining physical health (69 percent), (e) severe financial decline (66 percent), and (f) problems with family relations (53 percent). Repeatedly, respondents mentioned that whistleblowing undermined their trust in others. These numbers are extremely high; however, the numbers cannot convey the emotional distress that we heard from so many of our respondents.[25]

As important as recognizing the *extent* of the likely consequences of blowing the whistle is understanding *how long* it may take to make a difference—and how long you may pay a price for your actions. If your goal is to have an impact, it may require a marathon commitment to follow through on your charges and cost you hundreds of thousands of dollars in legal fees, lost wages, and other expenses. A retaliation lawsuit commonly takes two to three years and may last more than a decade for a complex, controversial case. The proceedings will drag out with investigations and lawsuits for years after the scandal, requiring you to relive the dispute in depositions and interviews. And you will learn that it is very difficult to stop midstream.

Even if your retaliation claims are vindicated and you are reinstated or compensated, the troubles do not end there. As a matter of law, it is often beyond a court's authority to address the underlying charges that gave rise to retaliation. Furthermore, long after the public has forgotten your courageous actions, your superiors will remember what you did to them and continue to view you as a threat. While managers come and go, a corporation has institutional memory. Admiral Hyman Rickover, founder of the nuclear navy, wisely observed that if you have to choose between sinning against God or the bureaucracy, pick God. That is because neither will ever forget, but only God will forgive. On occasion a third or even fourth generation of managers may continue the harassment campaign against a whistleblower—long after the original target of the dissent has left.

Sometimes it is better to have looked the other way than to have blown the whistle unsuccessfully or given up too soon. That is why GAP scrutinizes both merits and motivations before accepting whistleblower clients. We examine the availability of concrete evidence, timing, the whistleblower's commitment and vulnerabilities, and countless other factors affecting prospects for success. Sometimes we turn down whistleblowers seeking our representation because they are likely to face an adverse ruling that will make an example out of them, further embolden the employer, and intensify a pattern of institutional repression. After blowing the whistle, you can make a negative difference by quitting in the middle or by losing. The bureaucracy will have weathered the challenge to misconduct and be stronger in the aftermath.

Whistleblowers are in the news these days, held up as role models. In movies and magazines, the media glorifies those who risk everything to expose corruption, greed, and illegal activity. But for those who think that blowing the whistle is glamorous or a path to recognition, think again. The majority of whistleblowers suffer in obscurity, frustrated by burned career bridges and vindication they were never able to obtain. The prominent, lionized beacons of hope are the rare exception, and even most of them pay a horrible price with lifelong scars.

CHAPTER 2

The Red Flags

The previous warnings notwithstanding, if you are going to challenge the company that employs you, you must understand how large organizations operate. In particular, you should know how corporate bureaucracies function to target troublemakers and neutralize dissent.

Targeting Dissenters: Tactics of Retaliation

Corporate hierarchies employ intimidation and fear to convince their workers that the power of the organization is stronger than the power of the individual—even individuals who have truth on their side. Often, making an example out of one troublemaker is sufficient to keep the majority silent. The following section illustrates tactics your employer may use to "shoot the messenger" of bad news.

None of these techniques of retaliation is unique or new. More than three decades ago, the classic institutional response to whistleblowers was captured on tape in the instructions of President Richard Nixon to top aides H. R. Haldeman and John Ehrlichman. After learning that Pentagon cost-control expert Ernie Fitzgerald had blown the whistle on $2.3 billion in accounting irregularities in the construction contract of military cargo planes, Nixon said simply, "Fire that son of a bitch."[1]

In 1973 President Nixon took reprisal techniques to a new level. Fred Malek, director of the White House Personnel Office, issued the "Malek Manual," a secret report on how to purge the career civil service system of "unresponsive" employees—whistleblowers or Democrats—without running afoul of the law. The following reprisal tactics are drawn largely from the Malek Manual and apply equally to corporate and federal government employees, though we draw our illustrations primarily from the private sector. Ironically, whistleblowers exposed the Malek Manual, and it was published in the Watergate Committee's report.[2]

Keep in mind that the following list is not exhaustive; the forms of harassment are limited only by the imagination and, as in Orwell's *1984*, likely will be customized to strike at a whistleblower's unique vulnerabilities. Further, they vary in intensity. There is a direct relationship between the significance of a whistleblower's threat and the severity of the retaliation. Often the higher up the chain of command the whistleblower sits, the greater the perceived threat and the more vicious the retaliation.

Spotlight the Whistleblower, Not the Wrongdoing

This is also known as the smokescreen tactic, and it operates almost like a knee-jerk instinct. The first imperative of retaliation is to make the whistleblower the issue: obfuscate the dissent by attacking the source's motives, credibility, professional competence, or virtually anything else that will work to cloud the issue. The point is to direct the spotlight at the whistleblower instead of the alleged misconduct.

A typical initial management response to a whistleblower's disclosures is to launch an internal investigation and retaliate against the employee on trumped-up charges. Retaliatory travel, reimbursement, and time audits are so common they could be classified as bureaucratic knee-jerk reactions against whistleblowers. Allegations of everything from sexual harassment to stealing paper clips are possible—even charges that have already been investigated and discredited. Moreover, smears of alleged misconduct similar to what the whistleblower is exposing are not unusual.

Chutzpah in selecting the smear charges is a common tactic to demonstrate the organization's invincibility. Soft-spoken, humble individuals have been branded loudmouth egomaniacs. There is no limit to the petty and outrageous depths to which an unscrupulous employer may be willing to sink. An example is charging an employee with gambling at work for buying a charitable raffle ticket from a colleague.

Often a private security firm will be hired to do the dirty work of investigating a whistleblower. Sometimes investigations and surveillance are conducted by "babysitters," spies assigned by management to "assist" the whistleblower. Increasingly, employers also seek criminal prosecution for theft or misappropriation of company property—materials that are frequently the very evidence of illegality being used by the whistleblower.

Richard Parks and Wrongdoing at Three Mile Island

When Three Mile Island engineer Richard Parks challenged sloppy cleanup practices that could have triggered a nuclear meltdown, his employer's first reaction was to brush aside the safety issues and place Parks under investigation for an alleged financial conflict of interest. The company's search for incriminating evidence took on some extreme measures. Parks returned home one day to find that his house had been broken into and ransacked. Parks was not vindicated until he went public and sought help from the Department of Labor (DOL), Congress, and the Nuclear Regulatory Commission (NRC). All three acknowledged the substance of his claims, and after a six-month investigation the NRC ordered his employer to redo the entire cleanup with revised procedures and to conduct extensive safety tests.[3]

A related technique is to open an internal investigation—and then deliberately keep it pending for an indefinite period. The idea is to leave the whistleblower twisting in the wind, with the clouds of an unresolved, never-ending investigation hanging over his head. Indeed some whistleblowers endure a series of nearly seamless investigations for decades. The intent is not only to create uncertainty and stress but also to undermine the whistleblower's credibility. Potential media, government, and other officials may be discouraged from listening to and taking seriously the allegations of a whistleblower who is "under investigation." A related tactic is "chain witch hunts," in which a new investigation is opened as soon as an old one is closed without action.

Spotlighting whistleblowers, as opposed to their claims, often involves public humiliation—the bureaucratic equivalent of placing them in the public stocks. When Resolution Trust Corporation (RTC) enforcement attorneys Bruce Pederson and Jacqueline Taylor protested political sabotage of savings and loan prosecutions, they were publicly denigrated and assigned to work in buildings not staffed by any other RTC employees, such as the cafeteria.[4] Psychiatric fitness-for-duty exams are one of the ugliest forms of retaliation and have long been used as a way to spotlight the whistleblower. At the same time, companies can hide behind privacy laws to hint that there is a problem with the employee that the corporation is not at liberty to disclose.

"Crazy Like a Fox"

When Dr. James Murtagh, a physician at Atlanta's Grady Hospital, blew the whistle on fraud involving the hospital's federal medical care grants, an alert was issued that he was armed and dangerous. He was alleged to be mentally unstable and ordered to keep off the hospital grounds, with instructions to security that he could be dangerous. Eventually, Dr. Murtagh successfully settled a Federal False Claims Act lawsuit against the hospital for $1.6 million and organized other Grady whistleblowers into a relentless coalition that led to widespread white-collar prosecutions, including the felony conviction of a notorious Georgia state senator for his involvement in an extensive corruption scandal. Dr. Murtagh resumed his career and has become a leader in the whistleblower community, organizing two national conferences.

Build a Damaging Record against the Whistleblower

This tactic goes hand in glove with spotlighting the whistleblower. Not infrequently, companies spend years manufacturing an official personnel record to brand a whistleblower as a chronic "problem employee" who has refused to improve. The idea is to convey that the employee does nothing right. In truth, many whistleblowers have a history of sterling performance evaluations—*until* this tactic is used against them.

An employer may begin by compiling memoranda about any incident, real or contrived, that projects inadequate or problematic performance on the job. This is often followed by a series of confrontational "counseling" sessions, in which the employee is baited to lash back. Reprimands and comparatively mild disciplinary actions are taken first, in part because the employee has few (if any) due process rights in defense and in part because company policy may require progressive discipline. By the time something more serious such as termination is proposed, the employer is armed with a long and contrived history of "unsatisfactory performance."

The Wayward Whistleblower

Several years ago an individual herein pseudonymously referred to as John Doe began working at a major US pharmaceuticals production facility. This facility was charged with manufacturing a new infant vaccine for meningitis and pneumonia. Doe's role was to ensure that the facility's employees were sufficiently trained to the level required by Food and Drug Administration (FDA) standards. He soon became aware of gaps and shortcuts that were being taken both with the employees' training and with the manufacturing process itself. These shortcuts in the training program were particularly alarming because producing biological vaccines required more-complex processes than regular pharmaceutical production.[5]

Doe's concerns led him to send a written memorandum to his supervisor, explaining that the facility was not satisfying FDA regulations and the company's own code of conduct and that he would not be complicit in misrepresenting that fact. Doe filed complaints with both the company's Office of Compliance and its Office of Ethics and revealed the depth and the breadth of manufacturing, quality assurance, and product release problems to one of the company's attorneys. He was told that the resulting investigation found no problems with the facility, though internal memoranda unearthed later in discovery revealed a much different picture.[6]

Two months later Doe was placed on a personal improvement plan (PIP) for 90 days. The PIP stated that he had to stop making comments to anyone regarding the company's noncompliance with training requirements.[7] Doe was promptly suspended and fired two months later, after he had a hostile encounter with the human resources director at a holiday party.[8] It later surfaced that this manager was brought in to "deal with" Doe after his predecessor was terminated for refusing to fire Doe and that the manager himself was later dismissed for cause, including harassment, expense report "discrepancies," and unauthorized disclosure of proprietary information to a competitor.

Doe filed a lawsuit against his former employer under the then recently enacted Sarbanes-Oxley Act, claiming his termination was in retaliation for calling attention to the regulatory violations. It became a major test case warning of the new law's frailty. A federal magistrate dismissed the case, reasoning that the reported violations were immaterial to shareholders and therefore not within the scope of Sarbanes-Oxley. The Fourth Circuit Court of Appeals agreed. The law's new boundaries cancel protections for warnings, disclosures of risk, or even actual illegality unless the government punishes the company in a way that is severe enough to damage shareholder value. Under this standard, Sherron Watkins would not have had whistle-blower rights when she warned CEO and Chairman Ken Lay of the risks from Enron's fraud. Doe's fate was not an aberration. The devastated legal land-scape is discussed more fully in chapter 6.

In addition, the judge was swayed by the drug company's contention that Doe would have been fired regardless of his whistleblowing efforts—pointing to the hostile incident at the holiday party and the fact that Doe was reprimanded for professional misconduct prior to his initial memoran-dum.[9] Doe's advice to future whistleblowers: Don't rely on codes of conduct, agency investigators, or the courts to protect you. "The best way to blow the whistle is to gather all of the facts yourself and anonymously provide the evidence to a newspaper reporter. Then, walk away and find another job."

Threaten Them

Warning-shot reprisals for whistleblowing, such as reprimands, often contain an explicit threat of termination or other severe punishment if the offense is repeated. In some cases employees may have signed nondis-closure agreements as a condition of employment. The penalty for violat-ing these agreements, which typically fail to outline legitimate exceptions for fraud, waste, or illegality, includes the threat of criminal sanctions.

A Tobacco Scientist Blows the Whistle

Dr. Jeffrey Wigand was a scientist and a manager who had worked in dif-ferent aspects of the corporate world for much of his adult life, including at Union Carbide and Johnson & Johnson, before he was recruited for a position at Brown & Williamson Tobacco Corporation (B&W), one of the four largest cigarette manufacturers in the United States. Dr. Wigand was given a prestigious position as head of research and development, a large salary, and what he thought was a good opportunity to help develop a safer cigarette.[10] He was not blind to the moral difficulties that his position might entail, but the offer was too good to turn down.

As Dr. Wigand settled into his position, his illusions of helping the pub-lic faded. B&W's "safer cigarette" was not high priority, and research was can-celed. He discovered that the lab was sorely out of date and did not have any staff on hand to perform thorough toxicological and chemical analyses or to assess the propensity of a given cigarette formulation to start fires.[11]

He was sent to an orientation session on tobacco litigation and found out that B&W retained scientists only to help shield the company in the event of a lawsuit. In addition, "document management" was practiced to keep information away from any discovery process.[12] These practices and more made Dr. Wigand increasingly wary of his employer. Nevertheless, he continued working for B&W for four years until he was fired in 1993.[13] The company was not pleased with Dr. Wigand's efforts to determine the health effects of some cigarette additives and terminated him. While he was looking for other jobs, B&W sued him for breach of contract, eventually forcing him into signing a stringent confidentiality agreement to retain his medical benefits and severance package.[14]

The corporate bullying had the opposite of the desired effect. Dr. Wigand decided that instead of just walking away, he would fight back. Through an intermediary, he was connected with a *60 Minutes* producer, Lowell Bergman, who had a stack of internal tobacco industry documents that he could not fully understand.[15] This initiated a series of events that ended in the extensive tobacco industry trials of the midnineties. Despite threats and delays, and emboldened by the *Wall Street Journal*'s printing of Dr. Wigand's depositions, *60 Minutes* eventually ran multiple stories revealing the tobacco industry's flagrant disregard of the health of its customers. The industry did not want to make "safer" cigarettes or ones that were more resistant to starting fires.[16] The November 1998 master settlement agreement between US state attorneys general and the four largest cigarette manufacturers that resulted from the tobacco suits was one of the largest in US history, some $206 billion.[17]

These victories were not easy ones for Dr. Wigand, however. He received multiple death threats.[18] Every moment of his past life was scrutinized by B&W, which spent more than $8 billion on a 500-page smear campaign. Anything that could be twisted and used against him was put into the public record.[19] His marriage ended, and he was distanced from his family. Amidst the showdown of 1996, Dr. Wigand's attorneys hired a private investigation firm to dismantle the campaign against his character. Dr. Wigand was compelled to travel with a bodyguard.[20]

In the end, however, his testimony worked and was one of the linchpins of the government's prosecution. Dr. Wigand stood up to some of the biggest bullies of the corporate world and defeated them. After leaving B&W he began a new career as a high-school Japanese and science teacher and has been recognized as a Fannie Mae First Class Teacher of the Year. He also runs Smoke Free Kids, an organization to combat teen tobacco use.[21]

Isolate Them

Another retaliation technique is to transfer the whistleblower to a "bureaucratic Siberia." Similar to public humiliation, the isolation makes an example of the whistleblower while also blocking the employee's access to information and severing contact with other concerned employees. Moreover, like any good retaliation tactic, isolation puts pressure on the whistleblower to be compliant or resign.

Employers may also isolate whistleblowers by forcing them to work from home or take administrative leave with or without pay. They may be moved around within the same building to a new office with dim lights, dreary surroundings, and no desk or phone. Isolation does not necessarily require geographic relocation, however, as it may be sufficient to take away the employee's work duties, position, or clearance. This technique has been called the "potted palm" gambit because the employee's new post-whistleblowing duties are as extensive as those of an office plant.

Set Them Up for Failure

The converse of retaliating against whistleblowers by stripping them of their duties is the tactic of putting them on a "pedestal of cards." This involves setting whistleblowers up for failure by overloading them with unmanageable work and then firing or demoting them for nonperformance. This tactic commonly includes making it impossible to fulfill assigned responsibilities by withdrawing the necessary privileges, access, or staffing. Another variation of this tactic is to appoint the whistleblower to solve the problem he exposed and then make the job impossible through a wide range of obstacles that undercut any possibility of real reform. The employee may then be turned into the scapegoat and fired for incompetence when the problem is not solved. In extreme cases this retaliatory tactic may extend to setting the whistleblower up for criminal charges, disciplinary action, or even injury, such as by ordering people with poor backs to move heavy furniture.

Physically Attack Them

Karen Silkwood from Oklahoma's Kerr-McGee nuclear facility was killed after her car ran off the road on the way to meet a reporter under circumstances that led many to suspect murder. Shortly after Dr. James Murtagh successfully settled his False Claims lawsuit and made FBI disclosures in a political corruption case that sent the Georgia State Senate leader to prison, he was hospitalized for arsenic poisoning.[22] Dr. Jeff Wigand experienced anonymous death threats against himself and his loved ones. These whistleblowers' fates demonstrate the risk of physical retaliation for speaking out. Physical attacks on whistleblowers are not common but do occur. Sometimes organizations encourage or wink at "the boys" who do their dirty work, as the whistleblower gets beaten up by thugs on the work floor. Sometimes physical retaliation is more subtle. Whistleblowers at nuclear or chemical facilities may find themselves assigned to work in the hottest radioactive or toxic spots in the plant.

Eliminate Their Jobs

Another common tactic is to lay off whistleblowers even as the company is hiring new staff. Employers may "reorganize" whistleblowers out of jobs or into marginal positions. A related tactic is to eliminate—through reorganization—the structural independence of particular oversight units. A nuclear engineering firm may de-emphasize the quality control department by making it a component of the production staff.

"Reorganizing" Whistleblowers' Jobs at Fluor

Created as part of the Manhattan Project and operating in secrecy for more than 40 years, the Hanford Nuclear Reservation located in Washington State supplied plutonium for the federal government's nuclear weapons program. In 1989 all production ended and the Department of Energy, the Environmental Protection Agency (EPA), and the Washington State Department of Ecology began a concerted cleanup effort of the widespread hazardous chemical and radioactive waste.[23] Fluor Federal Services Inc. was hired by the Department of Energy to assist with the cleanup.

Fluor's crew at the Hanford site was instructed to install a particular kind of valve on a system of pipes used for handling the highly radioactive nuclear waste. The crew of seven refused to obey, however, because they feared that the underrated valves would burst, potentially causing the leakage of millions of gallons of radioactive waste into the surrounding environment.[24] Because of their protests, stronger valves were used, but all seven workers were laid off within days. They brought a retaliation claim against Fluor, which later agreed to reinstate them.[25]

Unfortunately, Fluor fired seven other employees to make room for the original workers.[26] This was both unexpected and unnecessary. It seemed to be an effort to cause tension between the seven rehires and the rest of the crew. One Fluor executive even spread a false rumor that the seven original workers agreed to the layoffs as part of their agreement.[27] In a matter of months, five of the original workers were once again laid off along with six others who testified on their behalf, were witnesses, or were merely too closely associated with them. The eleven newly fired workers filed another claim against their former employer for wrongful termination. The case came before a jury this time, and the workers were awarded more than $4.7 million in damages for both back pay and emotional distress.[28] The verdict was upheld by the Washington State Supreme Court and the case finally ended in 2008.

Paralyze Their Careers

An effective retaliation technique—and one that also sends a signal to other would-be dissenters—is to deep-freeze the careers of whistleblowers who manage to thwart termination and hold on to their jobs. These employees become living legends of retaliation when employers deny all requests for promotion or transfer. A related tactic is to deny whistleblowers the training needed for professional development. The message is clear: "She is going nowhere."

Bad references for future employment openings are common, and any whistleblower settling a legal case should be careful to take this into account. Sometimes this tactic can be subtle, using buzzwords to signal that a former employee should not be hired. Common examples are statements that an employee "is not always a team player" or "needs to work on maintaining cooperative relationships."

They Would "Make Sure I'd Never Work Again"

Inez Austin was a senior engineer–turned–whistleblower at the 586-square-mile former plutonium production facility in Washington State known as the Hanford site. An employee of Westinghouse Hanford, a company contracted by the Department of Energy at Hanford, Austin served as a member of a task group responsible for certifying the safety of cleanup procedures.

In June 1990, after her warnings about the dangers of a plan to pump radioactive waste from an aging underground single-shell tank to double-shell tanks went unheeded, Austin refused to approve the process. She was concerned that the ferrocyanide present in some of the tanks was potentially explosive and posed the risk of widespread radioactive contamination. In the face of pressures to meet deadlines and maintain productivity, Austin's proposal to postpone the pumping and conduct more research was met with threats of disciplinary action by company management.[29]

In further retaliation, Austin received the lowest performance rating in her 11 years at Westinghouse. She was labeled as mentally unstable and asked to see a psychiatrist. Her office was moved to a dusty trailer that provoked her asthma and where she was given inconsequential work assignments.[30] She was the target of illegal wiretapping, interception of her mail, and a house break-in.[31]

When Austin filed an official harassment complaint with the DOE, Westinghouse offered her a new position, a month of paid leave, a clearing of her personnel files, and attorney's fees if she dropped the charges. She accepted but then found herself isolated from any meaningful work assignments for the next three years. After being demoted in October 1993, Austin called a news conference and told the press of this continuing retaliation. Media pressure landed her a position as an environmental compliance officer for Westinghouse.[32]

In 1995 Austin again felt compelled to disclose questionable practices at the Hanford site, including allowing untrained workers access to restricted areas. Again her warnings were not well received, and she lost her job in February 1996. Austin finally took her story to the secretary of energy and filed a complaint with the Department of Labor, which ruled in her favor. She also sued Westinghouse Hanford in state court for harassment and wrongful termination and eventually settled out of court.[33]

Unfortunately, Austin's long-running problems were not over. "They [Westinghouse Hanford] told me that they'd 'make sure I never work again,'" said Austin in 1998, "and so far, that's been true."[34] Indeed it took her three years and hundreds of résumés to find another job, a position with the Oregon Department of Environmental Quality enforcing solid waste and water quality standards that entailed a daily 80-mile commute. Despite her troubles, Austin stands by her efforts to protect the health and the safety of the public and her fellow cleanup workers. "I can't see how I could have done anything differently, and believe me I have had time to think about it."[35]

Blacklist Them

Sometimes it is not enough merely to fire or make whistleblowers rot in their jobs: the goal is to make sure they "will never work again" in their chosen field or industry. After several oil-industry whistleblowers exposed illegal pipeline practices, for example, the company placed them on a list of workers "not to touch" in future hiring. It does not matter whether you are completely vindicated. As Professor Alford summarized the experience of a Medicare fraud whistleblower, "Her boss went to jail, but she couldn't get a job in the state where she worked. 'They were all afraid I might commit the truth.'"[36]

Blacklisting Dunn

Resolution Trust Corporation whistleblower Richard Dunn, a quiet financial management expert, blew the whistle on overbilling by contractors who were seeking to exploit failed savings and loans. After being terminated by RTC, he recounts trying to make a fresh start with a big-name accounting firm. A week into this new job, however, Dunn was summarily dismissed. He later learned that RTC had undermined him by telling his new boss that he had been fired for threatening a co-worker with a gun, thus making him ineligible for the new position. The firearms allegation lacked any substantiation in RTC's personnel records or elsewhere.[37]

Employers in scientific professions have exercised some of the ugliest forms of blacklisting. Dr. James Murtagh has endured a steady pattern of receiving new jobs in supportive environments just to get terminated without explanation within weeks. He subsequently found that his former employer had posted the equivalent of a smear dossier about him on its website. Another creative method is extradition. Whistleblowing foreign nationals at university laboratories, including students, have been warned that their visas will not be renewed and that the Department of Homeland Security is available to ensure their departure. Many other forms of retaliation against scientists have also arisen.

These experiences are not unique. They illustrate what you can expect. A massive study by Dr. David Welch, a pioneer SOX whistleblower whose seven-year ordeal illustrated the unreliability of those rights, summarizes what you can expect based on 27,000 whistleblowers' fates from 1994 to 2008 who filed retaliation complaints with the Occupational Safety and Health Administration (OSHA):

- 78 percent struggled financially for the first five years after blowing the whistle;

- 83 percent found it "extremely difficult to impossible" to find a new job in their field;

- 66 percent found it "extremely difficult to impossible" to find a new job after changing professions;

- 54 percent could not find work until they changed professions.[38]

Neutralizing Dissent: Tactics of Cover-Up

The point of the tactics just described is to overwhelm whistleblowers in a struggle for preservation—to undermine their credibility, career, family, finances, and even sanity until they are silenced and the issues that triggered the whistleblowing are forgotten. Typically, these tactics are only one of two fronts. In addition to "shooting the messenger," employers also strive actively to bury the message by covering up the alleged wrongdoing.

Employers often rely on longstanding secrecy tactics to camouflage institutional misconduct. Large corporations will devise systems and written or unwritten policies for keeping dissent—including information about possible wrongdoing—from surfacing or creating problems for the company. Some are standing policies. Others are adopted when companies become aware of their own wrongdoing and seek to avoid getting caught. Still others are put into place as a means of damage control after a whistleblower has publicly exposed an instance of misconduct. Illustrative tactics follow.

Gag the Employees

The most direct way to silence potential whistleblowers is to gag employees through repressive nondisclosure agreements as a job prerequisite or by excessively designating information as "proprietary" or with government contractors as "classified." Private employers often build gag orders into company manuals or employment contracts and then enforce them through civil suits for breach of contract or theft of proprietary information. More subtly, companies routinely order staff not to respond directly to the media or community but rather to refer all inquiries to an in-house public relations office.

Fighting a Gag Order on Nuclear Employees

At the Knolls Atomic Plant near Schenectady, New York, workers were threatened with termination, a $100,000 fine, and life imprisonment if they commented on operations at the facility. The gag order was issued sitewide following a visit by GAP attorneys who spoke to workers about radiation leaks.[39] Several plant employees and their labor union subsequently filed suit against General Electric, the plant's owner, and the US Department of Energy, seeking declaratory and injunctive relief.[40] They claimed the gag order violated their First Amendment right to free speech because GE was acting as a government contractor. Although the case was pending, the plant issued a second newsletter clarifying that any security policy "must be read in the context of the applicable statutes and regulations" and could not be used "to prevent proper reporting of matters involving compliance with health, safety, or environmental standards." As a result, the district court dismissed the case because this second newsletter rightly acknowledged the constitutional limits of the plant's ability to silence its employees.[41]

Study It to Death

A related tactic is to launch an investigation that is toothless or never ends, leaving the allegations of wrongdoing unresolved.

Roger Boisjoly and the O-Ring Taskforce

Roger Boisjoly was an engineer for the firm Morton Thiokol, which contracted with NASA to work on the solid rocket boosters of the space shuttle *Challenger*. Boisjoly claims that any engineer who worked on the *Challenger* knew it was doomed to fail, and so did NASA's upper management. By studying the solid rocket booster's O-rings, the engineers determined that they repeatedly failed to seal at 53 degrees or below. They also determined that if the primary seal was destroyed, the O-ring would almost certainly be destroyed.[42]

In January 1985 Boisjoly wrote a letter to his managers about the possible effects of the faulty O-rings and requested that Morton Thiokol take action.

Initially, his managers simply labeled his letter "private" and filed it away. Morton Thiokol was negotiating a new contract with NASA, and presumably Boisjoly's concerns might have compromised its renewal prospects.[43]

Nevertheless, after several more memos, the company commissioned a "task force" that included Boisjoly to investigate the matter further. Boisjoly soon found out that the task force lacked the power, resources, and management support to serve any meaningful purpose. No further tests were performed on the O-rings, and no further action was taken to address the issue.[44]

On the morning of the launch, Florida experienced record low temperatures that the O-rings could not handle. Boisjoly and his fellow engineers formed a group to petition NASA to stop the launch. Despite the findings about the O-rings, however, Morton Thiokol advised NASA that its data was inconclusive and NASA proceeded with the launch. The *Challenger* exploded 73 seconds after its launch and all aboard were killed—one of the worst disasters in NASA's history. After the crash Morton Thiokol managers tried to claim they did not know about the faulty O-rings, but Boisjoly testified against them. Boisjoly was then shunned by colleagues and managers until he eventually resigned.[45] Though too late to prevent the catastrophe, his concerns were ultimately validated.

Separate Expertise from Authority

The goal of this tactic is to ensure that corporate loyalists make all the important decisions, even technical judgment calls, with only a limited advisory role for the experts.

When NASA Sidelines the Experts...

As just described, Morton Thiokol's engineers were overruled by NASA managers determined to launch the space shuttle *Challenger* in 1986, even though all the company's practicing engineers opposed the decision.[46] Morton Thiokol's management admonished these engineers for not taking off their "engineering caps" and putting on their "management caps." Managers, of course, had their reasons not to postpone the launch of the *Challenger*, for one, so that President Ronald Reagan could refer to the orbiting space vehicle during his State of the Union address to Congress that evening.[47]

One variation of this tactic is to use a rigged version of "the democratic process" to control information and outcomes. Other experts— selected for their proven loyalty—are called in to "out-vote" the whistleblower, effectively overruling the scientific method. A more subtle version of this technique is to misuse the peer review process, either as a discrediting tactic by packing the panel with a particular bias or as a stalling tactic by instituting duplicative or unnecessary reviews. This has also become a popular harassment technique against medical whistleblowers. Whistleblowers, their charges, or both are condemned after secret hearings in which they are not allowed to know or respond to the specific issues or evidence. In some instances whistleblowers are not even permitted to participate, and no formal record of the proceedings is kept.

Institutionalize Conflict of Interest

Institutions accused of wrongdoing routinely initiate probes into their own misconduct. In many whistleblower cases, this is the equivalent of appointing the fox to guard the henhouse.

In one sense, it is only fair (and more efficient) to allow companies a chance to resolve allegations and straighten out internal problems. That is the point of internal checks and balances; corporations should be responsible for internal housecleaning. But when confirmation of misconduct could create liability or when individual business leaders are the direct cause of misconduct, this approach inevitably places in-house investigations in a conflict of interest.

Fannie Mae's Troubling Internal Investigations

In 2003 three Fannie Mae employees expressed serious concerns about their firm's accounting. For six years Fannie Mae had promoted a false image of financial security through the systematic use of inappropriate accounting and improper earnings management. This resulted in the company's overstating its income by an estimated $10.6 billion. The board of directors allowed the problem to continue by failing to exercise oversight of Fannie Mae's operations even after the three employees brought it to light.[48]

Roger Barnes, then a manager in the controller's division, made serious allegations about Fannie Mae's accounting for deferred price adjustments, which were promptly passed on to Ann Kappler, senior vice president and general counsel. Similarly, Michelle Skinner, director for e-business, expressed her reservations to Chief Operating Officer Daniel Mudd, which were echoed by Anthony Lloyd, a securities analyst in the controller's office.[49] Kappler was given a hand in the internal investigation of all three disclosures and was soon found to be making false and misleading statements about the issues raised and their disposition, even to the audit committee of the board of directors.[50]

In violation of Sarbanes-Oxley, Kappler then failed to ask the audit committee to conduct an independent review of Barnes's allegations. When the committee did investigate the complaint, it revealed that a $6.5 million adjustment had been made without explanation or documentation.[51] This was just one of several unexplained adjustments about which Barnes expressed concern. The auditing staff, however, said they could not determine one way or the other whether the adjustment was appropriate and ended their investigation.[52] Clearly, the Barnes Investigation should have been expanded to determine the extent of undocumented adjustments. Instead the investigation was abruptly brought to a close because of the purported immateriality of the amount involved.

Kappler's legal department also conducted an investigation into Barnes's allegations but completed its investigation in just four days. Fannie Mae was eager to conclude this investigation because of an approaching deadline regarding its yearly financial statements. If these statements were delayed, Fannie Mae would have to explain why. Kappler signed a letter for this statement that included the following:

> To the best of my knowledge, there were no omissions or misstatements of reported amounts or information in my area that would have had a material impact on the financial statements. For purposes of this statement, matters were generally not considered material if they involved an aggregate absolute value of less than $5 million of net income or $3 billion of balance sheet impact. However, I also considered all the factors in determining whether a matter was material and matters involving less than this amount were material if they would otherwise be of interest to a reasonable investor.[53]

As Kappler was well aware, Barnes had uncovered a flaw greater than her $5 million floor of materiality. It is unknown whether she realized this inconsistency at the time, but she never withdrew her certification.

In October 2003 Barnes's counsel sent a letter threatening to file suit against Fannie Mae for violations of SOX whistleblower provisions, discrimination, and retaliation. This letter included an anonymous letter Barnes sent in September 2002, listing questionable financial decisions with a possible impact of hundreds of millions of dollars. In November 2003 Fannie Mae hurried to settle the matter with Barnes. As part of the settlement, Barnes quit and returned all documents he maintained during his employment, including those kept to support his allegations.[54]

Though the documents included enough information for Fannie Mae to conduct an internal investigation, Fannie Mae still did not become the vehicle for accountability. About one month after Barnes's first complaint, Michelle Skinner made similar complaints to Mudd. An investigation into her concerns validated most of them, yet Kappler once again determined that Fannie Mae's accounting practices were proper and distributed a response to Skinner's concerns to this effect.[55] Fannie Mae was ultimately fined $400 million by the Office of Federal Housing Enterprise Oversight and the SEC.[56]

Keep Them Ignorant

Like government-classified national security information, companies' information may be restricted to a "need-to-know" basis. Taken to the extreme, this policy can be misused to hide the truth and thereby keep employees too ignorant to threaten the corporation. There is often a link between this tactic and various others, such as isolation and internal reorganization. Employers may seek not only to punish the whistleblowers but also to make it impossible for them to access information and evidence. When information is power, ignorance is anti-bliss.

Fostering Ignorance at Diablo Canyon

Managers at the Diablo Canyon nuclear plant also used transfers to enforce ignorance. Charles Stokes was an engineer who blew the whistle on falsification of results in the plant's seismic design review after discovery that blueprints for the twin reactors were backward, compared with how the facilities were constructed. His disclosures convinced the Nuclear Regulatory Commission to order that all the engineering calculations be redone. Management made sure that it would not fail again with a curious tactic. It transferred out Stokes and other dissenters, substituting replacements unfamiliar with the job history and obedient enough not to ask questions about unrealistic assumptions that made key calculations impossible to fail.[57]

On occasion, employers isolate whistleblowers from the evidence through a longstanding labor-management technique: physically locking them out. More subtly, employers can keep whistleblowers from gathering evidence of wrongdoing by strangling them in red tape. Managers may pull out technicalities and obscure subsections of procedures to paralyze efforts at gathering and disclosing information. Similarly, revoking an employee's security clearance is both a tactic of retaliation and a technique for hiding damaging information from those workers who would otherwise have access to it.

Procter & Gamble Keeps Its Researchers in the Dark

Depriving scientists of access to their own research is a common tactic for enforcing ignorance in that profession. Consider the case of Dr. Aubrey Blumsohn, a researcher at Sheffield University in England. Sheffield entered into a contract with Cincinnati-based corporate giant Procter & Gamble (P&G) to study the response to therapy involving the company's osteoporosis drug, Actonel. P&G sought to conduct research that would cast Actonel in a good light in comparison with Merck's Fosamax, the industry leader.

A double-blind study was conducted, where neither researchers nor patients knew if a patient received Actonel or a placebo. To make sense of the data, Blumsohn needed the randomization codes to identify which patients got the drug and which got the placebo. P&G instead gave Blumsohn its own incomplete summary of the data. Blumsohn repeatedly asked the company for the full data set.[58] P&G persisted in its refusal, however, asserting that the data was proprietary. To make matters worse, not only did P&G withhold from Blumsohn the information necessary to make sense of his own research but the company also began publishing abstracts ghost-written in Blumsohn's name, asserting various research findings about Actonel.

When P&G finally permitted him to review the data on a computer screen in England, Blumsohn observed that 40 percent of the data were missing in some of the graphs—data that later proved critical to the way in which P&G had misrepresented the study's findings.[59] When Blumsohn finally got the data, it showed that the results did not favor Actonel.[60] Blumsohn is now preparing to publish a corrected version of the findings. Incidentally, other researchers, most notably the research dean of

Blumsohn's institution, have admitted misinforming a medical journal about access to data in a related P&G study and acknowledged that key reported findings in that study were also false.[61]

Prevent the Development of a Written Record

When policies or suspect activities are indefensible, wrongdoing can best be obscured by keeping the evidence oral. This can be enforced by employer fiat, peer pressure, overscheduling (to ensure that there is not time to construct a written record), purging files—both electronic and hard copy—and "off-the-record" backdoor meetings. Managers recognize that it is difficult for whistleblowers to build a case against them without a paper trail. Verbal orders and agreements diffuse accountability over time and inevitably pit the whistleblower's word against that of his superior.

Rewrite the Issues

One of the more insidious corporate strategies is to trivialize, grossly exaggerate, or otherwise distort the whistleblower's allegations—and then discredit the employee by rejecting the resulting "red herring." A whistleblower who challenges that superiors overlooked problems on the job may, for example, find the concerns exaggerated into allegations of willful misconduct—thus stretched beyond credibility. The corporation then finds that, although mistakes were made, the employer committed no intentional violations. The charges are dismissed, the whistleblower is discredited, and the targets of the investigation promptly issue public statements that they are pleased to be exonerated.

Rewriting the record can degenerate into outright censorship. This may involve deleting evidence or issues that are too hot to handle—and therefore vanish from the ensuing investigative report. In other cases, the findings are "massaged" through edits that ensure that they will not be interpreted as significant. An investigative report—even one diluted by rewritten allegations, censorship, and neutered recommendations— can still be damaging to wrongdoers. As a result, a related technique is to issue a press release declaring that the investigation had concluded that there was no wrongdoing—but then refuse to release the report containing the record of the investigation.

Scapegoat the Small Fry

Just as corporations may trivialize allegations of wrongdoing by rewriting them, they may lower the scandal volume by shielding institutional leadership from accountability. Instead they target those who do not have a support constituency or who were only following orders from higher-ups.

How a Company Shifted the Blame onto a Government Official

Even regulatory bureaucrats are not immune from corporate attempts to shift the blame. Dr. Victoria Hampshire was an adverse drug event coordinator for the Food and Drug Administration, which required her to monitor animal drug–related problems reported by consumers and veterinarians. In 2001 the FDA approved the drug ProHeart 6, used to prevent heartworm in dogs. As part her postmarket review of the drug, Dr. Hampshire found the incoming data disconcerting. Between 2003 and 2005, more than 5,500 adverse drug event reports came in related to ProHeart 6, including almost 500 canine deaths.[62] Dr. Hampshire first notified other FDA officials of her concerns in 2003, and after a few more attempts succeeded in getting their attention. The drug was recalled in 2004.[63]

Wyeth Pharmaceuticals, the manufacturer of ProHeart 6, requested a review of the FDA decision and launched its own purported investigation into Dr. Hampshire, which, according to her, amounted to little more than an unsuccessful effort to plant evidence of a conflict of interest. After Wyeth presented the "findings" of its investigation to the FDA, the agency removed Dr. Hampshire from the ProHeart 6 review and, without notice or explanation, initiated its own criminal probe of Dr. Hampshire.

The charges were unsubstantiated, however, and the US Public Health Service awarded Dr. Hampshire an achievement medal for her work in 2005 and named her Veterinarian of the Year for 2006. The US Senate Committee on Finance launched its own investigation into the appropriateness of the actions taken by the FDA and Wyeth. In a February 6, 2008, letter to the heads of the FDA and the Department of Health and Human Services, ranking committee member Charles Grassley concluded that "by mishandling an investigation and submitting material to law enforcement that was rife with error, FDA not only wasted resources, it created serious doubts about the integrity of its processes."[64]

These are but a few of the techniques employed by corporate bureaucracies to contain and eliminate dissent. Knowing the potential responses to your whistleblowing will help you prepare for the worst. Nonetheless, remember that corporate ingenuity always creates new and unanticipated innovations reflecting creativity's dark side.

CHAPTER 3

What to Know
Before You Blow

Now that you understand what you may be up against in blowing the whistle, it is important to be well informed and proceed as carefully and deliberately as possible. In this chapter we offer advice on the next steps, derived from the experiences of countless whistleblowers.

Be Clear about Your Objectives

The first thing to know is yourself. What is your objective in blowing the whistle—what do you want to accomplish? What must happen for you to be at peace with your decision so that you can move on? Objectives can be relatively modest, like being a good citizen who honestly cooperates with a government investigation or makes a record of opposition to a questionable activity or decision. It may be constructive, such as warning corporate leaders of unforeseen consequences so that they can take responsible action. Or you may be seeking accountability by alerting the authorities to a corrupt official. Your goal may be to make a tangible difference by changing how responsibly your company acts toward the public. This can mean preventing a toxic spill from polluting the environment, an unsafe toy from reaching the market, or spoiled meat from contaminating the food supply.

Only you can make the choice from among these many different objectives. Make it carefully. It will define what you are getting into and the associated risks. A low-risk, anonymous hotline disclosure will satisfy a whistleblower's goal of being a good corporate citizen by getting necessary evidence or leads about possible misconduct into the right hands within the company. But it is unlikely by itself to make a difference.

Seeking accountability may involve being a witness in government criminal investigations. Seeking to prevent or expose a public health threat could mean becoming a public figure and debating your employer in the media.

What are the bottom-line lessons here? The more ambitious your goals, the uglier the retaliation and the more you will need to follow through. Be sure of your objectives and then draw and enforce boundaries so that you do not end up taking risks beyond what is necessary to achieve them. Remember to stay centered and true to yourself so that you do not risk even more retaliation for someone else's agenda.

In contemplating your objectives, do not forget your professional life. Map out where your actions will leave you a year, two years, and five years down the road. Plan out the route you want to take and how you reasonably expect your career path to proceed. There is no doubt that you are about to embark on a new chapter in your professional journey.

Anonymity versus Going Public

One of the first issues to consider when deciding how to proceed with your whistleblowing is whether you want to go public with your concerns or remain an anonymous source. This decision depends on the quantity and quality of your evidence, your ability to camouflage your knowledge of key facts, the risks you are willing to take, your willingness to endure intense internal and public scrutiny, and the likelihood of learning more if you remain anonymous.

Going public boosts the risks of whistleblowing. Before making that decision, you will find it worthwhile to carefully examine your motivations. Some potential whistleblowers expect recognition and glory after they become public crusaders for truth; most who have done it will advise you that the pain overwhelms any ego boost. If your main motivation is revenge or public recognition, you are blowing the whistle for the wrong reason. No matter how truthful or significant your dissent, when you blow the whistle you assume a real risk of being discredited rather than vindicated. And any positive public recognition is likely to be fleeting compared with lifelong enemies and scars.

It is also foolish to blow the whistle as a moneymaking venture. Publicity about multimillion-dollar awards in damage suits and "bounty" statutes such as the False Claims Act may lead some employees to conclude that blowing the whistle is likely to result in a financial boon. Realistically, the odds of cashing in on whistleblowing are akin to winning the lottery. The odds of painful and protracted reprisal, on the other hand, are almost a sure bet.

A public whistleblower should not expect justice. The only thing that you can count on is the personal satisfaction that you did the right thing and that you lived your values. If you approach whistleblowing with the idea that this is all you will receive, any other benefits will be a welcome bonus. As one now-anonymous whistleblower counseled in reflecting on his experiences:

> Unearth the paperwork showing the specific illegal and criminal conduct, forward that paperwork to appropriate law enforcement officials, send a copy of that paperwork to appropriate media investigators, and run away as fast as you can to secure other employment. You must not seek personal attention or financial gain . . . only take pleasure in the fact that you've acted in a legal and ethical manner and that you've contacted appropriate law enforcement investigators to find the source of illegal and criminal activity and directed media investigators to broadcast this activity to the general public.

The alternative to going public—blowing the whistle anonymously—has its own strengths and limitations. The positive side of being an anonymous whistleblower is that you may protect your career; and if you can keep the spotlight on the issue rather than on you, there might be a greater chance that the problem will be addressed. You often are limited in what you can expose, however, because you must ensure that the documentation you leak is self-explanatory and can stand on its own merits without your active public explanation. You cannot disclose any evidence that could be traced back to you. Many investigative bodies do not consider anonymous allegations credible. You may choose to provide another source—a reporter or your representatives at a nonprofit organization—with a fuller explanation of your documentation and trust your source to convey it without revealing your identity.

One pitfall is that your allegations may be traced back to you. The substance of the charges can be your "signature" if your job position makes you the only person, or one of just a few, who could be aware of the problem you have exposed or have access to the relevant records.

Although there are ways to avoid having documents traced back, it is virtually impossible to *guarantee* that the information will not lead back to you.

Anonymity offers the potential advantage of allowing you to maintain your insider's position, learn of more misconduct, continue gathering evidence to prove it, and witness how the company attempts a cover-up once problems have been exposed. Anonymous whistleblowers on the inside can leak information and still be placed on the "damage control" team assigned to cover up the fraud. Once public whistleblowers are exposed, they automatically find themselves outside the bureaucratic loop and usually isolated from the evidence. After the flow of information dries up, it is hard to rebut the system's evasions, denials, or disingenuous "reforms."

Keep in mind that it takes a certain personality to leak information anonymously while remaining cool enough not to draw suspicion. If you do not have a good poker face and you cannot think of a safe strategy for leaking information without having it traced to you, consider either going public or not blowing the whistle at all. How will you respond to your bosses if you are questioned about leaking information? Think about whether you are one of only a handful of employees with access to or custody of the leaked documents or of the initial information in question. Furthermore, you must consider the likelihood of being called to testify under oath or to speak with law enforcement officials about the substance of the leaked information or possibly about the leak itself. Lying to law enforcement officials or under oath is never a viable or recommended option. It could land you in jail.

To be a successful anonymous whistleblower, you must have an effective outlet and strategy for leaking the documentation. Chapter 4 of this handbook covers potential whistleblower outlets and the best way to approach them.

Whichever path you choose—anonymity or public disclosure—be decisive. The worst approach you can take is to remain semi-anonymous. If you are suspected of the leak but are not publicly known, you will experience the worst of both worlds. The company will begin to retaliate while denying any knowledge that you are a whistleblower. This can deprive you of your legal rights against reprisal. Perhaps worst, you will not have the benefit of outside resources to blunt the attack.

Questions to Help You Decide

The following checklist may help you determine if you are ready to blow the whistle either anonymously or publicly.

If you plan to remain anonymous, ask yourself:

- Am I in a position to know that what I see as misconduct really is improper in the bigger picture, or could tunnel vision be leading me to a wrong conclusion?

- Will my disclosure effect change, or will an anonymous disclosure simply give the wrongdoers an opportunity to cover up the problem?

- Can I prove my allegations with documents that do not require my public explanation?

- Can these documents be traced back to me because only a small group of people have access to them or because my copies are uniquely marked? (Beware of trace-backs through fax identifications or e-mail trails.)

- How likely is it that I will be the focus of suspicion because of my previous efforts to raise concerns?

- Can I act nonchalantly when these documents are disclosed so as not to attract suspicion? Do I feel comfortable and justified in being evasive or not telling the complete truth if confronted by my boss about the disclosure?

- If discovered, do my spouse and I have the ability to support my family without my job or even outside my current profession?

- Is my family prepared for and does it accept the possibility of stress from uncertainty and the possibility of a negative public profile if I am discovered?

- If discovered, what liability, if any, will I incur?

- Do I want to maintain anonymity indefinitely, or am I willing to provide testimony if a matter comes to government prosecution or other official action?

If you plan to go public, ask yourself:

- Does my job allow enough perspective to ensure that my conclusions are not the mistaken product of tunnel vision even if my information is accurate?

- Are my family and I financially and mentally prepared for a protracted fight with my employers to prove my allegations and to try to retain my job?

- Am I mentally ready to have my fellow workers and perhaps some friends turn against me because of my disclosures?

- Will going public cut off the flow of evidence necessary to prove my charge or more effectively make a difference, and, if so, what are the benefits?

- Am I ready for personal attacks against my character and to have any past indiscretions made public?

- Do I have enough evidence to prove my charges without having to go back to my workplace? Even if I can prove my initial allegations, would I be more valuable if I didn't go public and kept my access to new information?

- Am I sure that my motivations are to expose the wrongdoing on behalf of the public interest and not just for revenge, a quest for financial gain, or public attention?

- Am I financially and mentally ready to risk my career?

- Am I ready to have the professional reputation of someone who attacked his employer?

Thirteen Essential Survival Tips

If you have soberly confronted the questions in the preceding section and are still determined to blow the whistle, consider the following baker's dozen survival strategies before moving ahead. Whistleblowing is a dangerous business, but our experience has shown that a few simple tips can make the difference between success and failure. Review them before you make any irreversible steps that could cost you down the line.

1. Consult your loved ones   One of the most serious risks of whistleblowing is family breakup or alienation because the entire family suffers from the resulting hardships. Before taking any irreversible steps, confide in your spouse, family, and close friends—the personal support group you will need to depend on in the coming days—about your plan to blow the whistle. It may be necessary to adjust your whistleblowing objectives to meet their needs, not just your own. If you choose to challenge the system without your family's knowledge or approval, you may be risking a personal loss greater than the professional consequences. There is irony when whistleblowers help expose institutional cover-ups but keep it secret from their loved ones. Many do so to protect loved ones from experiencing anxiety or pressure. But they have a right to know and understandably may resent finding that their world has been turned upside down behind their backs. If you do not enfranchise your loved ones, your heart proceeds at its own risk.

2. Test the waters for support among your workplace peers   Through strategic but casual questioning and discussions with co-workers, you can learn whether your objections are credible and shared among your colleagues and whether you see enough of the whole picture to be certain that your suspicions are well founded. Beware the snapshot syndrome: the picture of a smoking gun has a different meaning if the context is a target range as opposed to the space over a dead body. Your colleagues may be important witnesses in the future and may have additional information about the problem or even confirm that it is more widespread than you know. Some co-workers may share your concern and be willing to join you in making a disclosure. Solidarity can make a tremendous difference in preventing retaliation. As you survey your workplace, remember not to give yourself away as a potential whistleblower, troublemaker, or other threat to the organization.

Teambuilding and the WorldCom Scandal

Cynthia Cooper was vice president of internal audits at WorldCom. When a senior manager brought to her attention that her boss, Chief Financial Officer (CFO) Scott Sullivan, was usurping large reserve accounts for unauthorized purposes, she became suspicious.[1] She asked WorldCom's accounting firm, Arthur Andersen, to investigate, and they did nothing.[2] She then took her concerns to Sullivan, but he warned her off. She needed evidence and a venue to report findings.

Along with her internal audits team, she worked in secret to decipher the cooked books. They found billions of capital expenditures that had never been authorized. They found that operating costs were being misrepresented as capital expenditures to boost the company's profits.[3] She and her team continued their after-hours search through the accounting system and eventually gave the information to WorldCom's board of directors, which promptly fired Sullivan and went public with the information.[4] Cooper and her team went above and beyond their duties to uncover the largest corporate fraud in US history and in the process were the catalyst to save MCI from Enron's bankruptcy fate.

---

3. Before breaking ranks, consider working from within the system
Challenges to institutional operations often are not taken seriously unless you can prove that you provided the proper authorities a chance to correct the problem and that they responded with indifference or repression. It is crucial, however, that your attempt to work within the system does not sound the alarm and trigger a cover-up or reprisal. You are in dangerous, hostile territory wherever the institution or individual officials have reason to be defensive. This can be difficult to avoid, especially if you are challenging significant wrongdoing. Working from within the system can expose you to retaliation without the benefit of support from a public constituency—the most isolated, and therefore vulnerable, position for a whistleblower.

The best initial approach to challenging potential misconduct may be to raise an issue casually, in an informal setting or meeting, as a contribution to prevent or solve problems. Your approach should be thinking aloud in a nonconfrontational way or asking for help in answering difficult questions. If management receives your concerns constructively without getting defensive, there may be no need for a whistleblower. Remember, however, that this is treacherous territory. Some corporate bureaucrats inevitably will get defensive at the "wrong" questions being asked, especially when they are part of the wrongdoing. They may lead you along to see if you "know too much" and want to take you out for that reason alone. Know whom you are talking to before you expose the truth.

If informal conversations do not work and you are not at peace with letting the matter drop, you may have to make the point more directly in as low-key and nonadversarial a manner as possible. This is best done in writing. You must state clearly what is wrong and what your position is on the matter, without being pushy or demanding. You will be risking exposure—but it may be important for your credibility later. If there is no record of your prior objection to the wrongdoing, superiors may respond by making you the scapegoat for the very misconduct that you attempted to expose. This would divert your energies to proving that you were not responsible for the wrongdoing. Review your employment contract and employee handbook for relevant internal complaint or whistleblower options as institutional channels. Be careful, however. As will be discussed further in this chapter, while some offices may be effective, others are traps. In either case, these outlets are a part of the company, so information is likely to go straight back to an alleged wrongdoer to get the other side of the story.

In many situations it is unwise or impossible to complain internally, especially when you seek to expose serious misconduct. It is hard to decide how far to protest within the system—even if you plan to remain anonymous. The decision whether to inform anyone internally must be made carefully on a case-by-case basis. If you make a record of protest in the system and then the problem is exposed publicly, you may draw suspicion to yourself. If you do decide not to go public or are informally discovered, however, you may lose your legal rights. Qualifying for coverage under the free-speech laws depends on being able to prove that your boss knew you were a whistleblower. Your legal defense may depend on some institutional record of your dissent.

Further, by not creating any record of your attempt to work within the corporate system, those responsible for misconduct have a better chance to retain "plausible deniability." They can undermine your credibility and boost their own by insisting that they would have acted if you had told them instead of going behind their backs to third parties. As a rule, it is a prerequisite for credibility that you create some record of notice, even if you have to be anonymous within the company.

Whenever possible avoid adopting the identity of a whistleblower. Act as a loyal employee who is simply telling the truth from as passive a perspective as credible, such as when the authorities summon you as a witness to answer their questions. It is more difficult for an employer to retaliate against a subpoenaed witness who reluctantly testifies about a problem when compelled to do so by the authorities. Of course you may have to take steps to convince authorities to seek disclosures from you—a task that could prove difficult but with which others may be able to help. For more-detailed guidance on working within the system of government authorities, see chapter 4.

4. Always be on guard not to embellish your charges   This is essential to maintain your credibility. It is far better to understate than to overstate your case because your employer will leap at the slightest exaggeration and use it to discredit you. GAP usually advises whistleblowers to stick to direct personal knowledge in telling their stories and then give congressional or media investigators ways to uncover the rest of the facts—including any broader implications of wrongdoing—for themselves. The less you exaggerate or jump to premature conclusions, the more credible you will be to people who have to trust you before they will help you.

5. Seek legal and other expert advice early   Do not wait until you are in the "career emergency room" to seek assistance in evaluating a range of important considerations. Consult those who know this territory when assessing the proper audience for your disclosure, the potential retaliation you could suffer, the odds for a successful defense, the approximate costs of defending your rights, whether legal restrictions exist for any of the evidence you plan to disclose, and the prospects for making a difference by blowing the whistle. Nonprofit organizations such as the Government Accountability Project can directly—or via referral—offer you advice and help you plan legal, media, and political strategies. GAP also can help you connect with various networks of whistleblowers so that you can get a reality check from others who have been through the experience. If you consult a private attorney, keep in mind that the ultimate decisions about whether and how to blow the whistle are yours to make, not the lawyer's. You are the one who must live with the moral, ethical, and professional consequences of your decisions.

6. Stay on the offensive with a well-thought-out plan   Develop your own strategy so that your employer is reacting to you and not vice versa. Do not premise your actions on some passive expectation that the truth will prevail. Because you are typically taking on an institution whose resources dwarf yours, generally it is more effective to wage a guerrilla legal war rather than merely win a lawsuit. The outcome may well depend on whether you have a proactive strategy or are just reacting to your employer's moves. Be clear-headed about precisely what you expect to accomplish and how. Strategically time your release of information and your meetings with the press and public officials to keep the company on the defensive. Always try to anticipate the responses to your charges and map out effective counter moves. Once you have stopped setting the agenda and are reduced to guarding against attacks on your credibility, you are in trouble. This strategic approach is unavoidable if you want to even the odds. The deck is too stacked for a fair fight if you play the company's game, responding to its moves.

An effective, proactive strategy provides you with three decisive advantages over your corporate counterpart despite any gross imbalance in resources. First, properly wielding the truth, you can cause a corporate disinformation and smear campaign to backfire disastrously in the court of public opinion. Second, you can capitalize on the solidarity and the protection that comes from an informed and enraged public as well as any associated institutions victimized by the abuse of power. Third, you can enjoy a degree of mobility that is absent in large corporate bureaucracies with their convoluted, multilayered decision-making process. You can run rings around these cumbersome adversaries with a proactive, effective strategy for turning information into power.

7. Maintain good relations with administrative and support staff The magic word for whistleblower survival is *solidarity.* It starts on the job with others who may feel mistreated. Managers who respond to dissent with harassment and repression may routinely use the same approach with secretaries, clerks, interns, and junior staff. Try to stay on good terms with them, as they are in a good position to know of impending management actions or, later on, to testify as to management motives.

8. Network off the job: identify potential allies such as elected officials, journalists, or activists with a proven track record Earning solidarity with the rest of society through information match-making is GAP's cornerstone strategy. When we succeed, whistleblowers win. Here is how the dynamic works. If the employer's bureaucracy isolates the whistleblower, the public remains ignorant and the whistleblower is surrounded by adversaries in a hostile environment. If whistleblowers connect effectively with all the stakeholders whose trust has been betrayed, it is a whole different reality. Instead of the employer surrounding the whistleblower, an informed, aroused society surrounds the company. The balance of power reverses.

Typically, a whistleblower is encircled and isolated
by traditional bureaucratic institutional employers—
corporations, legislatures, and executive agencies—and
the disclosed information is filtered or suppressed.

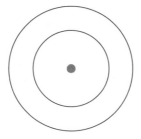

Beyond the bureaucracy are the sources of potential power outside
of the institutionalized power holders. These include the media,
public interest groups, and consumers—the commonweal.

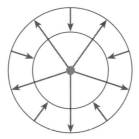

The challenge is to inform and educate the outer-circle constituencies
so that they exert power on the defined traditional power
holders—to build information spokes so that the commonweal
surrounds and holds accountable the bureaucracy.

There is strength in numbers, but with the exception of whistleblower support groups, do not contact any other outlet, the media, or Congress until you have categorically decided to blow the whistle and whether to do so anonymously or publicly. Then, particularly if you decide to go public, it is essential to develop a support constituency whose interests in your act of public service coincide with your own.

When the public remains ignorant because whistleblowers remain isolated, both are more likely to lose. Developing a support constituency not only breaks the isolation you may face but also exerts critical pressure on your employer. When wrongdoing is exposed, your employer will then be reacting to the media, Congress, the courts, and the public. Ensuring that your support constituency is informed and working with you will help you remain on the offensive. Do not underestimate your allies' advice and support. Seek out potential allies before your situation heats up and work through intermediaries whenever possible. Chapter 5 revisits this in greater depth.

9. Keep an ongoing, detailed, contemporaneous record as you go   There are three aspects to this tactic. The first is to thoroughly document the misconduct you wish to disclose to substantiate your whistleblower claims. The second is to thoroughly document your own job performance and reviews, as noted earlier. Third, even after you blow the whistle, it is essential to protect yourself by keeping a copious record of events as they unfold. Not keeping close, contemporaneous records of harassment and other activities is one of the biggest mistakes that whistleblowers make. The time you take now could be invaluable in any future investigation or court proceeding when you must have a grasp of the facts but your memory has faded. There are several good ways to document the wrongdoing, the cover-up, and any reprisals.

Keep a diary—a factual log of your work activities and the events at your workplace. Try to keep this diary as straightforward as possible, leaving out any speculations, personal opinions, or animosity you may have toward your fellow workers or your situation. The diary does not have to be kept on a daily basis, but it should become routine. It is important to write down events that relate to the wrongdoing you are planning to report or any harassment you are receiving. Record events that happen and the full names and titles of all people involved. Include the reactions of those with whom you communicate your concerns. Make sure that you date and initial each entry.

This process may seem like a burden, but it is an important investment in your professional survival. As legal evidence, the extra credibility from your straightforward written impressions at the time of disputed events may make the difference between winning and losing a future lawsuit. It is also an insurance policy against memory loss, and it helps piece together significant facts and patterns. Be aware, of course, that your employer will have access to the diary through the discovery process if there is a lawsuit.

Write memos of important events or conversations about which you want to make a permanent record. Place the date and title, "Memorandum for the Record" or "Memo to File," at the top and write down everything you can remember from the conversation or event. Then sign the memorandum, date it, and have someone witness it if possible. If you need to write a memorandum for the record about a conversation or event in which it will be your word against someone else's, the safest way to proceed is to write the memorandum, make a copy, seal it well in an envelope, and mail it to yourself. Once it is sent through the mail, it will be postmarked, and you should store it in your records without opening it. That way, when you need to prove your claim, the sealed envelope will show that you wrote the memorandum on the postmarked date. E-mails and faxes provide other ways to authenticate contemporary records, but, as discussed next, the electronic trail may be harder to camouflage or shield from surveillance. Do not use your office computer, fax machine, or postage equipment and materials for these purposes.

Watkins's Memos Preserve the Truth

When Sherron Watkins was looking for corporate assets to sell off during various mergers, she discovered that the company had been covering up significant losses. She was not certain what to do with this information, as she was not comfortable approaching either the CEO, Jeffrey Skilling, or her boss, CFO Andrew Fastow.[5] Once Skilling left the company, she took the opportunity to send an anonymous note to the new CEO, Ken Lay, hoping that some of her concerns would be brought to light.[6]

Her concerns went unaddressed at the next company meeting, so she cast her net wider. She ran her concerns past a friend—an employee at

Arthur Andersen, Enron's auditor—who tried to raise flags at that company. Finally, she wrote a second memo, faxing a copy to her mother as well as submitting it to the company.[7] Her efforts precluded Enron from successfully claiming plausible denial. Once everything fell apart, the company claimed that it was just a crisis of investor confidence that sparked unforeseen difficulties. Watkins's memoranda proved otherwise.[8]

Electronic mail systems in large organizations can be used to memorialize or confirm important conversations and, in some cases, press managers to put their thoughts into the electronic record. People tend to write more candidly in e-mails than in formal correspondence, yet an e-mail is just as much evidence as an old-fashioned letter. Moreover, electronic communications technology, including e-mail, chat, and text messaging, has the advantage of making messages easy to store and disseminate.

A note of caution: Do not put anything on your employer's e-mail system that you want to keep private. Do not allow your sole copy of a document to remain on the company's electronic system. In general, after you blow the whistle, your access to corporate records, including hard copies and computer files, will immediately be cut off, and the records that you left behind will be searched.

10. Secure all relevant records before drawing any suspicion to your concerns   Because corporate records may be destroyed or hidden, it is important to have a copy of all relevant documents before you expose the problem, even if you plan to remain anonymous. It is extremely difficult to blow the whistle successfully without credible documentation to back up your claims. Documentation generated by the organization itself is the best evidence to have. Secure your evidence early on because the flow of information will dry up once you are identified as a potential whistleblower. See "Gathering More Information" later in this chapter for more tips on gaining public access to information that may not be in your personnel file.

Many managers, when forced to do something that could later blow up in their faces, will keep a special file to demonstrate that they were only following orders. Those files can be valuable in trying to prove fraud or abuse of authority. If you cannot copy all documents, make copies of the best supporting ones and then make a list of the rest so that you can tell an investigator or court exactly which records to pursue.

Be forewarned, however, that when you make copies of the evidence incriminating them, some employers will accuse you of "stealing" their "property" or violating company policies or confidentiality agreements that you signed as a job prerequisite. Amazingly, prosecutors have agreed with the companies in some instances. Be sure that you do not take original records; you must limit your evidence to copies. Review your employment contract and employee handbook for confidentiality, along with nondisclosure provisions, regarding company records. Although most of these rules fantasize or overstate the power an employer has over evidence of its own illegality, the legal risk to you is very real. Even if you prevail, defeating an anti-whistleblower SLAPP (strategic lawsuit against public participation) suit can be draining, expensive, and scary. Be careful that any e-mails you maintain in a personal account do not include the company's proprietary information such as intellectual property and trade secrets, or privileged information such as communications between the company and its attorneys.

It can be foolhardy not to work closely with a seasoned lawyer on the lawful techniques for securing evidence. To start with, compared with working with government investigators, the risks are much higher if you take company records off-site for your retaliation lawsuit. In either context, you are most likely to be held liable for taking information that is "privileged" with communications between your employer and its attorneys or which concerns sensitive property such as patents or trade secrets. If you take classified information, the government may seek your criminal prosecution. On the other hand, your employer is much less likely to hound you for theft when you publicly disclosed information that the company had a legal duty to report to shareholders about high-risk activity.

If you are unable to disclose records legally because they contain proprietary information or other intellectual property, make a list of all the documents for your attorney to seek in litigation discovery or for congressional or law enforcement investigators to subpoena for their investigations. You can discreetly "misfile" in a different folder those records that are likely to be destroyed by the company, or rename and hide computer files within the company's network. You can then act as the mapmaker or navigator to guide law enforcement raids.

A tactic that has worked for GAP when whistleblowers want to reveal incriminating records is arranging for congressional or other government investigators to request supporting evidence for an investigation. The request should be memorialized in writing. If the employer subsequently demands to know what the employee took, we can then explain to the employer that the whistleblower cooperated with the investigation so as not to be guilty of obstructing justice. For the same reasons, we tell the company that we are unable to disclose what evidence the government has or anything else about the nature of the cooperation. Instead the company must seek the records and any further information from the relevant congressional committee or law enforcement agency.

This is hardly foolproof, however, as whistleblowers disclosing evidence to government investigators have still been attacked in court for "theft" of any information they learned on the job, even if the information is only in their minds and not in a document. Corporate proprietary claims to employees' minds as well as company records illustrate the ferocity you risk in proving your charges. In one recent case, the attorneys were held liable for receiving privileged company records.[9] Taping a conversation is another illustration. In 11 jurisdictions it is a crime to record without the other party's knowledge.[10] Consult a lawyer to be sure that you are on the right side of the law.

There *are* powerful legal doctrines on your side when you responsibly secure your evidence, especially if you are blowing the whistle on criminal conduct. As explained in chapter 6, newer whistleblower statutes like SOX explicitly override corporate gag orders to solidify legal disclosure rights. In court a cornerstone principle is that "public policy favors the exposure of crime, and the cooperation of citizens possessing knowledge thereof is essential to effective implementation of that policy."[11] This principle has even been extended to confidentiality agreements that otherwise would maintain secrecy of threats to public policy. This is the case especially if you are disclosing evidence of fraud against the government.[12] In those circumstances, protection may extend to your own investigative work within the company. An employee is protected while investigating what the employee reasonably believes to be fraudulent activity.[13]

The problem is that you cannot be sure. Courts often engage in after-the-fact judgments whether your behavior was reasonable, the damages to the employer, and "some form of balancing test to determine whether the employee's unauthorized dissemination of the documents qualified as protected activity."[14] It covers such criteria as whether you were challenging illegal conduct and whether you "innocently" acquired it while carrying out your job duties or just went snooping.[15] All of those may be factors beyond your control when you must make your decision on how to prove your charges.

These issues highlight the unavoidable dilemma you face when deciding whether to blow the whistle. If you do not have enough documentation or witness testimony, you may be risking retaliation for nothing. Under those circumstances you probably do not have a realistic chance of making a difference. On the other hand, there are severe, inherent risks in seeking to obtain enough evidence to be taken seriously. More than the evidence itself, how you gather it could determine your ultimate success. *If you are going to do it, do it right and be aware of the risks.*

In short, there are a variety of tactics that can work and numerous scenarios where copying evidence may be safe. But the territory is saturated with legal land mines. Advance preparation and careful planning are prerequisites for your professional survival. Again, the advice of a seasoned attorney can be invaluable.

Treating Evidence of Wrongdoing as "Property"

In early 2004 Stephen Heller was working as a temp for the Jones Day law firm in California. While there he came across information relating to Diebold Election Systems, a voting machine manufacturer and Jones Day client. The documents demonstrated that Diebold was knowingly violating California law by selling electronic voting machines that were uncertified by the state. Heller printed copies of all the relevant documents he could find—107 memos, charts, action plans, and e-mails—and handed them over to the elections watchdog group Black Box Voting, who then passed them on to then–California Secretary of State Kevin Shelley.[16] Shelley withdrew his approval of Diebold's flagship touch-screen voting systems, calling the company's actions both "fraudulent" and "despicable."[17] Two years would pass before Diebold would be able to sell its electronic voting systems in the state.[18]

Heller, meanwhile, faced unexpected consequences for blowing the whistle. In early 2006 the Los Angeles district attorney charged him with three counts of felony access to computer data, commercial burglary, and receiving stolen property. In November, Heller struck a plea bargain, stating, "My wife and I are very happy it is over. The deal will protect me and my wife and our assets (we have no assets left, other than our house, but whatever we are able to accumulate in the future cannot be taken away from us in civil court). My attorneys and I think this is the best deal I could get based on the circumstances."[19]

---

11. Engage in whistleblowing Initiatives on your own time and with your own resources, not your employer's   Employees can be fired for conducting "personal business" on company time using company equipment. Do not engage in whistleblowing activities during office hours or use office equipment unless you have specific approval, such as through a collective bargaining agreement. Avoid using a fax machine and other corporate resources. Know that your workplace computer terminal belongs to the corporation and that any e-mail or memo on it will be in the management's hands soon after you blow the whistle. Also be extremely cautious about using the office phone for "unauthorized" conversations, especially with the media. Make or take those calls on your own cell phone during breaks.

12. Check for skeletons in your closet   Be prepared to live with the "whole record" of your life. Any personal vulnerability or peccadillo you possess can, and most likely will, be used against you by your employer. You should always anticipate a smear campaign that aims to dig up your deeply buried skeletons, so be prepared. We all have them. Like candidates in an election campaign or nominees for political appointments, whistleblowers must develop thick skins. One practical step is to make a copy of the complete contents of your personnel file as insurance that new but back-dated "dirt" cannot later be slipped in. If there is something that is known about your past that you simply cannot stomach reading on the front page of a newspaper, reconsider blowing the whistle or at least proceed anonymously.

13. Do not reveal your cynicism when working with the authorities
With good reason, you may reflexively feel that any authorities assigned
to investigate your charges must be incompetent, corrupt, or involved in
covering up the wrongdoing. If you feel this way, it may be a fatal mistake
to wear your suspicions on your sleeve. For any investigator or auditor
who was not defensive to start with, your attitude may poison the well
and intensify preexisting biases against you. This is a key partnership with
whoever is on the front lines of enforcing rules. It helps to at least maintain the demeanor of presuming good faith. Further, it is only fair to give
an investigator the presumption of innocence until proven guilty. Some
of GAP's most significant government whistleblower clients have been
investigators who backed whistleblowers and refused to accept cover-ups
of their reports. Of course it would be foolhardy to extend blind trust
and spill your guts to those who may be agents of the wrongdoers, but at
least give third-party fact finders a chance to prove themselves by acting
appropriately on "test" evidence.

The rights and the responsibilities in your partnerships are a domi-
nant theme in upcoming sections. The tip here is to not sabotage what
may be your highest-stakes relationship by starting off on the wrong foot.

Maintaining Your Sanity

The foundation for these survival tips is a healthy attitude. To transcend
the stress, it helps to be fully aware of and accept what you are getting
into. This is a time to draw on and learn the extent of your inner strength.
You will need it. The constant, negative pressure that whistleblowers face
can color your judgment and make you paranoid about every event.
Paranoia works in the company's favor, helping it paint you as an unreasonable, unstable person whose charges should not be taken seriously. To
succeed you must be able to rise above this trap. The following suggestions elaborate on this idea.

Death of a Whistleblower

Blowing the whistle can bring with it tremendous emotional and psy-
chological despair. According to public reports, for Francis "Nick" Leonard
this was too much to bear. Leonard, a store clerk at a Florida Home Depot,

had come to loggerheads with his managers over inventory accounting issues—specifically "return to vendor" fraud, wherein a retailer falsely bills its supplier for lost, stolen, or damaged goods. Leonard was met with pressure to continue improperly billing vendors, reminded that in the current economic straits "anyone could lose their position with Home Depot at any time." Leonard quit his job in February 2009 and was found a month later hanging from an electric tower with a suicide message left for his attorney urging him to "pursue Home Depot for what had been done, and to take care of his relatives."[20]

Appreciate your values and keep your sense of humor It is better to stay calm—and even to laugh—than it is to seethe with anger when managers make a mockery of fairness or inflate their self-importance. It can be liberating to know that you have assumed responsibility for making your own decisions based on *your* values rather than accepting the company's line unquestioningly. While you need to respect the very real risks you are taking, laughing at fear is a good way to keep it in perspective and not be controlled by it. Along with the pain and the fear, there is real satisfaction inherent in taking control of your life. Take time to reflect on and enjoy the self-respect that comes from knowing that you are living your values. For many whistleblowers it's about being able to look in the mirror.

Watch your expectations of others You can reduce your own isolation by not being judgmental and by not expecting everyone else who is moral to blow the whistle. Even if you are doing the right thing and your concerns are accurate, it is enough to risk your own neck. Do not expect others to do the same. Your colleagues may sincerely hold differing opinions or may not be positioned to risk their only source of economic support for their families. They will resent you if you morally condemn them for failing to make the same difficult choice as you have—and this resentment will add to your isolation.

Keep your perspective Resist becoming obsessed in your whistleblowing cause. A measure of detachment is beneficial to your well-being and your effectiveness. It helps to have another job or a hobby that takes a good portion of your time so that your whistleblowing activity does not completely dominate your life. Letting it consume you can destroy you—and your credibility—over time. Similarly, although career reprisals may reduce your ability to support your family financially, only you can determine whether your whistleblowing will reduce or enhance your ability to provide your family with emotional support and guidance. You may have a lot more time and energy to give them. Through all these approaches, you can help turn the crisis of retaliation into a unique opportunity for personal growth.

Anticipate retaliation and surveillance   No matter how healthy your attitude, constructive your approach, or complete your ultimate vindication, facing some form of harassment is the rule rather than the exception for whistleblowers. Academic research confirms the pattern. In a study by Karen and Donald Soeken, 232 out of 233 whistleblowers reported suffering retaliation.[21] Similarly, 95 percent of whistleblowers in a study by Professors Philip Jos, Mark Tompkins, and Steven Hays said they faced reprisals.[22] Rothschild and Miethe's survey found that 69 percent of whistleblowers lost their jobs or were forced to retire as a result.[23] These results are not unique to the United States: a study of whistleblowers in Queensland, Australia, found that 71 and 94 percent reported official and unofficial reprisals, respectively.[24] Expect and be prepared for the worst even while you hope for the best.

It is particularly disconcerting to find yourself the object of surveillance by government, industry, or private investigators, but it comes with the territory. This experience can be very frightening and can exacerbate your existing anxieties. Although it is important to document any suspected surveillance through a diary or memorandum for the record, it is just as important not to let suspicious activity get to you. If you know someone is watching you, that person probably wants you to know. Often the purpose of surveillance is to intimidate you and push you into making a strategic mistake. For example, it benefits your detractors for you to sound paranoid to the general public by saying that your phone is tapped without having proof.

It is difficult to prove that you are being watched or that your phone is being tapped, so the best way to deal with this concern is to be careful about information you provide over unsecured channels like the phone and most e-mail services—without allowing yourself to be functionally gagged from communicating. One tactic that works is for both parties to communicate sensitive information solely through pay-as-you-go cell phones that can be rented anonymously from convenience stores. In fact, telephone communications or e-mail can serve to convey disinformation to listeners or to issue subtle, strategic warnings. Avoid inadvertently leaving sensitive information where it can easily be found—in office recycling or garbage, unsecured computer files, or the mail sent to your work. Employers have been known to go through whistleblowers' desks, confiscate computer files, and even open personal mail they receive at the office. If you operate from the premise that you may be watched and are appropriately careful, the surveillance efforts will be in vain. If you are cool enough to be strategic, the surveillance may backfire.

Charles Hamel and the Trans Alaska Pipeline Whistleblowers

Charles Hamel worked as an independent tanker and oil broker on the North Slope of Alaska, where he discovered environmental, health, and safety violations by Alyeska Pipeline and its consortium of oil company owners: ARCO, British Petroleum (BP), Exxon, Mobil, Unocal, Phillips, and Amerada Hess. In the early 1980s, Hamel began anonymously disclosing information about the companies' wrongdoings. Before long, sympathetic Alyeska employees who were fearful of retaliation worked through Hamel to bring more incriminating evidence to the attention of state and federal regulators, Congress, and the media without jeopardizing their careers. Hamel's network of sources provided him with information about Clean Water Act violations by Exxon and BP that resulted in citations by the Environmental Protection Agency. Through Hamel, who appeared frequently in the press and before Congress, Alyeska employees anonymously revealed air pollution violations at the Valdez terminal, a faulty system for detecting leaks in the Trans Alaska Pipeline, severe corrosion in the pipeline, the lack of adequate regulatory oversight, and oil discoveries held secret by the industry—costing the consortium millions in fines and environmental mitigation efforts.[25]

In 1990 Alyeska hired the Wackenhut security agency to undermine Hamel's successful whistleblower network. Wackenhut established an environmental front group, named Ecolit, to uncover Hamel's sources under the pretext of assisting him in litigation against the industry. Wackenhut monitored Hamel's home, rummaged through his trash, used sophisticated eavesdropping technology, obtained his financial records and personal family information, and even hired women to tempt him into revealing his sources. Ironically, Wackenhut's undercover surveillance operation disgusted some of its own employees, and disaffected agents secretly blew the whistle to Hamel, supplying him with enough information to bolster a lawsuit against Alyeska, Wackenhut, and Exxon for invasion of privacy.[26] During the 1993 US District Court proceedings, Federal Judge Stanley Sporkin described the spy operation as "horrendous" and "reminiscent of Nazi Germany." He declared that "no one should be subjected to the kind of treatment the Hamels were."[27] In December 1993 the Alyeska consortium settled with Hamel for an undisclosed amount that is reported to be in the millions.

Hamel has not ceased his work as a watchdog of the industry and an advocate for its workers. In a 2004 letter to the BP board of directors, he conveyed workers' concerns about pipeline corrosion that posed serious occupational safety, human health, and environmental risks in Prudhoe Bay, North America's largest oilfield.[28] BP ignored his warnings, so Hamel turned over the information to the EPA, prompting a criminal investigation. His evidence of faulty safety valves also triggered an investigation by the Department of Transportation. In August 2006 BP was forced to close part of the oilfield after discovering what it described as "unexpectedly severe corrosion" of the oil pipeline.[29] Subsequently, the price of oil rose $2 per barrel and BP stock fell.[30]

As remarked by US Representative John Dingell (D-MI), who has long been engaged with Alaskan oil issues, "Charles Hamel has provided important leads to Congress over the years, and he has served as a trusted outlet for many concerned workers."[31] Unfortunately for the company, our country, and the environment, BP did not learn its lesson. If there had been a Charles Hamel before the Gulf oil spill, that tragedy may have been averted.

Develop a personal support network   The outcome of your whistleblowing experience may well turn on a factor even more significant than the strength of your evidence, quality of your legal team, shrewdness of your strategy, or power of your allies: how you handle the pressure. Purely in terms of effectiveness, you always will be selling your own credibility to ongoing and prospective witnesses, partners, and the public. Your ability to be at your best is essential, but the strain and the pressure make it more likely that you'll be at your worst. And even if you hold up as a witness or public figure, the stress may have a severe impact on your behavior toward loved ones. This is a high-stakes test of the limits of your personal strength.

That means it is a real mistake to limit your support network to a legal team. Maybe extra support from family and friends will be enough. Maybe sharing experiences with other whistleblowers will help keep things in perspective. Professional therapy to cope with the additional stress may be an invaluable investment in yourself. Both GAP and the False Claims Act whistleblower support group, Taxpayers Against Fraud, have organized mentoring programs in which veteran whistleblowers volunteer support for those who need it.

Relationships, Relationships, Relationships!

Whistleblowing is something you should not do alone. Whether it is getting evidence, distributing it, acting on it, coping with life during high-stress periods, or getting a fresh start, you will need partners on whom you can rely. Even if you find them, you will not get their support unless they believe they can rely on you as well. Whether it involves a supportive family, witnesses with corroborating evidence, congressional staff, government investigators, the media, or the constituencies affected by the misconduct you challenge, establishing the right partnerships and building a strong relationship with them will be the most important factor over which you have control in determining your success or failure.

Building Partnerships

To varying degrees every one of these partnerships needs to be an intimate relationship in terms of openness, honesty, and trust. Relationships between you and your allies involve serious rights *and* responsibilities—it's a two way street. Responsibilities arise because, as a whistleblower, your relentless goal is for people to believe you and to believe in you. Without credibility you are doomed. The following are some of the lessons we have learned as to what you should expect and demand from any relationship throughout the whistleblowing cycle. The most common context for the following tips is partnerships with government investigators or nongovernmental organizations (NGOs).

Do no harm This is a first commandment you should both honor and demand. Your role is to tell the truth, not to use others or make judgments that the end justifies the means. A fundamental application of this principle is that each partner must respect the other's right to make informed choices about which risks to take and when.

Define your relationships through earned trust As a rule these are high-stakes, intimate relationships. You must open up and be vulnerable for them to work best. Yet as a whistleblower you will have to deal with many unscrupulous individuals. Before you confide in someone, they must earn your trust. This is no setting for blind faith. Test your partners as a prerequisite to risking trust.

First, get to know each other. At your introductory meeting, learn more about whom you are working with in terms of the background, responsibilities, attitudes, and values brought into the partnership and, most significantly, how your objectives overlap. Respect rather than judge or try to change those objectives, which may vary from person to person. For example, the mission of a government investigator and an internal corporate investigator will quite possibly be at odds—the former to learn what the evidence is and the latter to learn what evidence the government has obtained about a corporate client.

You also are entitled respectfully to seek the same information you would in a job interview. You have the right to ask, and to know, the potential partner's qualifications, experience, and background in other cases. Has a government investigator brought significant corporate wrongdoers to justice? Have a congressional committee's hearings had an impact? What is a reporter's track record in getting stories published in an outlet with enough prominence to get noticed? It is not out of line to ask for references to vouch for the person's track record. The stakes may be your professional survival, far higher than a mere job interview.

Air all concerns and establish the ground rules up front before divulging any evidence. The process of earning trust then proceeds with frank but constructive dialogue about each other's rights and responsibilities. Without being confrontational, share your fears and ask for the other's take on disparaging information or a bad reputation. Pin down clear expectations that you can each honor as well as commitments on any items that matter to you or your family. If others are impatient or do not seem to respect your issues, that is a timely alarm bell that they are only committed to using you. It may be unwise to trust them with your evidence.

Once trust is earned, remain vigilant. You and your partner must sustain the trust earned initially. It may be a fatal mistake to continue trusting a partner after some major development like a family medical disaster that makes a co-worker more susceptible to company demands or after mounting political pressure is brought to bear on a government investigator. It may just be that your first impression of your partner was based on transient efforts to earn your confidence. Has your partner earned more or less trust over time? Evaluating your relationships for trustworthiness is an ongoing commitment you should make to yourself.

Stay centered and in control of what risks to take   No matter how much you come to like, respect, and admire third-party partners, remember that blowing the whistle was *your* choice, not theirs. In most contexts you are the one who will live with the consequences of harassment, not them. Whether they are altruistic or have a hidden agenda, do not let others beyond those depending on you, such as your family or supporting witnesses you recruited, choose which risks you will take to further which objectives.

Remember that commitments are sacred   Once you are communicating openly, you need to learn whether you can count on your partners to deliver on their commitments. They must be both responsible and reliable, and so must you. It is not always necessary to create tests for prospective partners. Naturally, there will be many preliminary commitments to get your working relationship off the ground. Pay attention to whether and how they deliver on what is promised, before a broken promise means disaster.

Come clear on issues of confidentiality   You must be able to count on any third party to respect your request for confidentiality without justification. This is a ground rule to clear up before you volunteer anything. Clearly establish what information you are willing to have your partner share and with whom. It can be very tempting for a public interest group, for example, to pass your information along to the media or to use it as a teaser in such a manner as to give you away. Make sure there is no gray area surrounding your request for confidentiality.

Here are four cornerstone questions to ask anyone who promises confidentiality:

- First, *how broad is the commitment?* Does it only mean not disclosing your name, or does it also cover any identifying information? Often certain facts in the public record can betray your identity because you were the only one who knew them.

- Second, before it is released, *will you have a chance to review relevant portions of documents using your information so that you can ensure that your name and all identifiers are removed?* Only you know enough to judge whether publishing particular information would expose you.

- Third, *are there exceptions, such as an imminent crime or public safety threat, or limits, such as how long an authorized commitment extends, to the guarantee of confidentiality?* For example, a government investigator's promise may be valid for the investigation but not extend to an actual trial when your testimony is indispensable.

- Finally, *will there be reasonable advance warning if, because of exception or other reason, your identity must be revealed?* Few scenarios involve more unnecessary risk than going to work without knowing your anonymity has ended.

Remember that punctuality is a necessity, not a courtesy   In whistleblowing, time can be of the essence. Delays can leave you exposed and vulnerable to unnecessary risks. Disclosure can fail to keep pace with or take advantage of fleeting opportunities. Like broader commitments, this is a process where your partners show their hands from the first scheduled meeting. Closely monitor how they handle early administrative chores. It may be that minor tardiness or delays are predictable and can be compensated for with planning. But learn whom you are working with before there are consequences.

Know what protection you can count on   The bottom line of relationships is whether it is safe or dangerous to work with any potential partner.

You will need to make this evaluation in an endless series of partnerships until closure. Sometimes it is to assess factors like good faith and honesty. But equally important is whether a potential partner is willing and able to protect you. For example, choosing to go public through a frustrated, powerless citizen organization may be signing your professional death warrant. By contrast, solidarity from a coalition whose combined membership numbers in the tens of millions can be more valuable than conventional legal rights. So can a committed congressional champion. For example, Senator Charles Grassley (R-IA) has saved more government whistleblowers than have won official legal rulings under the Whistleblower Protection Act. Similarly, an aggressive phone query from *60 Minutes* can be more effective at nipping retaliation than 100 hours from a top lawyer billing $500 per hour.

One of the most common scenarios involves government investigators. A committed, respected investigator will know how to protect you by passing along advance warnings and not making mistakes or exposing you to unnecessary risks. A committed investigator can prevent retaliation by alerting an employer that witness harassment will lead to further liability for witness tampering or obstruction of justice. Discuss these issues with the investigator before assisting with the investigation. Also discuss whether the investigator can deliver on these commitments or needs further approvals to make them meaningful. Investigators can be overruled by their superiors. Ask for examples of incidences when the investigator and the agency effectively shielded a whistleblower from harassment.

Remember, protection of others is also your responsibility vis-à-vis co-workers or other witnesses who may face retaliation for disclosing supportive evidence or otherwise assisting you. Like you do with a reporter, legislator, or government investigator, you should commit to protect them and shield them from risks they assumed to help you.

Listen with your ears wide open   This is a two-way street. The relationship is doomed if you are not heard. It is reckless to trust anyone in a high-risk partnership who is not paying attention or who hears something different from what you said. The best investigator or reporter will take the initiative in active listening, repeating back what you said to make sure they heard you right on issues that cannot afford mistakes.

If they do not because of time pressures or personal style, politely test them a few times so you know they "get it" and "get it right," down to the essential specifics.

You also should be listening very carefully to what the third party says to you. You have to be grounded in reality, not just projecting or filling in the blanks with what you want to hear. Listen critically and ask questions whenever there is ambiguity surrounding something that matters, such as that person's agenda, the schedule for next steps, or the approval process for action. Pin matters down with active listening from your end.

Similarly, do not hesitate to ask questions to clarify professional jargon. Expect others to require such translations from you as well. Unless you are professional peers, a serious dialogue means those terms will have to be demystified or translated. Jargon in bureaucratese or legalese may have far different meanings than in everyday conversation. The professional terms in your trade can be a dialect that is impenetrable to those outside the profession.

From another angle, listen carefully to hear what the third party did not necessarily mean to tell you. Almost all of us reveal more than we intend to. The corollary is to pay attention to what the other party did *not* say. If there is any cat-and-mouse in the dialogue, where the other party does not want to go, that may be the best tip for where you *do* want to go.

Respect time burdens   One of the biggest costs of whistleblowing is your time and energy, and this does not cease once you have successfully blown the whistle. Interested third parties can drown you in an endless stream of follow-up activities, from public speaking to informal consultations. Remember that you already have done your share or more by sticking your neck out. Unless you choose a more active role, require that third parties respect you and your family's balance of priorities. Set boundaries that demand your time only when your contribution could make a difference for your own ongoing objectives.

Of course this responsibility applies to you as well. Do not expect or demand that others drop their prior commitments to work on your crusade. Overburdened congressional staffers, government investigators, or corporate compliance officers may not be thrilled to see you if they view your disclosure as "a lot more work." Indeed there is more resistance from government, legislative, and media institutions to following through on whistleblower charges because they constitute a tremendous burden in time and effort compared with cover-ups or ideological hostility. If you offer to contribute your own efforts toward transforming a draining, intimidating burden into something realistic, you can foster the recep tive attitude for a third party to really pay attention.

Minimizing the burden you pose for others generally means doing your homework in advance, such as screening your information and summarizing it in a user-friendly format. This is where teaming up with those who have prior working relationships in the field may be invaluable. A lawyer or whistleblower support group may be able to teach you which offices are open-minded and how best to package new information into fact sheets and introductory briefing packets customized for your audience.

Brainstorm and create synergy   Once you have a trusted partner, put your heads together to crack the mystery of what is still unknown. As a rule your own vision will be limited by some blind spot or you may miss the forest for the trees. Whistleblowing is an intense intellectual challenge and often like cracking a mystery. The synergy may well make a difference.

Pin down the durability of your current partner's commitments   The process of making a difference can require a marathon commitment. Determine whether a partner is in it for the long haul or at least for how long the relationship can be expected to last. For example, a media partnership may be intimate when breaking the story, but the reporter may be unable to sustain a meaningful commitment afterward. Will a public interest group be there for you to fight retaliation after it has used your evidence? Depending on your goals as a whistleblower, you may want to recruit partners who will be there for new developments and follow through on the work that a disclosure will spark, or you might choose to replace older partners whose commitments are fading or outdated due to evolving circumstances.

Contribute as an expert, not just a critic   Beyond your immediate disclosure, you are uniquely positioned to call the bluffs on any subsequent

cover-up. You may be able to point out the fallacies of a technical explanation, explain how it is inapplicable, or find evidence disproving false
statements. It is worth volunteering yourself for this role. You should
beware if a reporter or government investigator does not take advantage
of your offer, although it may be due to unavoidable time or logistical
constraints. A journalist may not be drawing conclusions, just reporting
both sides. But taking a company's defense at face value can be a symp-
tom of bad faith and a preview of coverage that will only parrot the corporation's denials.

Your value as a tutor may rival your value as a witness. You can help
congressional or other government investigators, the media, and public
interest groups translate murky data or confusing records that you are
used to working with. Your partners may need you to help navigate a
company's organizational structure. You may be the best equipped to figure out the right questions and to whom they should be posed. Again, it
may be a red flag if a partner wastes this potential contribution.

Put a premium on networking   This is a weathervane for whether a partner is willing and able to help in your most important survival objective—overcoming isolation. A government investigator should be press-
ing you for corroborating witnesses. To the extent you request and agree
to it, an NGO should be actively matchmaking you with media and other
citizen organizations. If you are anonymous or your goal is merely to be a
good citizen reporting evidence to the right authorities, networking may
not be relevant. But if you have gone public, a network distributing your
disclosure to all who should benefit from your knowledge is an essential
lifeline both for impact and professional survival.

Tend the professional relationship like you would a personal one   A
basic goal for any relationship is maximizing a positive attitude, keeping
your partner happy with you. This means respecting the rules of civility;
viewing your partner as a person rather than an object; and being supportive, even if that only means lending an empathetic ear. If you cannot
meet a commitment, respect your partner by providing a fair warning, an
explanation, and a possible solution. This is not just decent behavior. It
will have an impact on the outcome. Your partners really will do a better
job if they like you.

Your success in whistleblowing will depend far more on relationships—the all-important human factor—than on formal legal rights or resources. Relationships are equally significant as the quality of your evidence and the efficacy of your strategy in determining the outcome of your efforts.

Gathering More Information

How much information you know and can prove is a critical factor in assessing the strength of your case, developing a well-thought-out plan, and making a difference. In the conflict with a bureaucracy abusing its power, information is your arsenal. Are your personal experiences the only evidence of wrongdoing and illegal retaliation? Do you also have documentation or other witnesses to corroborate or supplement your story? An ample collection of incriminating documents may already be in your personal possession and your colleagues may be eager to back you up, but you will likely need to go hunting for more evidence. There are a number of resources available to get more information about your company as well as about additional documents and potential witnesses.

Corporate Filings

The financial information of publicly traded corporations is easiest to gather because these companies are legally required to make it available for public scrutiny. Compliance with the Securities Act of 1933 and the Securities Exchange Act of 1934 is the predicate upon which publicly traded corporations are granted access to public capital markets. Generally speaking, securities laws seek to protect investors through detailed reporting and disclosure requirements. In addition to the periodic reporting mandates of securities law, corporations must make nonperiodic disclosures of materially important events in a timely fashion.

All publicly traded companies must file disclosures of certain information with the US Securities and Exchange Commission, which then makes the filings accessible to the public. This is done through a service called EDGAR—the Electronic Data Gathering, Analysis, and Retrieval system—used by the SEC to collect and display corporate filing information. Virtually all corporate filing documents since May 1996 are available through EDGAR.[32] Unfortunately, this information is not always presented in a way that is comprehensible to the average person. In particular, EDGAR employs a list of forms whose purpose may be unclear. Here are descriptions of some of the forms that may be useful. For more-detailed information, consult the Internet links in Tool D of the Whistleblower Toolkit.

10-K   The first and most important document is Form 10-K, which is the annual summary of business activities. Shareholder reports are generated from the information contained in the 10-K. It is required to be accurate and is audited. It contains thorough operating statistics, financial information, information about legal proceedings, and management compensation. It has to be filed within 90 days of the end of the company's fiscal year for nonaccelerated filers and 75 days for companies that are designated accelerated or large accelerated filers based on size and history.[33] The 10-K should be the primary document you turn to when gathering financial information about a company.

10-Q   This is a quarterly equivalent of the 10-K. Unlike the 10-K, however, it is not audited. For nonaccelerated filers, it has to be filed within 45 days of the end of the quarter, and 40 days for accelerated and large accelerated filers—except for the fourth quarter, when the 10-K fills the role of the 10-Q.[34]

8-K   On this form companies are supposed to report and explain significant events that have an impact on the company's financial situation. Matters such as executive compensation changes, acquisitions, bankruptcy, and mergers, among other events, are reported in this document. These forms must be filed within four days of the change, and the information in them is for release to the public.[35] This is not as useful for general research but can be good for getting information about specific events in the company. Along with relevant 10-Ks, these should be thoroughly reviewed for any full or partial disclosures relevant to your whistleblowing disclosure. Whatever you find in this research cannot be credibly disputed by the company.

  With all these records, you also will be searching for what is *not* there. The SEC requires publicly traded corporations to disclose "material" information in these reports. The Supreme Court explained that a fact is "material" and its omission a violation of SEC rules "if there is a substantial likelihood that a reasonable shareholder would consider it significant in deciding how to vote" on relevant corporate decisions affecting the investment.[36] One example would be risking significant liability or government penalties for secret misconduct. If your whistleblowing exposes material information not in those legally required SEC disclosure reports, that in itself is illegal. As explained in chapter 6, it also triggers your legal rights under Sarbanes-Oxley whistleblower protections.

In addition to the SEC's EDGAR system, there are states with corporate disclosure laws that maintain additional databases of information about businesses operating in that state. This information covers only issues not included in federal disclosures, however, which may be comparatively minor. Companies also issue shareholder reports and investment information portfolios, but these contain dressed-up and interpreted versions of the information contained in the SEC filings. Nonetheless, these can be useful to see what the company is highlighting. For example, you may find the company taking false credit for an act of civic duty that is contradicted by the actual behavior you are challenging.

Other Information in the Public Record

It is more difficult to find nonfinancial information about a company that is official or verified. All companies issue press releases on items they want brought to the public's attention, but there are few mechanisms to provide public exposure of corporate misdeeds. Should an action bring a company to court, there may be public records relating to that case. There will often be useful information disclosed during the discovery process. Some of this data, especially proprietary information regarding patents or products, will be put under seal by the judge in the case. But there will be many documents and statements that will go into the public record. In addition, depositions taken as part of the legal proceedings may be available, either for free or for sale from the party who took the deposition. Information regarding court cases may be found through database searches using services like Lexis-Nexis or Westlaw, which may be available for a fee or through libraries, law schools, and universities. Legal actions may also be documented in the SEC documents noted earlier.

The Environmental Protection Agency and the Food and Drug Administration also collect and keep records of corporate information within their regulatory domains. The EPA maintains a number of databases and other information clearinghouses on topics related to pollution and the environment. These are Internet accessible and may be useful for finding out about a company's past behavior.

The FDA keeps track of companies that have had safety warnings or product recalls. There are a number of resources available on its website, *http://www.fda.gov*. Sections to pay particular attention to are "Recalls & Alerts" and "FDA For You," which have information for a number of categories of individuals, including health professionals and consumers. Also, *http://www.recall.gov* contains information about all product recalls issued by the federal government, regardless of department.

Freedom of Information Act

The enactment of the Freedom of Information Act (FOIA) in 1966 transformed the "need to know" stipulation for obtaining government records from federal executive-branch agencies into a "right to know" standard.[37] Virtually all states have since adopted some parallel form of public records law. The FOIA can be an effective way to gather supporting research for your charges. Under 2007 amendments, records received from government contractors are covered by the act.[38] Further, by seeking related requests already released to other parties, you can scour the publicly available record.

Using FOIA at Ground Zero

Five days after the collapse of the World Trade Center, both the mayor of New York and the administrator of the EPA declared "Ground Zero" at low risk of environmental contamination. A reporter for the *New York Daily News* supplemented his reporting on the disaster with documentation he received after filing a FOIA request with the EPA. Those documents verified other sources of information claiming that Ground Zero was contaminated with asbestos and other toxic chemicals and was endangering the health of both rescue workers and Manhattan residents.[39]

Making a FOIA request is a fairly straightforward process. Identify which agency has the desired information and formally write to its FOIA office with a reasonable description of the records sought. The more precise and narrow the request, the faster it will be satisfied. Be sure to make a separate request to every different office of the agency where records may be located. The FOIA offices will not distribute the requests for you. Also, provide your name and telephone number, as some requests can be resolved quickly in one call from the FOIA officer.[40] Otherwise, a FOIA letter need not be long or complex; no one should need a lawyer to draft one. For a sample FOIA request letter, see Tool B in the Whistleblower Toolkit.

The agency has a 20 day extendable deadline in which to respond, though you can request expedited consideration if you can show a compelling need. The agency is allowed to charge you appropriate fees for its time and money spent processing the request, but this may be reduced or eliminated if you work through a nonprofit organization or you can show that the information is in the public interest.[41]

You should address the six criteria that an agency considers when reviewing a public interest waiver:

- the subject of the requested records concerns government operations and activities;

- the disclosure is likely to contribute to understanding of these operations or activities;

- the disclosure will likely result in public understanding of the subject;

- the contribution to public understanding of government operations or activities will be significant;

- the requester has a limited commercial interest in the disclosure; and

- the public interest in disclosure is greater than the requester's commercial interest.[42]

An agency may refuse to disclose a record that falls within any of FOIA's nine statutory exemptions, including national security, personal privacy, trade secrets, and law enforcement records.[43] The law also provides administrative and judicial remedies for those inappropriately denied access to records.[44]

FOIA offices are not independent of the respective agencies that they serve. They typically work with agency bureaucrats to hunt down the documents you are requesting. This warrants a word of warning. If the government agency from which you are requesting records is complicit in the corporate malfeasance, it may tip off your employer as to your inquiry. Making a FOIA request through a third party can alleviate the risks of retaliation; however, no degree of care can prevent a corrupt agency official from informing your employer that someone is up to "no good." A government agency will frequently warn a company that it is about to release documents obtained from that company to give it an opportunity to object to the disclosure.

Unfortunately, during this millennium FOIA has often been more a source of frustration than a credible open-government law. At the end of 2007, however, Congress enacted an amendment to make the law more user-friendly, impose penalties for delays, mandate a tracking system for requests, require notification of redacted information and the exemption justifying the withholding, and establish an ombudsman at each agency to help mediate disputes.[45] Further, the Obama administration has shifted FOIA's presumptive response from withholding to disclosure[46] as part of a policy reversal toward transparency in an Open Government Directive. For details on the pace and the strength of the act's revival, see *http:// www.openthegovernment.org*.

Public Interest Organizations and the Media

When government enables rather than regulates corporate interests, nongovernmental organizations and the media become the primary watchdogs of the public interest. Thousands of civil society groups and journalists are constantly scrutinizing threats to the common good, conducting informal oversight of a wide variety of government and corporate activities. When you seek information from an NGO and, to a lesser extent, the media, it is important that the organization be well established and reputable—many groups may hide the sources of their funding, operate under deceptively benign names, and intentionally present biased or misleading information. Bearing that in mind, there is a wealth of information that NGOs are ready to share, beginning on their websites.

For example, a large amount of product-related information, as well as useful links, has been gathered and posted by the Consumers Union (*http://www.consumersunion.org*). OMB Watch (*http://www.ombwatch.org*) and the Project on Government Oversight (*http://www.pogo.org*) also maintain databases that track regulatory and law enforcement actions against government contractors. The National Security Archives (*http://www.gwu.edu/~nsarchiv*) has a library of information through FOIA releases, often declassified through its efforts, that includes information about misconduct by government contractors. It can be very helpful to demonstrate that your charges are consistent with a confirmed pattern of misconduct. OMB Watch's website also provides navigational help for the EPA's publicly available research. For the Internet addresses of a range of public and private resources, see Tool D in the Whistleblower Toolkit.

Don't rely on them alone, however. The Internet has given people ready access to news and information about the private sector and civil society. Popular search engines, such as Google, Yahoo!, and MSN, allow users to easily explore the NGO universe. Similarly, these search engines often have news services that can track down multiple articles pertaining to your issue by keyword. As with anything on the Internet, the sites indexed by search engines vary greatly in quality, so make certain that any information that you rely on gained through such a search is credible and verifiable. Respectable, established news providers such as the BBC and the *New York Times* show up alongside local papers and opinion blogs, with no evaluation given of the source. Libraries will give you access to older periodical information, and services such as Lexis-Nexis can provide historical searches of news stories.

A Note on Defamation

When disclosing information to the media or the public, be aware that there are legal restrictions on statements that harm another's reputation. Although the Supreme Court has granted defamatory speech a significant amount of First Amendment protection in the interest of free and open disclosure about persons and issues of public importance, even speech that is slightly defamatory can lead to a lawsuit that is filed to cow the whistleblower into silence.

Public Figures versus Private Citizens

Defamation can be written (libel) or spoken (slander). To determine whether your disclosures are potentially defamatory, you must first consider whether the subject of your speech is a public or private figure. Those who have injected themselves or been drawn into the public spotlight on specific issues are considered public figures. By voluntarily accepting high-profile involvement with a matter of public concern, public officials and celebrities enjoy lower protections from defamation.

A public figure must establish that a false statement was made knowingly or with a reckless disregard for the truth.[47] This inquiry requires proving the subjective state of mind of those who generated the speech. On the other hand, a defamation case by an individual who is not a public figure need only show that the whistleblower was at fault—usually negligent—in making a false statement.[48] Once a comment is deemed to be defamatory and made with the requisite mental intent, the plaintiff need only prove that the statement was conveyed to a third party and resulted in damage to the plaintiff.

Truth as an Absolute Defense

Generally, truth is an absolute defense to any charge of defamation in US jurisdictions.[49] Other aspects of defamation law vary from state to state. For example, some states distinguish statements of opinion as being incapable of having a defamatory effect, while others allow them to be defamatory if there is an implied factual basis for the opinion.[50] Statements made in the course of court testimony generally are privileged, that is, protected from charges of defamation.[51] This is an area where you should use care and, again, seek the input of an attorney.

Although this primer on strategies may seem overwhelming, it is only an introduction to the art of whistleblowing. Careful strategic planning may be the most important investment you make in your professional survival. Taking on the system can be the wisest or worst decision of your life. If you intend to win, you must prepare and be smart about how you blow the whistle. For additional Internet and academic resources, see Tool D in the Whistleblower Toolkit and the bibliography.

CHAPTER 4

Where to Go
When You Want to Blow

Once you are prepared to blow the whistle, the central concern of your strategic plan is where to take your story. What avenue is most likely to expose and correct the wrongdoing you plan to reveal? Which is best able to protect your interests and concerns? Whistleblower outlets range from company management and corporate hotlines to Congress, law enforcement and regulatory agencies, the courts, the media, and affected constituencies—all of which have the decision-making power or public sway to effect meaningful change. But not all outlets are created equal. Some provide greater confidentiality than others. Some are well positioned to expose wrongdoing; others tend to discourage dissent. Still others are known for being their own source of retaliation against whistleblowers. Delivering your message to these outlets is often made much easier and safer with the help of outside advocacy partners such as public interest groups and employee organizations. In this chapter we discuss the different outlets available for blowing the whistle.

Blumsohn's Media Campaign for Accountability

Frustrated that Procter & Gamble was withholding the data necessary to make sense of his own research study on P&G's drug and that P&G was publishing inaccurate results of the study under his name without his consent, Dr. Aubrey Blumsohn took his concerns to the British Broadcasting Corporation (BBC). In response his direct employer, Sheffield University—ever mindful of its financial ties to P&G—suspended Blumsohn and threatened him with termination.[1]

Blumsohn was undeterred. With GAP's assistance, National Public Radio, the Associated Press, and the *Wall Street Journal* reported on his case.

He met in Washington with a number of congressional offices and public interest groups concerned with health and scientific integrity. He also gave a talk at the National Institutes of Health, drawing attention to P&G's role in suppressing honest science. All of this negative publicity paid off for Blumsohn and for researchers everywhere.[2]

Blumsohn and the university settled their dispute, and P&G finally released the full data set, confirming Blumsohn's suspicions that the corporation had misrepresented the data on Actonel. P&G took the extraordinary step of issuing a "Researcher's Bill of Rights," affording researchers full access to their data and the right of approval for anything written in their name.[3] Blumsohn's actions brought about important change within the drug industry that promises to make the jobs of future researchers easier and their analyses more credible.

On balance, GAP's experience suggests that making strategic disclosures through all available audiences—internal in-house channels, nonprofit groups, Congress, the media, and government regulatory agencies—is the most effective means to expose and address the most significant institutional wrongdoing. For more low-level corruption, in which the corporation itself may be victimized, in-house advocacy may be most effective and actually less likely to spark retaliation than going outside the company. The False Claims Act is the best outlet for the narrow purpose of recovering fraudulent profits in government contracts. The relatively new whistleblower hotline provisions in the Sarbanes-Oxley Act may also provide avenues to address wrongdoing. Nonetheless, keep in mind that every whistleblowing situation is unique and calls for its own approach.

Whistle Where You Work: The Corporate Channels

It is noteworthy that each of *Time* magazine's three Persons of the Year for 2002—whistleblowers Sherron Watkins, Cynthia Cooper, and Coleen Rowley—attempted, like most other whistleblowers, to bring wrongdoing to light *within* their organizations only to be discredited and punished. None sought the limelight or money. Each sought to have the wrongdoing stopped and the problem corrected for the good of the institution.

You should generally make an internal record of your concerns in some form, even if integrated into job assignments. This is necessary to bolster your credibility and to avoid claims down the road that the company did not know about the issue. The more difficult judgment call is whether you can seriously work for change from the inside. The answer will depend largely on the degree to which your company is committed to truth and reform. A genuine commitment means that the company will welcome the opportunity to address your concerns quietly, effectively, and early on, instead of pursuing cover-ups that risk media frenzies, federal agency investigations, congressional hearings, and liability from various directions. In that case, there are a number of possibilities for working effectively through corporate channels.

In-House Disclosure Programs

According to a survey by the United Nations Office on Drugs and Crime, all Fortune Global 500 companies recognize that employees may not, out of fear of retaliation, blow the whistle.[4] As a result, many have set up anonymous hotlines, Internet-based whistleblower systems, or a third-party ombudsman within an in-house ethics office. Unfortunately, many internal oversight and enforcement systems have been used by corporations to conceal wrongdoing and for bad-faith damage control. In some cases, however, they have been successful channels for whistle-blowers. In chapter 7 we discuss a number of policies and guidelines that if implemented would provide a promising sign of corporate reform. These can serve as useful criteria in judging whether it is safe to pursue an internal disclosure under the protection of a corporate whistleblower program or whether it is better to bypass internal channels in favor of external mechanisms.

Voluntary corporate disclosure programs became popular during the 1970s as a way for the Securities and Exchange Commission to address illegal, shareholder-financed political contributions or bribes at home and abroad.[5] In the 1980s they became common as an alternative to direct government investigations of whistleblower charges in the nuclear power and defense industries.[6] In the 1990s the US Sentencing Commission's "Guidelines for Organizations and Entities" called for mechanisms to report potential illegality as a way to demonstrate that the misconduct violated institutional policy as well.[7] Now, with the passage of Sarbanes-Oxley, audit committees of publicly traded companies are required—under threat of delisting their securities from the market—to establish procedures for the receipt, *retention, and treatment* of employee complaints,[8] and for an anonymous complaint submission system for concerns about "questionable accounting or auditing practices."[9]

Internal disclosure mechanisms allow companies to identify, disclose, and correct violations of institutional responsibilities. Check your contract or employee handbook for more information. They often take the form of 24-hour employee hotlines that an employee can call toll-free to report an allegation of fraud, waste, or mismanagement. The allegation is then reviewed to determine if follow-up is necessary, in which case an investigator is called and, if the case is not dismissed, corrective action is contemplated.

Nonetheless, even under SOX, there is considerable potential for abuse. SOX does not specify what reporting mechanisms are required, whether complaints are to be routed directly to the audit committee of the corporate board or channeled through management, if the system should be managed by an independent third party, or how complaints should be investigated. It leaves "retention" and "treatment" of complaints undefined.[10] The act requires members of the board of directors to serve on the auditing committee.[11] Although the complaints are ostensibly anonymous, the continued, nonnegligible risk of being exposed and experiencing reprisal may discourage employees from using the system to begin with. Of some dubious comfort, a hotline disclosure would trigger SOX corporate whistleblower protections, as discussed in chapter 6.

While an imperfect start, SOX has spawned a cottage industry of whistleblower hotlines with promising results, as seen by the 2007 PricewaterhouseCoopers study's primary conclusion: hotline tips beat corporate security, auditors, and law enforcement as the primary means of detecting corporate fraud.[12] The new hotline industry is developing professional standards as well. For a summary of industry best practices, see Tool H in the Whistleblower Toolkit.

Although it is still too early to tell what effect the broadly worded compulsory provisions of SOX will have, voluntary measures are inherently no more reliable than the good faith a corporation brings to the process. As discussed earlier, they can be very effective for detecting fraud against the corporation. Structurally, however, internal reporting systems are vulnerable to the unavoidable conflict of interest inherent when an institution is responsible for investigating or disclosing its own misconduct. The investigation is often conducted by attorneys whose professional duty is to the client corporation—rather than to the public. The same attorney who interviews whistleblowers and serves as a liaison between the corporation and the government during a voluntary disclosure may later act as counsel for the defense in the event of enforcement action or a whistleblower-initiated lawsuit.

As a result, voluntary disclosure programs have failed to serve as an effective substitute for external oversight and too often serve as a shield for liability. Summarized below are lessons learned about corporate hotlines and voluntary disclosure programs from a review of whistleblower cases since 1979. Depending on how the courts and rule-making agencies elaborate on and enforce the SOX requirements, these same problems could plague compulsory mechanisms as well. Programs have been:

- incomplete in scope because institutions set the boundaries for investigations, which at times have been limited to exploring the "tip" of the misconduct and ignoring the rest of the "iceberg";

- incomplete in their findings of fact because companies elect not to disclose the most significant instances of fraud or abuse;

- inadequate even for government oversight because firms can and do rely on claims of "commercial or proprietary" information and the attorney-client privilege to withhold key records in corporate investigative files from government auditors;

- a rationale for delaying formal proceedings while a company's self-investigation proceeds—taking 2.8 years on average and more than 10 years in some of the cases surveyed by a Government Accountability Office study;[13]

- a form of advance discovery for future litigation, which at worst creates opportunities to intimidate or influence witness testimony and at best provides early knowledge of—and a corresponding opportunity to rebut—significant, threatening testimony;

- a method for evading government scrutiny where regulatory agencies such as the Nuclear Regulatory Commission decide to view internal corporate "reform" programs as substitutes for direct over-sight and off-limits to encourage their creation and use; and

■ openly advocated in industry speeches as a way to avoid harsher government enforcement action despite official disclaimers that the programs' purpose is good corporate citizenship.

These programs can be useful structures for a company that wants to do the right thing, but they can also serve as easy cover for corporate wrongdoers. There is no substitute for independent accountability.

Going up the Chain of Command

Depending on your situation, you may consider taking your complaint directly to your supervisor or to management, in-house counsel, one or more members of the board of directors, or even shareholders. When-ever possible, working with your supervisor is best for solving the prob-lem quickly and quietly. If your supervisor is the problem, however, or is sympathetic to or intimidated by the wrongdoers, you may need to aim higher. Consider Cynthia Cooper, the WorldCom whistleblower who took large-scale internal accounting irregularities past her complicit CFO and directly to the board of directors.

Remember that where responsibility rests will determine how much of a threat you pose to the institution. Wrongdoing in minor day-to-day operating decisions does not implicate the higher levels of authority as do large-scale corporate activities creating significant risks. The higher the problem's source is in the chain of command, the greater the motive to silence and retaliate.

Going to corporate counsel   Theoretically, corporate counsel owes its ultimate allegiance to the corporate entity and not its officers or directors. This makes it a seemingly attractive outlet for complaints about conduct that jeopardizes the financial health and the well-being of the company, including risks that open the company up to legal sanctions. Nonetheless, attorneys do not wield any formal decision-making power when it comes to addressing such problems. They cannot initiate an internal investiga-tion, reverse a crooked business deal, or terminate corrupt officers. At best lawyers will diligently follow their ethical duty to make reports of misconduct to their corporate clients through the chain of command, with corresponding recommendations. But as the attorney's client is the company and not its employees, you will enjoy no guarantee of anonymity. In practice many view their client as the company managers who control their career advancement and so could become the architects for retaliation.

Going to the shareholders In the context of corporate governance, shareholders suffer from some of the same problems as even good-faith corporate counsel. For one, shareholders may be powerless to solve the problem other than with blunt and drastic action. Depending on the particular power-sharing arrangement established by the law of the state of incorporation and in the company's own corporate charter, shareholders are typically empowered to approve—but not initiate—major corporate decisions. They cannot force a company to investigate a whistleblower claim, cancel a fraudulent transaction, or desist from suspect activities. They can vote to fire an officer or to pass shareholder resolutions regarding corporate operations, but these are not binding on the board of directors, which retains decision-making power. Direct shareholder actions are rarely a sound investment of energy for immediate change. The targeted officers frequently hold major blocks of stock, and cautious institutional investors, who are closed-minded to disruption, control most of the rest. A shareholder challenge of any type that receives 10 percent support is considered a dramatic moral victory.

Going to the ethics office or ombudsman Corporate ethics offices and ombudsmen generally are available. The former is a nonauthoritative, institutional conscience. The latter is a nonauthoritative mediator seeking "win-win" problem-solving resolutions as an alternative to conflict. Depending on the issue and the organizational support, both can be helpful to broker a lower-key resolution. Both potentially represent a constructive liaison within the corporate organization.

Both still work for the institution, however, so they can be no more effective than its own good faith. Ombudsmen, for example, may be buried within the organization and powerless to obtain necessary records. They frequently have no anti-retaliation rights in a job whose duty is to question authority, and numerous GAP whistleblower clients have included ombudsmen fired for pursuing the wrong issue. The lack of independence also enables scenarios where bad-faith ethics offices or ombudsmen act as scouts for management to identify whistleblowers early, enabling cover-ups and preemptive reprisals.

In short, if you choose this channel to act on concerns, the principle of earned trust is all important. In addition to trusting your liaison, learn whether the program's structure is trustworthy. For the professional best-practice standards for ombudsmen, see Tool F in the Whistleblower Toolkit.

Pursuing shareholder and consumer litigation   In contrast, shareholder litigation, such as through derivative lawsuits, can be a significant resource for accountability. Whistleblowers and litigants who generate information for the public record can reinforce each other's efforts, even without direct partnerships. Many whistleblowers among professionals, such as tobacco whistleblower and scientist Dr. Jeffrey Wigand, come to occupy niches as expert witnesses in shareholder and consumer litigation. Disclosures to counsel for shareholder derivative litigation can be a way to even the odds by recruiting reinforcements for your dissent from the large law firms that pursue those cases, and at least initial communications could be shielded by legal privileges.

Pointers for Taking It up the Chain

If you have considered your situation, feel confident working from within the company, and have decided where to take your disclosure up the chain of command, here are a few pointers to keep in mind.

Identify the right person   As discussed in the context of ombudsmen, some corporate audiences will be more open to your information than others. Take some time to research the right supervisor, manager, director, or shareholder. Discreetly probe your colleagues about these individuals' reputations for handling complaints and controversy. It may not hurt to peruse a news database to see if they have been involved in similar situations before. Finally, if you do not already share a comfortable working relationship with the individual, consider getting to know each other more before raising any issues—or raise concerns casually and informally, such as asking questions about a hypothetical problem during discussions at meetings.

Prepare for the moment   If you plan to blow the whistle through a formal meeting or letter, try to verify your facts and organize them into a professional, succinct two-page memo or five-minute presentation. The busy corporate officer will appreciate brevity and structure. Even if you plan for an informal conversation or a quick note, make sure you have your story ready so that it comes out coherently and confidently. This means knowing all the facts as well as having the evidence and the witnesses to support them. Do not surrender any original documents, however, until you are sure of the person's intentions; and, if you do surrender documents, keep copies. For complicated scenarios it may help to prepare a written timeline and notes for your own reference.

Maintain the perspective of a loyal corporate citizen. Instead of moralizing, emphasize your concern about the potential harm the wrongdoing would risk for the company and its employees. Wherever possible, do not cast judgment or even draw conclusions. Rather you should simply be following through on information that raises questions or concerns. Try to determine whether a person's initial defensive response may be truly hostile or simply a case of playing devil's advocate.

Maintain your composure   Although you may be outraged, try to remain calm when you communicate your concerns to someone in the company. This will make the message less threatening and dramatic and thus easier to listen to, digest, and deal with. Staying neutral will also give you a better opportunity to gauge the other person's initial response. If the response is truly negative or evasive, at least on the surface, back off immediately and reassess the situation. Your demeanor should be to proceed thoughtfully from a perspective of trying to understand. Do not start arguing. Even if the response is positive or enthusiastic, keep up your guard, as the person may not be revealing his true stripes.

Follow through with your complaint   Often it is easiest for your contact to respectfully smile and nod—and then completely ignore your disclosure and hope that the problem goes away by itself. Try to build a next step into the end of your initial conversation. If you notice that the problem persists or that there is a lack of company response, try to follow up without raising the ire of that company officer. You may want to contact someone else, but avoid the appearance of "spreading rumors" by letting the second contact know whom you have already talked to and why. If you are continually stonewalled or feel a rising risk of retaliation, step away and reevaluate your whistleblowing strategy. Depending on the response, you may want to take a time out to let suspicions defuse, or you may need to break ranks immediately due to a cover-up's imminent consequences.

Whistleblowing to Regulators and Law Enforcement

If your employer is engaged in illegal practices, the obvious audience for your disclosure would be the government entity responsible for regulating such activities. This includes a range of executive-branch agencies and departments at both the state and federal levels. You will want to thoroughly research these, or seek competent legal counsel, to find out all rules, regulations, and laws that are implicated by your employer's actions and what agencies have jurisdiction to enforce them.

Criminal violations may be reported to local police, state and federal attorneys general, or the Federal Bureau of Investigation. On the other hand, breaches of federal securities laws; workplace, nuclear, and food and drug safety codes; and environmental regulations can be reported to, respectively, the Securities and Exchange Commission, the Occupational Safety and Health Administration, the Nuclear Regulatory Commission or the Department of Energy, the Food and Drug Administration, or the Environmental Protection Agency and their state-level counterparts. These executive bodies are diverse, so their effectiveness and trustworthiness will vary.

Birkenfeld and the Government's Bait and Switch

After taking a job at the Swiss banking giant UBS in Geneva, Brad Birkenfeld discovered that UBS's secret dealings with American tax evaders violated the bank's written policies and agreement with the Internal Revenue Service (IRS). He resigned in 2005, leaving UBS executives with written notice of the bank's illegal cross-border practice pursuant to UBS's own policy of

"Whistleblowing Protection for Employees." UBS dismissed his allegations following an unobtrusive internal investigation.

Back in the United States, Birkenfeld turned to the IRS to expose the wrongdoing. In June 2007 he registered under the IRS's Whistleblower Reward Program and proceeded to tender sensitive and detailed information about UBS's underground world of offshore tax shelters to the IRS, SEC, DOJ, and US Senate. Though the DOJ does not participate in the Whistleblower Reward Program, it assured Birkenfeld that it was not seeking to prosecute him.

Facing charges based in significant part on Birkenfeld's disclosures, UBS entered into a historic Deferred Prosecution Agreement with the DOJ to avoid criminal indictment for tax evasion. The agreement promised to keep UBS out of the US tax shelter business, thereby saving the US Treasury $100 billion a year, and to provide the names of thousands of American tax dodgers. Senior Justice Department tax trial lawyer Kevin Downing stated, "I have no reason to believe that we would have had any other means to have disclosed what was going on but for an insider in that scheme providing detailed information, which Mr. Birkenfeld did."

Regardless, while the implicated UBS senior executives paid fines and freely returned to their homes, the DOJ pressed charges against Birkenfeld, who pled guilty to a single count of fraud conspiracy. In a chilling move for potential financial whistleblowers everywhere, Birkenfeld was sentenced to 40 months in prison.[14]

As a result, it becomes important not only to research which regulatory or law enforcement agency has legal jurisdiction to take action but also which is capable and willing to do so. Some agencies are rendered incapable by a lack of adequate funding or competent personnel.

The Problem of Regulatory Capture

Agencies may have hidden agendas or become dominated by the interests of the industries that they are supposed to oversee. This "regulatory capture" is achieved through the hiring of industry loyalists, a policy shift from agency oversight to cooperation with the regulated industry, or even bribery. A recent survey at the FDA—the agency responsible for regulating the safety of drugs, food, medical devices, cosmetics, and the blood supply—by the Union of Concerned Scientists revealed that 60 percent of agency scientists knew of cases "where commercial interests have inappropriately induced or attempted to induce the reversal, withdrawal or modification of FDA determinations or actions."[15]

In instances of regulatory capture, whistleblowing on corporate misconduct is a threat to the regulatory agency as well. Whistleblowing to the agency may thus not only be ineffective but may invite severe retaliation in the aftermath if cozy or corrupt government-industry collusion is behind the misconduct you disclose. In those circumstances the agency likely will conduct a sham investigation that finds your claims lack merit, leaving you without further protection from employer retaliation. Sometimes you will find yourself a target, instead of or in addition to your allegations, and the subsequent report openly attacks your actions or credibility. This can set you up for further retaliation from your employer that has not yet occurred and can undercut you in any independent channels.

Take care to identify those agencies that have genuine independence and integrity by investigating how extensively they have actually regulated your employer's industry and company. How often have they found violations and issued significant fines or other sanctions? Does the agency head have any prior or ongoing relationships with the industry or company? Assess your employer's attitude toward the agency; a sense of indifference or friendliness toward the agency may not be a good sign. State regulators or attorneys general may have incentives and influences that differ from those of federal agencies, so they may be a promising alternative.

New York State Attorney General Comes to the Rescue

Illegal trading of mutual funds escaped the attention of the SEC for years until whistleblowers brought it to light, prompting state law enforcement to file suit. The first mutual fund whistleblower, Noreen Harrington, worked for Stern Asset Management, which housed the Canary Mutual Fund. She learned about illegal trading occurring at Canary because people in her office were bragging about how much money they had made through these trades.[16] Though Harrington made internal complaints about the asset management to Stern, her complaints were ignored. Harrington eventually resigned from Stern. She stayed quiet at first, hoping that regulators would discover the illegal trading. She came forward a year later, compelled by the harm she saw inflicted on ordinary investors, including her sister, who lost substantial savings in a 401(k).[17]

Harrington blew the whistle through an anonymous call to the New York State attorney general's office.[18] They didn't have just her word to go on—her allegations were fully substantiated with documentation. Harrington showed the attorney general a paper trail that led him to an Internet chat room, where her colleague made his trades.[19] Her actions triggered a massive investigation, the effects of which have had huge repercussions throughout the mutual fund industry. Corporations have paid billions of dollars in fines and restitution. Fraud charges have been filed against several firms and executives.[20] Managers and stockbrokers from some major mutual fund firms have faced criminal charges, several CEOs have resigned, and at least one company has been shut down,[21] In addition, mutual fund companies are reevaluating their practices, and the SEC proposed new regulations for overhauling the industry, which manages $7 trillion in assets for investors.[22]

Pointers for Taking It to an Agency

The good news is that, once identified, a willing and capable regulatory agency will be receptive and legally empowered to address the problem. Here are a few tips for approaching its office staff.

Keep your letter short   Due to their high workload, many agency officials do not have the time to read more than a page of your complaint. If it is impossible to condense your letter to two pages or less, it is a good idea to prepare a one-page fact sheet or an executive summary. Enclose copies of only the most important supporting documents; do not send a large stack or the originals. At the end of your letter, make suggestions on where officials might go to pursue follow-up investigations or find further corroborating evidence.

Make it clear whether you consent to having your name or documents shared with the company   In your letter you should state outright and early whether you need to remain anonymous; otherwise, your letter is likely to be processed right back to your employer during the agency's investigations. If you want to preserve confidentiality, request that the recipient take the precaution of talking to you before acting on your letter. If confidentiality is an issue, however, you lose control until and unless your requests can be granted. Hold off on even identifying issues until the ground rules are established to protect your own identity and any identifying information that could be traced back to you.

Focus on the relevant legal violations   An agency has a mandate to address certain legal violations. It will be less interested in claims that lie outside its jurisdiction as well as the retaliation you may have experienced. Present the agency with information that can help it do its job with less time and effort.

Make sure that investigators have a way to reach you during working hours   If you cannot talk to the agency from your workplace, find a discrete way for someone to take a message for you and return the call from an outside telephone or cell phone during your break or off hours.

Calling State Regulators to Action

Whistleblowing at the state level can sometimes be a successful stepping-stone to federal regulators. An internal whistleblower first informed the SEC about market timing at Putnam Investments, but when SEC investigations fell short, he turned to state regulators.[23] After state regulators got on the right trail, the SEC stepped in again and charged Putnam Investments, a subsidiary of Marsh and McLennan Cos., with securities fraud.[24] Putnam settled with the SEC by agreeing to adopt steps to closely control trading activities. Putnam was also required to pay $110 million in fines and restitution.[25] Customers withdrew $61 billion in assets after the charges of market timing surfaced, a quarter of total assets under Putnam management.[26]

Whistleblowing to Congress

Whistleblowers often have been successful by triggering legislative oversight of executive-branch abuse or its acquiescence to the wrongdoings of industries it should be regulating. This oversight includes congressional authority for committees or ad hoc bodies to conduct investigations with full-fledged subpoena power. Members of Congress may also initiate probes by the Government Accountability Office (GAO), the investigative arm of Congress.

Real Public Relations: A Journey from Company to Congress

While vacationing in July 2007, Wendell Potter, head of corporate communications for the health insurance giant CIGNA, decided to visit a free touring health clinic in rural Virginia. Potter was appalled by the crowds of desperate people driving as far as 200 miles for basic medical treatment provided in the open air and free of charge. He eventually resigned from CIGNA in May 2008 and decided to go public. With the help of an old acquaintance and former reporter, Potter connected with Senator Jay Rockefeller, who invited him to testify as a whistleblower before the US Senate Commerce Committee. In his June 2009 remarks, he told the committee, "I worked as a senior executive at health Insurance companies and I saw how they confuse their customers and dump the sick: all so they can satisfy their Wall Street investors."[27] Though he was careful not to breach his post-employment confidentiality agreement with CIGNA, Potter's cool-headed testimony of underreported, though publicly available, industry practices has had a major impact on the healthcare debate and launched his new career as a high-profile pro-reform advocate.

Risks and Rewards of Taking It to Congress

The congressional spotlight on corporate wrongdoing can draw intense public attention and exert direct pressure on corporations to change their ways. Members of Congress, however, are also influenced by all types of constituent groups, including major political contributors in their states or districts, so it is important to do some research on particular members of Congress before soliciting their help.

For corporate whistleblower disclosures to Congress, there are no sweeping legal protections like there are, albeit underenforced, for federal employees. Even worse, in practice legislators may simply pass complaints about corporate misconduct back to the company for self-investigation, which rarely brings about much good. A congressional office may not safeguard your identity even if you request it, either because of a congressional staffer's inexperience in dealing with the bureaucracy or due to the individual member's unwillingness to stand up to a powerful corporation.

That said, members of Congress have included the most committed, effective champions for whistleblowers. Mutually earned trust in this context can make all the difference in having an impact and surviving professionally in the process. A Senate "angel" represents far more protection than any formal set of legal rights. This protection can be extremely important but often requires persistence and tact. Congressional allies also will be easier to find if your dissent is supported by a solid constituency base or promises opportunities for public visibility on an important political or public interest issue that matters to the voters.

Pointers for Taking It to Congress

When going to Congress, remember that it has an investigative arm, the Government Accountability Office. It is helpful if a member of Congress initiates a GAO probe on your behalf. Although GAO investigations may take several months or longer to complete, their findings are generally considered authoritative and do influence policy. GAO also protects the identity of employees who speak with investigators.

Unfortunately, sustained congressional protection of individuals is the exception. You should not assume that you will be able to secure such protection, particularly for what may be a multiyear harassment campaign. If you are counting on a congressional shield from ensuing retaliation, pin down whether and how far the congressional office is willing to go. Here are a few tips to keep in mind when contacting members of Congress.

Thoroughly check their track records   Before you write to members of Congress, make sure you have checked their past records of supporting whistleblowers. Do not divulge any information to them before you take this important step. Find out not only if they have helped whistleblowers in the past but also if they followed up once the headlines faded. You can do this by researching their past work in back issues of newspapers, by talking with NGOs that have ongoing relationships with offices and staff, and by directly discussing those issues with the member's staff person. Be sure to identify the right member by seeking recommendations from those familiar with the office. Frequently, however, the best you can do is call the member's office and ask for the name of the staffer who works on your issue.

Senators generally have more clout than members of the House of Representatives, but they cover a broader range of issues and are difficult to get engaged in constituent matters. On the other hand, senators are less likely to be influenced by a corporation than a House member whose district is home to the company. If your research suggests that all three of your home state legislators are unlikely supporters, reaching out to the congressional committees with jurisdiction over your disclosure may be a better first approach. The appropriate congressional committees should always be a potential target audience, provided they have a favorable track record with whistleblowers. They have the authority and the resources for oversight as well as legislative solutions. The primary outlet, however, is the authorizing committee due to its oversight function.

Keep your letter short   Like regulatory agency officials, congressional staffers likely do not have the time to read more than one or two pages from you, so use the technique described earlier for executive summaries here as well.

Limit your initial contact to a request for confidential communications Just as with law enforcement or regulatory agencies, if you require anonymity, it would be a mistake to leave yourself vulnerable to how a stranger handles your request for confidentiality. In that circumstance it is generally best to call so that there is no paper trail and you do not have to be melodramatic in camouflaging your name. In whatever form you communicate, begin by summarizing the issue and the topic, without identifying specific misconduct or the wrongdoer, and request a confidential meeting. If the staffer agrees, start off your meeting by requesting a commitment to generic confidentiality safeguards for any whistleblowing relationship and proceed accordingly.

State your factual case from the beginning   Enclose copies of the most important documents, but do not send a large stack. Be clear and concise. Make a list of your documentation, and *do not send originals*. Keep your description free of jargon or unsubstantiated conclusions. Do not assume that the staff member who reads the letter will understand how your company works. Again, if you need to send a longer statement, separate it from your cover letter or fact sheet. The short version should be no more than a two-page summary.

Focus on the public interest issues raised   It is all right to talk about harassment or retaliation, but put it at the end of the letter and do not dwell on it. A congressional office is much more likely to offer support if there is something in it for the public good—and not simply for you. Particularly if you are not a constituent, it is in your interest to be perceived not merely as an individual victim of injustice but as an important source of information on an issue of concern to the voters, such as a public health or safety hazard you are exposing.

Offer guidance for follow-through   At the end of your letter, make suggestions about where congressional staff might go to pursue follow-up investigations or further corroborating documentation. Tell them if any investigative agencies are working on your case and whether you think they are successfully uncovering information of value.

Make sure that staffers have a way to reach you during working hours   If you cannot talk to them from your workplace, find a discrete way for someone to take a message for you, and return the call from an outside telephone or cell phone during your break or off hours.

If you have not received a reply within a week, call to follow up   Ask whether the staffer has received and had a chance to read your correspondence and, if so, whether you can be helpful in answering any questions. Congressional staff members are very busy, and the most successful whistleblowers know when to keep calling a staff member and when to wait. Do not be a pest, but make sure that you do not fall through the cracks. Do not demand excessive attention, and be polite at all times. Members of Congress act out of their broad discretion and are not required to perform on your behalf. Threatening political embarrassment for inaction is almost always a disastrous strategy, and congressional offices know the political risks of an issue anyway. More relevant is their respect for you. Staffers have a responsibility to make sure their bosses aren't taken by surprise. As a result, if you assert yourself responsibly, they likely will want to at least understand the issue, whether or not they are ultimately supportive.

Offer to act as a ghostwriter Offer to draft communications for congressional staffers who are open to pursuing your allegations and are interested in a working relationship with you. This ensures that the accuracy of your message in the first draft will not be threatened by having it pass through another person with less background on the issue. Further, it is less burdensome for a staffer to revise and edit what you write than to draft the material from scratch. Be aware that the finished product will be more toned down than you might have wanted. It is usually best to live with this compromise as you begin the process of building support for stronger congressional advocacy on your concerns. This is an opportunity to help draft a message in which your concerns are being aired by Congress, instead of one employee. It is a significant opportunity, so do not abuse it when it's available.

Consider watchdog groups Watchdog groups have good working relationships with various members of Congress, and you may be more successful funneling your evidence through them. Such groups can play the role of advocate and often keep your identity anonymous. They may know more about a specific politician's relationship with your company or industry as well as his or her record on whistleblower cases. You may want to team up with the advocacy group for meetings with a legislator's staff to draw support from the organization's credibility, connections, or clout on Capitol Hill. At a minimum ask the NGO for insights and recommendations on relevant staffers.

Blowing the Whistle on Fraud through the Courts

The Federal False Claims Act[28] offers a proactive avenue for whistleblowers to expose corporate fraud through the courts. Additionally, 28 states, the District of Columbia, New York City, and Chicago have similar statutes to combat fraud perpetrated against state and municipal governments.[29] It is a private attorney general statute that allows whistleblowers to do more than make noise. They can file lawsuits on behalf of the taxpayers to challenge fraud in government contracts. If they win, they keep a portion of the recovery. This is a law that combines doing good with doing well, in terms of recovering fraudulent profits, and it works at that level. Ironically, however, the price for its financial recoveries may be locking in secrecy for years about fraud with potentially devastating public consequences.

Note that the False Claims Act "does not apply to claims, records, or statements made under the Internal Revenue Code."[30] Thus, if you are blowing the whistle on tax fraud, consider calling the IRS Fraud Hotline (800-829-0433) instead or participating in its rewards program for information.[31] The Dodd-Frank Wall Street Reform and Consumer Protection Act of 2010 also established bounty provisions for Commodity Futures Trading Commission (CFTC)[32] and SEC[33] disclosures that lead to enforcement actions recovering more than $1 million. As Brad Birkenfeld's experience demonstrates, however, these payment programs can be treacherous for those who try to collect.

The False Claims Act, by contrast, provides court-ordered payments only to those whistleblowers who fight and win battles against corporate fraud in government contracts. Nicknamed the "Lincoln Law," the False Claims Act was first passed during the Civil War. By facilitating a partnership between whistleblowers and government, it has become the nation's most effective resource for citizens to challenge fraud in federally funded contracts with the private sector—including inappropriate billing, falsifying records, bribery, and misrepresenting products and services or their value. Through this law, individual whistleblower "relators"—corporate employees or nonemployees who are original sources of evidence of such fraud—can challenge the company directly before a jury of taxpayers. Keep in mind that the Justice Department has the right to take over the case once you bring it. In fact, whistleblowers rarely prevail without DOJ support.

Origins of the False Claims Act

President Abraham Lincoln knew that standard government oversight mechanisms could not keep pace with unscrupulous defense contractors. In 1863 he discovered that the same horses were sold to the cavalry two and three times. In another case, sawdust was added to gunpowder, causing Union guns to backfire and kill federal soldiers instead of Confederate troops. As a result, Lincoln won the right for citizens to serve as the government's enforcers through False Claims, or *qui tam*, lawsuits. These are private-citizen suits, literally those filed "in the name of the king" that allow whistleblowers to force the return of fraudulent earnings to the US Treasury and to keep a portion of the recovery for themselves.[34]

The law was amended during World War II at the behest of military contractors and gradually eroded by the Supreme Court until it lost much of its effectiveness. But by 1986 renewed interest in the prevention of fraud and waste, together with determined leadership by Senator Charles Grassley (R-IA) and Representative Howard Berman (D-CA), led to an amendment that put the teeth back into the Lincoln law.

Deputizing whistleblowers to file antifraud lawsuits has become the most effective anticorruption measure in our nation's history. In 1985, before the law was modernized, the Justice Department recovered $26 million in civil fraud recoveries—a good year compared with the usual $6 million to $9 million total. Recoveries in the next 21 years totaled nearly $24 billion. If combined with corresponding criminal recoveries, False Claims lawsuits led to $5.6 billion in fraud recoveries during fiscal 2009, including $2.3 billion in combined civil and criminal penalties from the Pfizer Corporation alone for fraudulent drug promotion.[35] Initially, most suits involved Pentagon contracts, although over time the balance has shifted into other arenas such as healthcare, where the government is recovering $15 back for every $1 invested in investigations and prosecutions.[36] Moreover, the law's two congressional champions have noted:

> Studies estimate the fraud deterred thus far by the *qui tam* provisions runs into the hundreds of billions of dollars. Instead of encouraging or rewarding a culture of deceit, corporations now spend substantial sums on sophisticated and meaningful compliance programs. That change in the corporate culture—and in the values-based decisions that ordinary Americans make daily in the workplace—may be the law's most durable legacy.[37]

The False Claims Suit against Gambro Healthcare

Gambro Healthcare will pay more than $350 million in criminal and civil penalties to settle allegations of healthcare fraud in Medicare, Medicaid, and TRICARE programs. This includes alleged kickbacks paid to physicians, false statements made to procure payment for unnecessary tests and services, and payments made to Gambro Supply, a sham durable medical equipment company.[38] The investigation into Gambro's suspect practices began in 2001 when a whistleblower, Gambro's former chief medical officer, filed a False Claims suit alleging fraudulent billing practices. The settlement also requires Gambro to allocate $15 million to resolve potential liability with various state Medicaid programs.[39]

How a False Claims Suit Works

There is a six-year statute of limitations within which the whistleblower must act.[40] Contracts have been defined broadly to include corporate commitments in exchange for government licenses or regulatory approval required by law.[41] This means, for example, that a whistleblower "relator" can challenge a government contractor's fraudulent cover-up of violations of environmental or other laws in which compliance is a condition of the contract or a licensing prerequisite. If the *qui tam* lawsuit is successful, the wrongdoing contractor must repay to the government three times the dollar amount of proven fraud.[42]

After a whistleblower initiates a suit, the Justice Department has 60 days to investigate the claims and decide whether it will take over the case or let the whistleblower prosecute it alone.[43] In practice, the DOJ often takes six months to a year or longer to decide. The entire cycle for a False Claims suit may range from two to five years or more. If the government takes over a case and proceeds to recover money for the taxpayers, the whistleblower is guaranteed an "original source" award of at least 15 percent of the recovery. If the government joins a suit to which a whistleblower has substantially contributed, the incentive award can increase up to 25 percent of the amount recovered[44] (although the government has never agreed to the maximum). For individuals prevailing without government intervention, the award is 25 to 30 percent of the amount recovered, plus attorney's fees.[45]

Not surprisingly, the success of the False Claims Act has earned it powerful enemies among large contractors, such as General Electric, who have repeatedly been caught on the losing side of the act. Several defense companies struck back by attempting to have False Claims cases against them dismissed on the grounds that the law is unconstitutional. So far these attempts have failed.

The fraud lobby In 1993 a coalition of 22 contractors, nicknamed the "fraud lobby," launched a campaign to gut the law. Since 1990 nearly all of those contractors had pled guilty or paid fines totaling hundreds of millions of dollars for fraud, 17 of them on multiple incidents. During their legislative efforts, the lobby's members faced 28 active, unsealed *qui tam* suits. As Senator Grassley summarized, "They hate the act because it is very effective at exposing their fraud."[46]

The fraud lobby's legislative campaign failed—but not without stirring up significant debate over the law within the Justice Department and Congress. Ironically, the DOJ served as industry's advocate at the outset of the legislative battle, backing proposals to impose various limits on False Claims cases. In brief, the debate centered on industry's plan to ban relevant citizen suits once a company had announced it was investigating itself through a voluntary disclosure program. The goal was to restore a corporate and government duopoly on uncovering and challenging fraud.

Industry's concern about a conflict between the False Claims Act and voluntary disclosure programs was unfounded, however. A 1996 GAO report found that only four out of 129 voluntary disclosures involved overlapping *qui tam* suits.[47] The GAO concluded that the two disclosure channels complement each other and that *qui tam* suits help keep voluntary disclosure programs more honest.[48]

In the end, the campaign to gut the False Claims Act failed. Indeed it was the catalyst for a media spotlight on whistleblowers and big-business fraud. Despite all its wealth and resources, the fraud lobby could not find any office to introduce its proposals. But the fight was not over. A few years later, good government groups fought back a similar effort by the healthcare industry. Understanding the background and the controversies behind the False Claims Act is important for any whistleblower considering it. But it is only the first step. For state-of-the-art research on this important whistleblower law, check the Taxpayers Against Fraud website at *http://www.taf.org.*

Considerations before Filing a False Claims Suit

Bringing a False Claims lawsuit is both complex and expensive. You need to find a competent lawyer (see chapter 5) who has the financial resources to fund a case that could run into five or six figures in costs and fees. If the government decides not to take your case, to continue the lawsuit you and your lawyer must be prepared to go through the long and costly process of legal discovery. Do not underestimate a company's ability to finance a large number of lawyers to fight you. You and your lawyer must be mentally prepared to follow through on a case that could drag on for years. Most frequently, law firms will agree only to limited representation—filing a complaint and advocating that the Justice Department take over the case—but not commit to litigate independently if you are turned down.

Cost   The price tag of litigation is often the greatest constraint facing whistleblowers who seek to file a False Claims action. In the end, most False Claims suits are filed as contingency fee cases, wherein the attorney gets 30 to 40 percent of the recovery. As a prerequisite to taking a case, attorneys may also "double dip," asking to take $500-per-hour charges off the top of the whistleblower's recovery to pay for accumulated hourly fees.

Time and blanket secrecy   The False Claims Act imposes a number of notable limitations. During the 60 days to more than a year that the case typically is "under seal" for DOJ review, you cannot disclose that you have filed suit or discuss the evidence. This estimated time lag is conservative; delays have exceeded five years.

This means that after filing a claim, you are essentially gagging yourself from public dissent until the Justice Department makes a determination. You must make any media disclosures *before* filing the case, as courts will dismiss a case if a whistleblower "breaks the seal" by talking to the press. If you do speak to a reporter before filing a False Claims suit, be aware that if the reporter does not credit you with exposing the fraud, you may be disqualified from credit as the original source of the evidence in any story before you go to court and thus not maintain eligibility as the original source to file suit. In a very real sense, the seal turns False Claims litigation into a "money for temporary but prolonged silence" lawsuit.

That is not such a problem when only money is at stake. But the de facto cover-up can have serious consequences for fraud involving ongoing public health and safety threats. In at least one instance, a court has enforced gags even on disclosures with public health and safety consequences.[49]

Unfortunately, the False Claims bar has not actively challenged blanket interpretation of the gag orders to exclude facts about ongoing public health and safety threats. In fact, it has defended them.[50] This raises real questions about whether the False Claims Act is being litigated as a public interest statute or whether it is fostering another form of lawsuit where the public's right to know is rejected when it obstructs a big payoff.

Voices for Corporate Responsibility   Not all False Claims lawyers defend blanket secrecy for those whistleblower lawsuits. In December 2009 two highly successful, visible, and prosperous trial lawyers, Cyrus Mehri and Reuben Guttman, the latter a False Claims specialist, founded Voices for Corporate Responsibility to promote responsible and safe corporate whistleblowing. Among those assisting them are whistleblowers such Dr. David Welch, the pioneer SOX litigant turned scholar. In addition to oversight of Department of Labor programs, they have used the organization as a platform to strengthen the False Claims Act as a public interest law. Guttman has been particularly persistent and vocal in advocating that the act should promote disclosure rather than blanket secrecy and that *qui tam* settlements should not forgo corrective action against public health and safety threats in exchange for more money. In settling *qui tam* litigation, he has aggressively and successfully negotiated for corrective action against public health and safety consequences from prescription drug fraud.

Government preemption   The government also can engage in the False Claims equivalent of plagiarism. Even if the government is ignorant of the fraud before you expose it to the relevant officials independently of a lawsuit, once it knows of your disclosure, the Justice Department can preempt you from bringing a *qui tam* claim by filing a False Claims suit first. The lesson to be learned is to be ready to file expeditiously and then remain mum after making any disclosures to the government or the public.

Government acquiescence   Other factors may limit the effectiveness of using the False Claims Act to blow the whistle, particularly in cases in which the government itself has acquiesced to the company's wrongdoing. Often, when a favored contractor finds itself in trouble over procurement, the government agency is more interested in hiding the problem than solving it. Scandals in government contractor programs can create problems for the government's program managers. Therefore, if there is any credible discretion, a government agent may hand out waivers or some other form of approval of a company's misconduct, even though it formally violates the agency's regulations. Even passive government compliance that winked at fraud can trigger the legal doctrine of "acquiescence," a common defense that there can't be fraud if the victim does not care.

The Department of Justice, moreover, rarely tries to prosecute a government agent for giving waivers and often uses the waivers as an excuse not to prosecute the companies. The normal practice is that if a federal government agency opposes a False Claims suit, the DOJ will not pursue it. As a practical matter, the DOJ cannot succeed without the regulatory agency's expertise and supportive testimony.

A caveat   A final note of caution is to be sure that you know and understand the rules and regulations that you believe are being violated. Government regulations are sometimes written so loosely and vaguely that it is difficult to prove illegality. An illustration of this problem is the case of the now-infamous $435 hammer. After Congressman Berkley Bedell was tipped off to the overpriced hammer by a whistleblower, he asked the US Navy to audit the program and expose the fraud. The navy responded that the price for the hammer was "exorbitant but legal" because the company used "government-approved purchasing and estimating systems."

Janet Chandler's False Claims Suit: A Whistleblower Epic

In 1995 Dr. Janet Chandler blew the whistle on Cook County Hospital's fraudulent mismanagement in the implementation of a $5 million federal grant to provide comprehensive, one-stop "Cadillac" treatment for pregnant drug-dependent women and their children. She was fired within months and so began an incredible journey from near–professional ruin to a federal investigation validating her concerns and a favorable landmark Supreme Court decision under the False Claims Act. Chandler did not stop there, and she has been an active contributor to the whistleblower community, from sharing her expertise with others to providing personal support.

Dr. Chandler, a highly credentialed psychologist, challenged a program that supposedly provided state-of-the-art, one-stop services to addicts, from child care through therapy. She joined the grant midstream and eventually found that the hospital was not fulfilling commitments made in the grant application. Among the concerns were issues of random assignment, ghost subjects, and quality of care. Concerned for the welfare of the indigent women and children, having a research background and aware of high-quality medical and research integrity, Dr. Chandler felt that the rights of this vulnerable population were being compromised and that the hospital was not doing what it had contracted to do. She protested within ranks and was promptly fired, but Department of Health and Human Services investigators later confirmed her concerns for the protection of human subjects.

Six weeks after being fired, Dr. Chandler testified at a Congressional Commission of Research Integrity hearing in Chicago. After a verification study, GAP successfully recommended her for the 7th Annual Joe A. Callaway Award by Claire Nader in Washington, DC, "in recognition of her resolute insistence on integrity in science, concern for humane treatment of human subjects, her honest assessment of treatment and research under her purview and her readiness to testify publicly about scientific misconduct despite the pain it caused her and her poignant summary of the buck-passing she experienced by asking the Congressionally mandated Commission of Research Integrity—'Won't anyone take responsibility?'"[51]

Despite GAP's help, it took two years to find a law firm willing to file a False Claims suit challenging the fraud. Few Chicago lawyers were willing to take on the Cook County system. The civil rights firm of Miner, Barnhill & Galland eventually took on the case. Dr. Chandler persisted and eventually defeated Cook County in a 9-to-0 Supreme Court decision, setting a precedent that county governments are liable for fraud in government contracts under the False Claims Act. In the process, she united Barack Obama and then-president George W. Bush in a common cause. Obama was then a firm lawyer and an author for her successful Seventh Circuit Court federal brief, which was appealed to the Supreme Court. President Bush's Justice Department supported her lawsuit and eventually joined the successful action.[52]

In 2007 Taxpayers Against Fraud made Dr. Chandler and Jim Holzrichter the Co–Whistleblowers of the Year. In 2008 she was similarly honored by the National Grants Management Association. She and Holzrichter are currently volunteering their time with mentoring programs at Taxpayers Against Fraud and GAP to help whistleblowers deal with the emotional stress and the personal crises that come with the territory of whistleblowing.

If you are confident that you can meet these various challenges, a *qui tam* action may work for you. Nonetheless, it is a marathon roller coaster. Even if you ultimately win, are vindicated, and receive a multimillion-dollar judgment, you may well hit bottom and get stuck there for years.

A Whistleblower Epic: Part II

Consider the experience of Jim Holzrichter, Dr. Chandler's mentoring partner and 2007 Co–Whistleblower of the Year. As an auditor-turned-whistleblower, he knows a lot about surviving emotional stress. In 1989 he and a former test engineer, Rex Robinson, filed suit against California-based defense contractor Northrop. Holzrichter served as a valuable witness for the US Attorney's Office, the Defense Criminal Investigative Service, and eventually the FBI. His disclosures exposed fraud surrounding Northrop's electronic systems for the B-1 and B-52 bombers as well as the radar jammers for the F-15 fighter jet.

Sixteen years later he won when the defendant, now Northrop Grumman, paid the federal government $62 million to settle the charges. During the interim, however, Robinson died and Holzrichter's family faced incredible struggles. They had to live in a homeless shelter after company blacklisting. After the Justice Department joined the False Claims lawsuit, Holzrichter and two of his children had the tires inexplicably shear off their cars on separate occasions over a period of three months. Ultimately, $12.4 million was divided between Holzrichter and Robinson's estate. Proving adept at survival and bouncing back, Holzrichter went on to get a degree in paralegal studies, and he now works on multistate fraud litigation.

Whistleblowing and the Media

News Media

One of the most obvious whistleblower outlets is the print or broadcast media. Public exposure can be extraordinarily effective when handled properly by a responsible reporter. The media is indispensable for making a difference when the stakes are high for company management, government regulators, or the general public. None of the success stories listed at the beginning of this handbook could have occurred without the active role of the media and the public pressure created by its news stories. By ending the cycle of secrecy that sustains corporate misconduct, the media is usually indispensable for turning information into power.

The media helps level the playing field. News reports can take disputes outside company walls and into the glare of the public domain. Media coverage can transform a workplace "troublemaker" into a public hero or reduce a powerful executive into an embattled figure whose resignation is demanded. But public exposure can also cause a company to change its stance on negotiations with you from favorable to unwilling if it finds itself shamed and on the defensive.

At first glance, going to the media may appear to be the easiest and quickest way to warn the public about a threat to their health, safety, or investments. But it should be a last resort, not the first. Remember that the public's attention span can be distressingly short, especially when dealing with stories that are complex and technical rather than sensational or scandalous. The company might well wait for public attention to wane before launching an internal counterattack against the whistleblower. Further, in the short term a media attack will force the corporation into a defensive posture. If you are making real progress working quietly and constructively within the corporate system, an unnecessary media attack can backfire badly. Even when it is necessary, it must be integrated into a larger campaign strategy.

Also remember that the news media is a competitive business, driven by economic interests as well as informational dynamics. Reporters may give your employer equal time and introduce a "he said/she said" slant to the story. Similarly, corporate public affairs offices can preempt bad press by releasing news announcements that neutralize or drown out your story. Thus media coverage can be thin or, worse, put the company in a good light.

If sustained coverage is necessary, the employee activist must plan for an entire campaign involving a stockpiled series of stories released over time so that each reinforces the effects of the one before it. Time intervals between releases give the company ample opportunity to do something counterproductive, such as putting forth a demonstrably untrue fact in its defense, instituting a gag order forbidding employee contact with the media, or otherwise overreacting—each of which may attract more media attention. For example, a whistleblower may choose to divulge only one aspect of a complaint so that there is more information left to counter the company's ensuing claims of an otherwise "impeccable" safety record.

Breaking the Dead Silence

Posing for a photo op next to a company van, Robert Ranghelli told the *Washington Post* about the mishandling of bodies by his employer, National Funeral Home. The *Post* published Ranghelli's accounts, corroborated by another former employee, that National Funeral Home regularly left decomposing bodies unrefrigerated in the garage and the back rooms of its premises in April 2009. A few months later, the company declined to release the results of an internal investigation that cleared it of any wrongdoing and fired Ranghelli—a new father and the sole wage earner in his family—for violating company policies restricting contact with the media. Again, the *Post* covered his termination, quoting his attorney, "This is a cover-up and a whitewash. . . . Their concern is to send a message to their workforce: 'Don't disclose information, or you'll end up like Robert Ranghelli.'"[55]

If it is done successfully, the company's deepest wounds will be self-inflicted. Nevertheless this time-interval approach is difficult to carry out. If one divulges all the facts to a reporter at the onset, the journalist is under no obligation to follow your preferred strategy and may decide to report everything in the first article. In the alternative, feeding reporters only certain information in the beginning may undermine your relationship in the long run when it comes out that you withheld information. They may begin to wonder what else you have not divulged and treat future claims with more skepticism. Yet another tactic is to work with a different reporter on the second piece of the story, provided that the story is big enough to be covered by more than one major news outlet in your area. You should never try to work with different reporters from the same news outlet in an attempt to play them against each other.

Pointers for Taking It to the News Media

There are ground rules in the media that participants should know and respect. Not all reporters are willing to take the time and the effort required to publish your allegation or to maintain your anonymity unless you assert yourself. You should be upfront with the reporter at the initial meeting, making sure that the information cannot be used without your go-ahead. Going to the media often is a serious and significant part of the whistleblowing process. It may not be sufficient, but it is frequently a necessary part of any effective whistleblowing effort. It is worth your time and attention to design a careful media strategy. Here are some considerations to keep in mind.

Identify the right outlet   You will need to figure out whether the national or local press is the best fit for what you are trying to accomplish. Both have advantages and disadvantages. A local reporter will be more interested in your story because of its hometown implications but may also face more pressure to stay away from your allegations if the company has a powerful economic base in the community. Local reporters may be better able to follow up on leads—or have immediate access to witnesses who can back up your claims and provide additional documentation. If you do place a good local media story, it will get the company's attention. But if the story does not make a significant enough splash in the larger, national media, the net effect may be detrimental. The news may trigger a cover-up or reprisals against you rather than serve as a catalyst for real reform.

A national story inherently has the greatest potential for impact, but it is often hard to make the national press pay attention to issues that do not have a clear and immediate resonance nationwide. To be confident that a national outlet will be interested in your story, you must be able to identify the ways in which your allegations directly involve or affect a major corporation, have a substantial impact on broad national issues, or significantly affect a slice of the public. Keep in mind that it may be more difficult for out-of-town reporters to verify your story. Do not assume that they will have the time or money to travel to your area. Whether a story is local or national, try to research the kind of coverage a similar issue has garnered in the past and what the outlet's relevant editorial policy has been.

In some cases, your best approach to the local/national question might lead to a compromise as you consider whether to work with a local paper that is a part of a national newspaper chain, with a newswire network, or with a national news syndicate such as Associated Press, United Press International, or Reuters. This will give your story a hearing both within and way beyond your local news orbit. Newspapers in a chain are less likely to be intimidated by local political or economic pressures, and your story may appear nationwide. Well-known chains include Cox, Gannett, Hearst, Knight-Ridder, Newhouse, Scripps Howard, and Thompson syndicates. Examine your local papers (particularly the front or editorial pages) to find out if any of them belongs to a chain that has a national office or is on a major newswire, such as the *New York Times* or the *Washington Post/Los Angeles Times* newswire.

Another important consideration in selecting a media outlet is how time-sensitive your information is. Are you trying to ward off an imminent disaster, or do you have the luxury of allowing the reporter more time to research and develop your disclosure? If you have time to spare, a magazine writer, a broadcast producer for a weekly investigative show, or an investigative reporter may be your best option. If you need an immediate turnaround, network news or a daily newspaper reporter are good choices.

Identify the right reporter   To protect yourself, you need to choose a reporter carefully. Research journalists who cover your area of concern in the newspaper, radio, or television outlets you are considering. Pay particular attention to the ways they have treated similar stories in the past. Were they sympathetic to people in your position? Compare the stories of competing reporters. If you are thinking about working with a broadcast journalist, you may have to request videos of some of their work, because most libraries do not routinely keep this kind of material on file. Many stories will be available on station websites.

It is important to develop an idea of how a reporter will handle your story before you initiate contact. If you find that the reporter's past stories seem largely to echo reports from the relevant corporate public relations office without being adequately critical of statements or assumptions, that journalist is not likely to ask the tough questions or conduct the thorough investigation you want. Even a story that lays out all the facts may still be biased in its tone. Try to find a reporter whose track record and reputation reflect what you hope to achieve by blowing the whistle. The best reporters can take a story far deeper and with much greater impact than you ever thought possible.

Establish the ground rules for your working relationship   Once you have selected a media outlet and a journalist, it is important to understand how best to approach the reporter or broadcast producer and determine what he can and cannot do for you. Before providing the reporter any information, be sure to clarify and reach agreement on the terms of your working relationship. One crucial issue to clarify is whether you expect anonymity. Good reporters will not reveal their sources, even before a court of law.

Before you tell your story to a reporter, you must set rules for how you want to be identified. Be clear about whether or not you are speaking "on the record." If so, the reporter can identify you by name and position in the industry. If you choose to speak on the record, be sure to state that you are speaking only for yourself and not as a representative of your company. If there is any chance of confusion on this point, you might want the story to include this disclaimer. You can also decide to speak "off the record," which means that the reporter cannot use your name but can characterize your position (for example, "an outside auditor for XYZ Corp."). Unless you are careful, such characterizations can be revealing to anyone trying to identify the source of the leak. You should come to a mutual agreement on such characterizations in advance.

When you provide information "on background," the reporter is not supposed to characterize you in any way but must write about the information generically. This approach is the safest but makes it harder for the reporter to write a story that will be interesting, credible, and specific enough to get published. Be clear with the reporter about your choice of attribution and be very specific when necessary. Sometimes particular facts alone are the functional equivalent of your signature. This is the case, for example, when only a few people (including you) could possibly be aware of the information you have released. In that case, if a reporter uses your information at all, your identity will be revealed. Similarly, if you are the only one who has raised concerns about a problem, you will be the person thought to have disclosed the information.

If you want to remain anonymous in those circumstances, it is wisest to communicate only on "deep background" when educating a reporter about the issue. This agreement generally means that none of your information is to be used except as a foundation for asking more-generalized questions. Of course, this means the information is much less likely to ever be disseminated. It still may prove valuable for an independent investigation, however. Knowing what questions to ask in pursuing a lead or interviewing a key player can be very useful. Further, the extra knowledge from deep background can facilitate a reporter's ability to judge the veracity or reliability of statements made by witnesses and corporate officers in the reporter's investigation.

Reporters prefer to speak with you on the record and will assume that you are speaking on the record unless you specify otherwise. Be aware too that many reporters have different definitions for these disclosure terms, so it is critical that you define your terms *before* you release your information. Do *not* expect the reporter to accept retroactive limitations on information you have already shared. Make sure that the terms of your agreement apply to your entire conversation and clarify whether you expect them to apply to subsequent conversations. Above all, you must weigh your need for protection against the need to tell the reporter enough to write the article. This is invariably a difficult but important judgment call.

Reporters have no shortage of items competing for their attention. If your story is time sensitive, give a specific deadline for its use; otherwise it may be put on the back burner. You also need to pin down whether you are offering an "exclusive." This means that you will not talk to other members of the media until your reporter airs or publishes the story. Obviously, it is in the reporter's best interest for you to make that commitment. This can be useful for you because the reporter's sense of ownership may be motivation to work harder on it. But the reporter may also think that by owning the story there is unlimited time to work on it. Meanwhile, your whistleblowing initiative can be overtaken by other events.

If the reporter requires an exclusive arrangement that limits what you can share with others, restrict the first interview to deep background until you have made up your mind. If and when you decide to grant the exclusive, protect yourself by working out the terms of the arrangement before going further. For example, limit it to a reasonable period of time, depending on the story. In general, you should agree on a time frame that is long enough to allow the reporter to cover the story thoroughly but does not drag out until the issue becomes stale. Imposing a deadline may irritate the reporter, so be sure to suggest it in a courteous and reasonable way. Remember that you can always agree to extend the deadline. One approach for a particularly hot story is to grant a temporary exclusive while the reporter seeks approval from editors to make a desired commitment, such as front-page publication within a specified period. Usually, the reporter can only give his best judgment as to front-page placement.

Another item that may be important to pin down is whether the reporter is willing and able to commit to follow-up coverage. Most significantly, what is the reporter's role if there is any follow-up harassment of you, your family, or your associates because of disclosures through that outlet? Even if a story does not get published, an aggressive query from a *New York Times* journalist or *60 Minutes* producer can be effective to prevent retaliation by convincing a corporate bully that harassment is not worth it and will just make the company look worse. If retaliation occurs anyway, seeking accountability will be more personal for the reporter. Determine up front if the reporter can commit to being there when you are on the ropes, but do not be upset if that is not an option. The media outlet has no responsibility to you other than honoring the commitments you carefully hammered out in advance.

Often you can pursue print and broadcast reporters simultaneously. You must be sure that each knows the other is also covering your story. They may agree to release their stories close together to reinforce the story even though their audiences are different. This reduces the sense of competition.

Have your story prepared   Start by visualizing the headline and the lead paragraph of the news story you are trying to produce. The key to publicizing problems is to make the story interesting and clear, to present reporters with a compelling description of the actions and their ramifications for the public. Write a short, focused summary and back it up with definitive documentation. Have your documents organized in an understandable order; and when speaking to the reporter, use an outline that you have prepared and practiced beforehand. Respect the reporter's limited time by being organized and avoiding excessive detail. Open with a basic overview, offering documents as you go, and then go into detail in areas in which the reporter expresses interest. A good rule is to limit introductory summaries to a minute in a phone call and to 10 minutes in a face-to-face meeting. The conversations can go on much longer, but your prepared summary should not.

Practice delivering your message, taking into account the suggestions offered here. Although these tips will help you communicate more effectively, in most cases they will not come naturally. Practice is especially useful to help you get over the jitters and allow you to become more familiar with your material. Often someone from a concerned nonprofit group or congressional office can help you prepare for your media interviews by asking you tough questions and giving you feedback on your answers.

This does not mean memorizing or preparing a script, unless you decide that that is the best way for you to communicate. Relatively spontaneous, extemporaneous speaking is usually best. It is more credible, sounds more natural, and, because it is easier to listen to, is more effective at communicating the point. A good balance can be struck by speaking from an outline, where concepts are listed and reinforced with key facts, punch lines, and statistics.

Provide a timeline　　A skeletal chronology organized around dates can be a concise, easy-to-understand summary that highlights milestones in your story. The spotlight on dates is particularly useful to identify patterns or causal relationships. Reporters, congressional staff, and lawyers alike generally appreciate a timeline to help them organize the facts of your narrative. Prepare the timeline before your initial interview.

No matter what, keep your cool　　The calmest person in the room is usually seen as the most credible. That demeanor reflects self-confidence, with no need for defensiveness. The point is not to be emotionless or uncaring but to stay poised. It leaves the impression of self-confidence. This is extremely hard because you are probably nervous about being made a public figure, about opening up to a stranger, and, above all, about the public policy and personal issues at stake. But there are few tips more important for media interviews—or in other settings in which credibility is essential. Especially if a reporter tries to bait you, strive to stay unruffled and unflappable. Respond thoughtfully, even to provocative challenges. Remember too that the reporter is not doing his job if he fails to ask you the tough questions that are at the heart of what your opponents and hardest critics might say about the situation.

Never exaggerate or dramatize   Never embellish your information. A common mistake made by whistleblowers, once they have finally convinced someone to listen to them, is to tell the reporter 110 percent of the story to make their point. This is extremely problematic because once the reporter—or another source, such as a company official—detects the 10 percent that is embellished, the rest of your information becomes suspect. Depending on context, be cautious about your conclusions, no matter how logical, especially if they involve speculation. Your initial contribution is as an eyewitness to significant facts. At the same time, do not shortchange the significance of your whistleblowing. In particular, focus on the consequences known or reasonably expected. Identify all the issues and provide leads so that reporters can make their own judgment calls on tougher questions. It helps your credibility when investigators conclude for themselves that the situation may be even worse than you initially asserted.

Once you have reviewed and prepared your information, refrain from delivering an overly dramatized presentation. High drama erodes the patience of veteran reporters, many of whom feel that they have "seen it all." Television reporters will be particularly concerned about your delivery if they are trying to judge how credible and articulate you will be on camera. Similarly, be wary of reporters who seem to exaggerate or dramatize. Do not let yourself be lured into action for the sake of sensationalism. That could be ruinous in other, more sober contexts. If the story needs a hook, avoid having it buried in your back.

Be an advocate for the story, not for yourself   Do not try to convince reporters that you are a hero or martyr. The relevance of your personal stature, or even reprisals against you, will depend on how the reporter evaluates the significance and the credibility of your evidence. Emphasize the ramifications for the public. Do not start your conversation, for example, by reciting all the injustices that you have had to endure. The best way to impress a reporter with your story (and your motivations) is to emphasize the facts about and the consequences of the misconduct that you witnessed; let the journalist ask about your personal hardships. If the reporter has not asked, volunteer the personal problems that you have had only in the context of pinning down confidentiality or at the end of the meeting, and keep your statements brief.

Even if reporters ask you about your personal fight with the company, try to keep the focus on the subject of your whistleblowing—the threat to public health or safety, or the fraud and the abuse you seek to expose. You can discuss incidents of repression by raising questions about why the organization is trying to silence you or others (e.g., what is the employer afraid of?). If and when you do discuss retaliation, do not come across as bitter, defensive, or paranoid, and do not dwell on the subject.

A reporter may well decide, however, that the harassment is a part of the story, so be ready and able to summarize what happened to you—and why people should believe you despite your employer's efforts to discredit you. If you go public, part of the territory is successfully defending yourself when reprisals have occurred.

Speak in "sound bites" Few things are more precious to a reporter than time and space. If you cannot make a point crisply in 15 to 30 seconds, you may lose the opportunity to share it at all with the public. Because this is probably your only chance, practice and prepare sound bites—clear, concise, and catchy statements about the issue at hand. They represent the thought you want to leave behind for any given point. View the sound bite as analogous to the topic sentence in a paragraph or the lead in an article. In-depth explanations may help educate the reporter, but a detailed discussion seldom will be practical to broadcast or print as is; the reporter will most likely condense and paraphrase that part of the interview. In many cases, all you will be permitted to communicate directly to a public audience is a sound bite or two, so offer several good ones to provide the reporter with a menu of points you want to make. Practice your sound bites before meeting with the reporter.

Think consequences　Impact is the point of everything—for you, the reporter, and the audience you both want to engage. You are taking the risk to make a difference. You will gain both a media outlet and public solidarity for your dissent only if you demonstrate the impact on their lives. That means emphasizing the consequences of whatever abuse of power you are exposing. Maybe it is the risk of life-threatening injury or the waste of public funds in a government contract. You will earn solidarity only if the public is concerned about the consequences, and that means the point of your message is to warn them.

Start with the bottom line　Contrary to what we have been taught at school or on the job, when approaching an interview it is usually better to start with the conclusion and then explain its basis. Otherwise, reporters and public audiences feel you are trying to evade a question. Or they may get restless waiting for you to get to the point.

Demystify technical jargon and paint a picture with your words　Try to express yourself with words that create a picture in the reader's or listener's mind. Creating a mental image is generally more compelling that an abstract or wordy academic approach, even if the audience understands your point. More commonly, your audience may not comprehend the significance of your words, particularly if you are a scientific or technical expert and prone to jargon. Often an analogy to everyday ideas and situations can demystify technical language and create a clearer picture of what is going on. Think about similar situations in real life that people can relate to. For example, a complicated corporate price-gouging scheme can be likened to a vendor's selling bottled water significantly above market prices on the hottest day of the year. Similarly, a technical deficiency in the construction of a nuclear power plant could be compared to making a teakettle out of wax.

Get it right the first time　You rarely get a second chance to make a first impression. After your initial contact, do not assume that you will have the opportunity to correct inaccuracies. Be certain of the facts and stay in command of them. One false fact is likely to bury the truth in doubt.

Make your time available   Within reason, reporters should have ready access when they need to reach you. This may take effort because most employees are restricted from speaking with the press for "personal reasons" on company time. Return the reporter's call during your next break or let the reporter call you at home after hours. Avoid using your company's phone when dealing with the press.

Make your expertise available   Your expertise is another unique contribution you have to offer, demystifying technical jargon for the reporter or explaining the hypothetical consequences of some abuse of power. Your role as a teacher may determine whether a reporter both fully understands the story's implications and gains confidence that it can be communicated effectively. It is also an opportunity to earn the reporter's trust and to demonstrate your mastery of the subject matter of your disclosure.

Monitor the story without being pushy   This advice applies both before and after the story is completed. If you have not heard from the reporter for some time during the research and writing phase, it is acceptable etiquette to call with an offer to be helpful and answer any questions that may have accumulated. Do not assume that you own the reporter's time and back off if your offer is not accepted immediately. After the story is written and published, you should keep the reporter informed about how the scandal is progressing but avoid becoming a pest. Reporters are often pressured by their editors to move on to the next story. They frequently have to fight for the time and newspaper space for any follow-up stories.

Do not attack the reporter if you have to correct a mistake   Realistically, reporters must absorb far too much information to get everything absolutely accurate the first time. Often their job is to develop functional expertise about a subject, starting with a zero knowledge base. The most fortunate receive a few months' time; more often they have only a few days or even hours to tell the whole story. If something is inaccurate or an agreement in your working relationship is breached, assert yourself but do so civilly and without getting personal. Keep the reporter's circumstances in mind and respect the hard work that almost all reporters invest in their profession. A good journalist will want to get it right and will appreciate your initiative so that an inaccuracy is not repeated.

Be prepared for the story's not being published   There is no way around a serious, inherent wildcard when working with the media. Many factors important to you may be out of the reporter's control and instead decided by people whom you will never meet. Reporters have to sell their stories to editors and publishers. The more controversial the issue, the more the managers of the newspaper or television station will get involved. Sometimes owners or key institutional stakeholders may be tied in some way to the targets of your whistleblower disclosure or even implicated directly. In the absence of a conflict of interest, the owners and managers of newspapers and television stations may still feel political and monetary pressures. They may fear a lawsuit, for example. Often stories are edited to fit allotted space, and the edits may leave out key facts or analysis. Reporters do not usually write the headlines, which may end up off target, disappointingly sensational, or outright inaccurate. When reporters invest a significant amount of time and resources, it is a good indicator that their employer wants to break a major story. But do not count on it. Not infrequently, stories have been canceled even after being written for the front page and having obtained several layers of preliminary approval. Remember, however, that in terms of making a difference, sometimes the most effective stories are those that are never printed or broadcast. That happens when media queries convince wrongdoers to change their minds before there is a scandal.

Keep the reporter's purpose in perspective   Reporters are not there to provide assistance, crusade for your cause, or be your friends. Though some reporters may offer to help locate a lawyer for you or to contact your company, most will remain uninvolved in your personal concerns to safeguard their independence, objectivity, and credibility. Their focus is on reporting the relevant facts of the case. When your dissent is clearly on behalf of the public, there may be common ground. If reporters believe that your information is credible and significant, they may seek more information from attorneys with relevant expertise. They may contact the company to find out what is being done about your allegations. You should not expect reporters to take these steps, however.

Most reporters will resent it or withdraw if you pressure them to editorialize or to act as your advocate. Of course, they will form opinions about the issues and who is playing straight. These judgments may be reflected subtly in the article. Which facts are emphasized? Who gets the better of "he said/she said" exchanges? Who gets the first and last word? In most cases, however, the professional standard is to let the facts speak for themselves.

Do not assume because you are working closely with a reporter that he is your friend. Part of a reporter's job is to put you at ease so that you are willing to speak openly and preferably on the record. Regardless, your interactions with a reporter are above all a business relationship. A reporter who is gracious and understanding is being a professional. Be sure to be professional in turn. Friendship may evolve, but do not presume.

Be ready for the aftermath   As a final note, you should be prepared for what may come *after* you have successfully blown the whistle to the media. If you have been anonymous in your whistleblowing, it is important to remain calm and not do anything that casts suspicion on yourself. Once a story hits the media, your company will begin damage control. Depending on your position, you may be asked to sit in on meetings to address the issue or even to help plan a cover-up. This would put you in a good position to continue telling the reporter whether the company is legitimately trying to solve the problem.

If you are going public with your whistleblowing, you may receive more publicity and requests for interviews after the story appears. It is good to take advantage of the extra publicity to shed more light on the subject of your whistleblowing, but approach your new-found status with caution. It may be flattering to suddenly receive all this attention, but remember that a company can discredit you by portraying you as a self-glorified publicity hound. A little humility goes a long way in making your case.

New and Social Media

Facebook. YouTube. Twitter. The blogosphere. Computer-enabled platforms are the wave of the communications future, with a new generation of Americans growing up online. In contrast to traditional print and broadcast media, this "new media" offers the possibility of on-demand, real-time creation, manipulation, and consumption of content anytime, anywhere, by anyone. Wikipedia is a shining example of the new-media phenomenon. It harnesses interactive, openly editable web-based technology to form a virtual community of participants who use, contribute to, edit, fact-check, and financially support a multilingual, free-content encyclopedia that has grown to be one the world's largest reference websites, with more than 16 million constantly revised articles accessed by more than 78 million visitors every month.

What does this mean for whistleblowing? In short, a lot. The democratization of media means that whistleblowers are no longer at the mercy of the mass media in reaching the public with their disclosures or in recounting the retaliation they have suffered.

Social media such as Facebook and Twitter offer a lightning-fast and efficient way for whistleblowers to communicate news updates and calls for action to supporters. Tools like blogs not only offer a forum for whistleblowers to express their views but also afford access to the mass media and much greater exposure. That said, whistleblowers need to use new media carefully and strategically, or they risk a negative boomerang effect.

It wouldn't seem like 140 characters sent via Twitter could mean this much. But employees have been fired for "tweets" critical of their company. How would your supervisors find out? They can check your online diary, showing that you were posting personal messages during working hours. Likewise, Facebook posts note the date and the time that comments are made. The company will say it is firing you not for dissenting but because you were conducting personal business on company time or misusing the company's computers for personal purposes. Of course, that is just an excuse, a pretext, as everyone handles personal matters at work from time to time. But your boss will claim that it is a legitimate business reason for firing you, and a court may just agree.

This is no abstract threat: a July 2010 poll by online e-mail and data security firm Proofpoint of 261 communications professionals found that 7 percent of companies with more than 1,000 employees terminated employees for posting proprietary information on social media sites. Among new media sites and blogs, the number is even larger.[54] The point is, what you post online—and what others post online about you—is public and can be used by you *and* against you. While it is a good practice to document the wrongdoing you witness at your company, when you do it via social or new media you are also making a record for the world. Make sure it is not a gift to your legal adversaries.

You might think that online diaries, blogs, and other content management and storage platforms, if kept private, are an effective means of documenting and selectively communicating wrongdoing. But are you certain this media will remain private? Are you positive you have not left an electronic paper trail? If you are at all in doubt, consider consulting an attorney, consumer privacy organization, or whistleblower protection group for advice. There have been plenty of controversies to raise suspicions about the private sector's handling of our private information. Consider Facebook's attempts to revise its Terms of Service to assert broad, permanent, and retroactive rights over users' personal information even after they deleted their accounts. Or consider Google's automated public listing of e-mail contacts upon the launch of its social networking tool, Buzz.

Our point is not to scare you away from using new and social media. We all know how powerful viral YouTube videos are and how effective social media can be, like in raising millions of dollars for Haitian earthquake relief. And just as employees post mistakes, bosses post mistakes, too. Be cognizant of this—you never know what you might find. The upsides of new and social media for whistleblowers have yet to be fathomed. By all means, make use. But be smart and strategic.

Going Viral: The Story of Allan Zabel and Laurie Williams

Laurie Williams and Allan Zabel worked at the Environmental Protection Agency for years. As enforcement attorneys and environmental experts, they had the job to know what did and did not work. In their opinion emissions trading, or "cap and trade"—a system designed to curb the harmful emissions of corporate polluters—did not work to curb global warming. Zabel's specific duties were to monitor climate change policies in California, where cap and trade has been in place for years.

Yet this method was to be a cornerstone of then-pending national legislation aimed at tackling this enormously important issue. Williams and Zabel felt compelled to act. Very clearly disclaiming their beliefs as personal, they penned an op-ed in the *Washington Post* and coupled it with a YouTube video explaining their position. In the video they noted their government jobs and experience to help viewers assess their credibility.

Although Williams and Zabel were not compensated for the video, and they made clear that they were speaking in their own capacities and not on behalf of the EPA, the agency accused them of ethics rules violations and demanded they take down the video under penalty of termination. Williams and Zabel complied. Agency officials also ordered them to gain EPA approval prior to any further personal postings or public opinions— a clear gag order on their free-speech rights. Again they were threatened with termination if they did not get in line.

Williams and Zabel fought back, going over the heads of the EPA administration with the help of the Government Accountability Project. The White House took the lead for a generic solution beyond EPA and, in late 2009, the Office of Government Ethics issued new guidelines for all government agencies, banning censorship for noncommercial speech and forcing the EPA to withdraw its ethics-based gag policies.

Pointers for Using Social and New Media

If you are thinking about blowing the whistle, here are some tips about using your personal social media pages:

Set your privacy settings high   Often users of social media want to "live online," wrongfully assuming that only friends are interested in what they are doing. But if you bring a lawsuit against your employer, your bosses will undoubtedly become the most interested audience of your future (and past) updates. For starters, make sure your privacy restrictions on these platforms are set to the highest level.

Watch who your friends are   Are some of your online followers co-workers? Just casual acquaintances? Friends of friends? Try to be selective as to who is following you online. Never allow anyone you do not know to follow you.

Avoid posting during business hours   Unless you are a communications professional, posting is not likely in your job description. Do not serve your employer a legitimate business reason to fire you on a silver platter.

Watch what others post about you   On Facebook it is common for friends to take pictures at parties and "tag" the attendees. Have you been tagged in an unflattering light? Doing something professionally inappropriate or morally questionable? People have been fired for less. You can remove the tags but not the photos. Perhaps you should ask your friend to remove them.

CHAPTER 5

Getting Help in Blowing the Whistle

You may feel helpless and alone, isolated in a stifling work environment where your supervisors use power and deceit to punish you and cover up the truth—while even your most trusted colleagues are forced to rally to management's side for fear of retaliation. You may be shunned; labeled a traitor, troublemaker, or liar; and left to fend for yourself. The board of directors, the courts, Congress, and the media may all seem like an intimidating and uncaring, if not altogether hostile, audience to your claims. But take heart: there are sources of strategic, moral, and material support in numerous communities that can make the experience both less harrowing and more effective.

Advocacy Partners: A Whistleblower's Best Friend

Advocacy partners can be a vital resource for whistleblowers. These groups can provide advice and support as well as resources and connections, can share their own research and knowledge on issues of concern to you, and can even serve as your main channel for blowing the whistle. Consider calling on them, particularly if the idea of blowing the whistle to a hotline, a member of Congress, or the press seems too intimidating. They are an essential link in the chain of accountability that can turn your whistleblowing information into power. Most of the success stories in this handbook would not have occurred without the solidarity and the support of advocacy partners.

Advocacy partners can also be key to an anonymous whistleblower strategy. If you plan well and implement strict confidentiality procedures up front, they can help you communicate evidence to the public while hiding you as its original source. For example, whistleblowers can speak through advocacy partners by ghost-drafting comments, appeals, letters, and Freedom of Information Act requests. Public Employees for Environmental Responsibility and the Union of Concerned Scientists have been particularly adept at working with whistleblowers to develop the right questions for employee surveys that generate credibility through anonymous confirmation for an individual's dissent.

Whistleblowers can define the issues, and then advocacy partners may produce and release issue reports, or "white papers," based on whistleblowers' findings that provide the public and the media with a lay translation of technical terms and a context for the current details of corporate malfeasance. Bolstered with well-documented facts, citations to publicly available reference materials, and photocopies of internal memos not readily accessible, these reports are an effective vehicle for disclosing what conscientious employees know, without exposing their identities. Similarly, advocacy partners can harness the media by issuing news releases or trying to place supportive articles in local or national newspapers.

There are relatively few experienced organizations that specialize in working directly with corporate whistleblowers using such strategies. In addition to the Government Accountability Project, which has a more than 30-year track record of whistleblower advocacy, other sources for help are listed in Tool C in the Whistleblower Toolkit. These include whistleblower self-help organizations that are multiplying at a heady pace, often organized around particular issues.

Beyond these groups there is a range of advocacy organizations that may not work extensively with whistleblowers but can help nonetheless. These range from issue-oriented public interest groups to labor unions and professional associations. They vary in their approach to whistleblower concerns and in the type and the degree of assistance they offer—generally depending on the extent of your shared agenda. A public interest environmental group may choose to help you fight your battle because you have information critical to exposing industry contamination. A consumer organization may view your information as important in warning the public about unsafe products. A union may work with you because you are a dues-paying member or because you have information about a corporation that can be used in collective bargaining or an organizing campaign. A professional association or society is likely to be concerned about issues affecting the profession's credibility.

These nongovernmental organizations are the keystone of your solidarity networks. They know who the significant actors are in the public and political arenas and can be matchmakers with the partners you need to make a difference, from responsible government officials to knowledgeable journalists. They often specialize in monitoring and combating precisely the type of misconduct you are exposing. In that context they may know of analogous corporate misconduct and may recognize your experience as part of a larger pattern. They can channel, cloak, or amplify dissent through solidarity tactics, such as the surveying discussed earlier. In short, NGOs are the natural leaders to follow up on the work you begin by disclosing a corporate abuse of power.

Babak Pasdar and Civil Liberties NGOs: Teaming Up to Make a Difference

Babak Pasdar is a nationally recognized expert on computer security. In 2003 he discovered a circuit operated by one of the major telecom companies that joined every customer's family with an unknown party in Quantico, Virginia—the company town for the FBI. The "Quantico circuit" provided unfettered access, both targeted and en masse, to all communications in the company's mobile network, including location tracking of any mobile phone user, any mobile telephone calls, e-mails, text messages, photos, and videos. The system was structured so that there would be no record of what information Quantico received.

After agonizing for more than two years, Pasdar tried to engage with some private attorneys that claimed specialization in constitutional privacy matters. After an initial interview with these attorneys, Pasdar decided that his efforts would be better served by a different group. Despite their oath of privacy, the attorneys filed a $233 billion lawsuit against the major telecom organizations, with Pasdar's story as an anonymous witness.

Pasdar eventually found the Government Accountability Project and made a series of anonymous disclosures in 2006 and 2007 to civil liberties groups and congressional offices but got nowhere. Alarmed by media reports of imminent House acquiescence to legislation that granted telecoms blanket immunity for prior domestic surveillance, he decided to go public. On March 4, 2008, he submitted an affidavit to Congress, which GAP shared with civil liberties organizations on the front lines of the struggle to maintain privacy rights.[1] They distributed his affidavit throughout their well-developed network of congressional supporters, and it ended up sparking a counterattack by House of Representatives leaders who rallied behind Representative John Dingell to temporarily defeat legislation granting telecom immunity against lawsuits challenging illegal domestic surveillance.[2] Unfortunately, follow-through from this reprieve was unable to stop subsequent approval of telecom immunity.

This section describes the most common types of advocacy partners.

Public Interest Organizations

Public interest groups cover the spectrum of issues. Think through the types of groups that might be concerned about the wrongdoing you have witnessed. Once you identify them, check that their position on the issue is in line with yours. If it is, you may be able to establish a mutually beneficial relationship in which your information helps their cause and vice versa. Do not be discouraged if you cannot find help right away. Even if a particular group cannot help you, be sure to ask for referrals to other organizations as well as subject matter experts and pro bono lawyers who specialize in your issue.

Some public interest organizations offer awards for courageous individuals who have contributed to their cause. Being nominated for these awards can be helpful because it increases your visibility and credibility to be publicly honored for your whistleblowing. Sometimes the recognition includes a modest cash award, and almost all awards generate at least some publicity that can put pressure on your bosses not to retaliate. Here are a few of the awards that have honored whistleblowers:

- Cliff Robertson Sentinel Award

- David P. Rall Award for Advocacy in Public Health

- Gold Whistle Award

- Goldman Environmental Prize

- Index Whistleblower Award

- Joe A. Callaway Award for Civic Courage

- LennonOno Grant for Peace

- Project on Government Oversight's Beyond the Headlines Award

- Ridenhour Truth-Telling Prize

- Right Livelihood Award

- Special Counsel's Public Servant Award (for federal whistleblowers)

- Transparency International's Integrity Awards

Employee Organizations

Labor unions, employee federations, and professional associations are the primary employee organizations. All have employee-based memberships and work to further their members' interests. Although managers can punish individuals for simply bringing up problems, both retaliation and smears are more difficult to carry out when a group of employees speaks with one voice—and the bigger the group, the stronger the voice. Unlike public interest groups, employee organizations are generally not wedded to furthering a particular issue but rather to serving their members. Therefore it is likely that you would need to be a member before securing assistance from such organizations.

Unions can be a natural ally for whistleblowers. They have established political access, deference among legislators, and working relationships with regulators. In exchange for paying dues, union members are often entitled to tangible services as well. For example, a union may provide legal counsel to members facing employment disputes. Membership in a union may also trigger legal options you would not otherwise have, such as binding arbitration through a hearing in which you have equal say with management in choosing the arbitrator who will decide your case.

As potential allies in your whistleblowing, unions vary tremendously. Some can be counted on to stand up for members who blow the whistle. They may also work in partnership with other groups, to link whistleblowers with affected constituencies. Other unions are so closely aligned with management that they would be reluctant to challenge your employer. Still others may support you in principle but may make a strategic decision not to push on the ethical issues you raise because they are in a protracted battle with management over pay, benefits, or other issues of higher priority.

Supportive local union leaders may not be able to come through for you if their efforts are vetoed by superiors who are cozy with management on the regional or national level. As you would with other groups, you should check out your union's track record in assisting whistleblowers before you approach it for help. Be aware that if the union is unsympathetic to whistleblowers, a union official might alert management to your activities.

You may be faced with the decision to trade statutory rights against retaliation with those available in a union collective bargaining agreement. In the latter context, the union is the official party and controls the case, not you. To illustrate the risk, it is not unusual for whistleblowers to be frustrated because the union abandons their litigation short of receiving even an informal day in court through an arbitration hearing.

Employee Support Organizations

There is a rare hybrid that combines the missions of an issue-oriented public interest group and an employee organization. These groups consist of employees from a particular industry that have joined together to champion a common agenda. For example, for many years the Center for Women's Economic Alternatives was a North Carolina self-help group for women working in the poultry industry. Because such groups are employee-focused, they are more likely to understand and be sensitive to whistleblower concerns. If an employee support organization exists in your field, it may be especially useful in connecting you with other like-minded professionals—including current and former whistleblowers—in your area of expertise.

Professional Associations

Depending on your job, you may also consider approaching a professional association, such as the Union of Concerned Scientists, National Association of Social Workers, American Association for the Advancement of Science, American Society of Limnology and Oceanography, or a state bar association. These associations vary greatly in size and mission. Most provide dues-paying members with up-to-date information about developments in the profession, through newsletters, educational events, conferences, and job listings. Others, such as the Union of Concerned Scientists, will go further in defending the interests of members and the integrity of the profession. Those organizations that are independent and have large memberships can be credible and powerful friends in your battle to tell the truth and keep your career intact.

A note of caution: professional associations often have large budgets, but many acquire some of their funding from industry. Be sure to investigate where the association gets its funding by requesting a copy of its annual report. These reports should list the primary contributors and provide general information about the association's program. Check with your peers to see what they think about the association and its leadership and if they have ever sought help from it. Often even the most cautious and conservative associations have an ethics committee whose members may be kindred spirits.

Considerations before Working with Advocacy Partners

Remember, the principle of earned trust still applies to advocacy partners. Although many groups do admirable and important work, they can also be self-serving. These organizations do not have any inherent loyalty to you; it is to their mission. They may be sorely tempted to use you as an "information object." They may not have any time for your retaliation struggle once they have vacuumed your brain. They may breach your confidentiality. This is not a context for blind faith.

Ground rules The question of how much control you have over the public release of your information is something you need to negotiate in advance. For example, it may be acceptable to you for a group to use your information in framing tough survey questions based on your disclosures, even if you would object to the group's asserting that it knows the answers. Remember that, unless you have approached the group's lawyers to represent you, your disclosures to them are not automatically covered by the attorney-client privilege. Unless you work out a confidentiality agreement first, your information becomes theirs to use. As such it is advisable to research their reputation and how effectively they have worked with whistleblowers in the past. If you already have a lawyer, ask for advice about whether it is wise to approach a particular organization.

Initial approach   After identifying the right advocacy partners, how you approach them can be decisive in establishing a good working relationship. Never go in with demands. Although your issues are important, remember that there are a lot of competing issues and priorities for these groups. You do not want to alienate staff by being too pushy, expecting them to drop long-term projects for the honor of taking on your agenda.

If a whistleblower organization that you trust has established intake procedures, follow them. That generally means writing up the basis of your whistleblowing concerns and the details of your case in a standard two-page, single-spaced summary. If an organization does not have an established intake procedure, your summary can be sent to the appropriate contact person. If you are not yet sure you can trust the organization, however, do not share your summary or confidential information until you have a mutual agreement and a commitment from the group about how your information will be used.

Confidentiality   As you begin communicating with an organization, remember that protecting your attorney-client privilege is critical if you want your information or identity to remain confidential. Advocacy groups are not automatically covered by the privilege. Therefore you may be waiving this legal right unless you talk only through the group's lawyers, or someone supervised by a lawyer, on the condition that the conversation is covered by the attorney-client privilege. If you fail to protect your privilege by disclosing your information to a nonattorney, you could be deemed to have waived your privilege rights, and in legal proceedings that person could be required to share your disclosures.

Follow-up   Your next step is to make a follow-up call to the contact person to ensure that your information was received and to set up an in-person meeting. Be firm and politely persistent in your conversations. These groups generally are understaffed and overextended. They appreciate your sensitivity to what they are coping with; patience is an investment in your longer-term working relationship. If they are not interested, ask for referrals to other organizations. If the group is concerned and wants to help, be sure to establish clear parameters for defining your relationship. The sooner you communicate your mutual expectations, the less chance there will be for misunderstanding and potentially career-damaging mistakes.

Questions to Ask before Taking on an Advocacy Partner

Making an organization a valuable ally takes work and patience. The following are some questions you may want to research or ask:

- What are the organization's funding sources?

- Has the organization worked with whistleblowers before? If so, who, and may I contact them about their experience?

- What is the organization's track record in making a difference with respect to issues raised by my disclosure?

- How wide of an audience can the organization reach? How many members does it have? What is its capacity to mobilize them? Do relevant news outlets, congressional or local legislative offices, and government officials take its message seriously?

- If it is a union or professional association, what benefits does it provide to members?

- How will the organization use my information? What are the organization's goals in using my information?

- If applicable, is the organization willing to protect my identity as the source of the information?

- To ensure accuracy, will I be able to fact-check public documents that the organization produces? (This is especially important if disclosures are of a highly technical nature.)

- Is there one person who will be my primary contact?

- If applicable, is the organization comfortable working with my lawyer?

- What sort of financial commitment, if any, is expected of me?

Whistleblowing on the Web

The Internet has increasingly become a popular tool for persons of conscience and their advocacy partners, particularly when an employee wants to leak a "smoking gun" document that speaks for itself. Scanned photos or internal memos can set the record straight in a powerful way. Advocacy groups' websites double as bulletin boards to post such documentation. The documentation can be supplemented with outreach to relevant management officers, decision-makers, and media outlets, with links back to the scanned documentation, a brief description of its significance, and even the public record of corporate bluffs surrounding it. As with white papers, these web links can be a resource confronting companies with a well-documented message while keeping the messenger safe.

WikiLeaks and Similar Sites

WikiLeaks.org offers one such vehicle for the anonymous posting of disclosures about corporate and governmental wrongdoing. It boasted more than 1.2 million documents within a year of its winter 2006–2007 launch. According to the site, WikiLeaks was founded by Chinese dissidents, journalists, mathematicians, and start-up company technologists from the United States, Taiwan, Europe, Australia, and South Africa interested in exposing oppressive regimes and unethical behavior without risking prison for whistleblowers and journalists. The site won the 2008 *Economist* Index on Censorship Freedom of Expression Award and the 2009 Amnesty International Human Rights Reporting Award (New Media). It gained the financial support of the Associated Press and the *Los Angeles Times* for releasing such headline-generating documents as human rights abuses in Iraq, Guantanamo Bay standard operating procedures, Sarah Palin's Yahoo! account e-mails, and the Minton Report on toxic dumping in Africa.

The website became famous, or notorious, in 2010 with multiple notable releases. First, in April it posted a video titled *Collateral Murder,* apparently recorded from an American military helicopter gunship that fired on and killed 12 innocent Iraqis, including two Reuters reporters. The pilots exhibited a "video game" mindset, laughing and joking in firing their weapons. When a van full of individuals showed up to help the wounded, the van was attacked as well. It subsequently released hundreds of thousands of documents related to the American occupation of Afghanistan, including information on a CIA "black ops" assassination squad, the systematic US suppression of Afghan civilian casualties, and US officials' belief that the Pakistan military was aiding and guiding the

Afghan insurgency. That was followed, with worldwide controversy, by the release of hundreds of thousands of pages of classified documents on the Iraq War and State Department diplomacy. As of this writing, the website is previewing similarly ambitious corporate releases.

Financial constraints and court injunctions have periodically led to the suspension of some of WikiLeak's activities, and it is under cyberattacks to shut the site down by overwhelming its servers. Moreover, while the website purports to promise anonymity (and to this point it has not divulged any sources), a whistleblower should never assume that sending these types of materials online means they are not leaving tracks. In general, electronic communications leave footprints—even after you delete them. At the time of this writing, the US Army has charged and is holding one private with the leaking of the *Collateral Murder* video. His legal prospects are not strong, as military whistleblowers enjoy extremely limited protections.

Whistleblowers should be cautious of something else: there is no buffer between you and WikiLeaks-type websites that simply post materials. No one at WikiLeaks offers its sources legal advice about the risks the sources are running. Are you sure that what you are releasing won't incriminate you? How many other people might have had access to the files you are releasing so that the trail does not lead directly to you? Could you be fired in retaliation? WikiLeaks alongside similar sites such as Cryptome.org has proven to be a powerful, though not risk-free, option for whistleblowers wishing to remain anonymous. Wikileaks does not purport to do more than dump anonymous documents into the public domain. It does not get involved with follow-up investigations or advocacy. The good offices of an attorney or advocacy group are still advised prior to blowing the whistle via the World Wide Web, if for no more reason than to provide a broader context for the web disclosure.

Whistleblowers and Their Lawyers

Employees who decide to blow the whistle or have already done so need a strong support network that includes legal expertise because—as discussed in the next chapter—whistleblowing can take on complex legal dimensions. Regardless of whether your experience leads to a lawsuit, an attorney can prove invaluable. Nevertheless, financial considerations or the particulars of a case may lead some whistleblowers to deal with the matter independently, or *pro se.*

A well-informed and sympathetic attorney can offer assistance at every step of the whistleblowing process, not just in the courtroom against retaliation. An attorney can help you prevent reprisals from occurring in the first place by supervising and monitoring your disclosure through the safest channels. If retaliation is inevitable, an attorney can ensure that you are on solid legal ground by screening your whistleblowing disclosure to provide an expert opinion on whether it is legally protected speech. If you say too much or do not have enough corroborating evidence, you may forfeit your rights against harassment.

Considerations before Selecting a Lawyer

Of course, effective legal counsel depends on picking the right lawyer and maintaining an effective working relationship. In the eyes of the law, the attorney and client are one. The attorney is the client's mouthpiece, and the client automatically receives both the benefits and the liabilities of the attorney's statements and decisions. Your choice of a lawyer is as significant as any other decision in the whistleblowing life cycle. Unfortunately, many whistleblowers are so eager to get their cases into the hands of an "expert" that they accept the first lawyer who will take them on affordable terms, entrusting their whistleblowing experience and their professional future to someone they really do not know. Such an arrangement poses unacceptably high risks to future happiness, financial well-being, and legal success.

Instead, create a list of lawyers with whom you might want to work. Ask your friends, family, colleagues, and anyone else whose opinion and judgment you trust. Get specific information from these sources. Find out what legal issues your contacts had in mind and what made a particular lawyer a good choice. Additional resources that may help you find representation are the websites of the National Employment Lawyers Association (NELA; *http://www.nela.org*), the Public Justice (*http://www .publicjustice.net*), and your state and county bar associations. Whistleblower support groups like the Government Accountability Project, the National Whistleblower Center, and Taxpayers Against Fraud (*http://*

www.taf.org; for False Claims suits) have attorney referral programs and a familiarity with other lawyers' track records.

Both NELA and the bar associations list local lawyers who specialize in employment law. In addition, bar associations keep records of disciplinary or misconduct issues that a given attorney has had. Public libraries should also have a copy of the *Martindale-Hubbell Law Directory*, which describes the specialties of attorneys under a variety of cross-references; it is also available online (*http://www.martindale.com*). When seeking a referral, ask for attorneys who specialize in wrongful discharge. If that fails to produce an adequate list, broaden the scope of the search to employment law. Be aware that you want a lawyer who mainly represents employees, not employers! The employment bar is highly divided.

Once you have a list of attorney prospects, you should set up meetings to get a feel for how it would be to work with them. Find out ahead of time whether the attorney charges a fee for an initial consultation. Pin down who would handle the case, as it may not be the same attorney assigned to discuss your case initially. Do not make a decision until you meet and have confidence in the specific attorney who will be responsible for defending your rights and interests.

Also consider consulting whistleblower organizations such as GAP or other public interest legal organizations that have an interest in the particular issues behind your whistleblowing. Remember that the attorney-client privilege does not apply during discussions with lay representatives unless they are supervised by an attorney. By pointing out that you have suffered retaliation for pursuing issues of public concern on the job, especially ones that relate to the organization's mission, your need for legal help will be clear. In some instances they may be able to provide legal assistance directly. In most cases they can refer you to other experienced attorneys who can assist you. Referrals are a routine part of GAP's service to whistleblowers.

Ultimately, trust and intuition are as important as a catalog of do's and don'ts in selecting and working with an attorney. Like any partnership, to be effective the attorney and the client should like each other and have a rapport based on mutual respect, at least within the context of their professional relationship. After all, they must rely on each other in a high-stakes conflict in which they are both underdogs by any conventional measure. Being open with each other is a prerequisite for success.

Pointers for Choosing a Lawyer

The smart whistleblower will follow both intuition and the guidance of this section, which is based on lessons learned by others who have gone through the same experience. The first set of factors concerns finding the right attorney; the second focuses on maintaining a good relationship and terminating a bad one.

Summarize your story in writing beforehand   Again the first step is your two-page summary. Prospective attorneys will appreciate the time they save by reading it before meeting with you. They can then get down to asking you the hard questions with some background knowledge of the dispute and its context. Remember that your case summary supplies an attorney's first impression of you and your communication skills. It allows the attorney to test your credibility by revealing whether you tend to exaggerate. Stick to the facts and avoid overstatements or unnecessary conclusions.

Ask about experience and conflicts of interest   It is important to have a guide who has been down this difficult legal road before. Lawyers have different training, interests, and expertise. You need an attorney who has handled whistleblower cases before, ideally with favorable outcomes for the clients. Attorneys without relevant experience may be excellent lawyers, but you need an advocate who knows where all the potholes and pitfalls on this road are and how to avoid them.

You should also be aware of any possible conflicts of interest that a lawyer might have in taking your case. Conflicts of interest arise when a lawyer has had dealings with the other party in your case; has an interest in the outcome of your case other than as your representative; has prior knowledge of, or connection to, your case; or is representing other clients whose interests conflict with yours. Lawyers are ethically obligated to investigate any possible conflicts of interest and report them to you, but it does not hurt to ask and to get your lawyer's response in writing. If you remain concerned, you can check the Martindale-Hubbell database or use a web search engine to investigate the attorney's history and past clients.

Conflicts of Interest Lead to Foul Play

One whistleblower at a poultry slaughter plant later learned that his powerful lawyer represented the state's poultry trade association. Not surprisingly, the lawyer allowed the statute of limitations to lapse on the whistleblower's case. Also not surprisingly, the employee could not find anyone to take a malpractice case against the lawyer because the state was dominated by the poultry industry.

Do not disregard the importance of getting to know each other No matter how experienced or skilled a legal practitioner your attorney is, he is also your employee and someone you will need to get along with at least on a professional level. Throughout this process, you will need to supply your attorney with information, make requests, and cooperate in a variety of ways, so it is important that the two of you can work together effectively. One common reason that attorney-client relationships sour is that each entered into the partnership with differing expectations of their relationship. An essential step in deciding on an attorney is to clarify—and then communicate—your own expectations in as much detail as possible. Consider whether you wish to remain as detached as possible without compromising your interests or whether your active involvement in the lawsuit is important for emotional vindication. In case of the latter, it would be mutually frustrating to hire the equivalent of a brilliant surgeon with no bedside manner.

Another area to clear up is who's in charge. While clients are officially the bosses, many just want a lawyer to tell them what to do. And many lawyers will not have it any other way. Other clients want to actively retain control of choices that are fundamental to their lives, such as which risks to take, after listening to their lawyer's recommendations. Compatibility on issues like this will make or break your working relationship.

Prepare to show your evidence Make a list of relevant documents currently or potentially available for your whistleblowing case. Identify solid candidates as supporting witnesses, and be prepared to describe how their testimony could help. You are not likely to win without either documentary evidence or strong supporting testimony. With that said, have your evidence available, but do not swamp a prospective attorney with too many documents during the initial consultation. Whistleblowers who show up with multiple binders of documents at the outset may simply overwhelm the lawyer.

Be clear about each other's goals and objectives   This includes not only issues involving the attorney's representation but also matters concerning the larger public policy issue that triggered your whistleblowing. Not all employees want or expect the same thing when they initiate legal proceedings as a result of employer retaliation. Employees may seek reinstatement, reversal of other retaliatory measures, monetary damages, adequate resolution of the originally reported misconduct, increased public awareness of an issue, or variations on and combinations of these aspects.

When hiring a lawyer, ensure that he understands and shares your goals. If you just want the situation to go away quietly and to get your job back, a lawyer or legal organization that wants to raise awareness about whistleblower issues may not be the best match for you. If you want to take a stand and make a statement, make sure your lawyer knows this and is prepared for a public campaign rather than a quick monetary settlement. Lawyers and legal organizations vary tremendously in their values, priorities, and work styles. There is limited overlap between the tactics and the outcomes of an attorney whose primary goal is to make money compared with one whose primary goal is to make a difference. It is important that you be clear and make sure your lawyer is willing to pursue your goals.

Determine the lawyer's willingness to work with your advocacy partners
Some attorneys are unwilling to relinquish control of valuable information they learn from legal depositions or subpoenaed documents until the lawsuit is over, leaving groups who helped champion your cause holding the bag. This could mean that evidence may not reach the public for years—even if that evidence could prevent needless tragedies or scandals. This issue is a complex one. There are often valid legal reasons for keeping significant evidence secret. The use of secrecy is a necessary tactic in litigation.

For example, premature public disclosures may rule out future voluntary cooperation by your former employer or colleagues in pretrial efforts to gather necessary facts for the lawsuit. In some instances willingness to keep damaging information "under seal" could increase the value of a settlement in your case. But that could have the ironic result of sustaining a cover-up that you lost your job trying to expose. Instead of getting the truth to the public, you will just be trading money for silence—getting paid to help keep the misconduct secret. In the process, you may have burned your professional bridges within the corporation, the industry, and your profession.

In short the best way to win damages in a lawsuit is not always the best way to expose and correct the wrongdoing that led you to blow the whistle. These dilemmas are inherent in whistleblowing. They are tough choices and, ultimately, yours to make—*not* to let your lawyer make for you. The important point here is that you should pick an attorney who shares your perspective as much as possible, to avoid the possibility of serious conflicts at a critical juncture in the case when they could be highly damaging.

Be clear about each other's role in the process   Make sure you and your lawyer see eye-to-eye on your respective roles in the case—about how much of the work you expect to be doing and how much is your attorney's responsibility. Find out how much time the attorney is willing to commit. Even the best lawyers are inadequate if they are too overburdened with work to give your case the attention it needs. On the other hand, many clients have an entirely unrealistic expectation of how much time is necessary. Remember that each task you complete is a task that you will not have to pay your attorney to do. Committing your own time and energy to the case can help keep costs down.

Developing clear and consistent lines of communication is an invaluable element of any attorney-client relationship. Depending on what you decide about your respective roles, figure out how much notice you will receive of developments, information, and decisions that make a difference for your case. An attorney who withholds key developments from a client can poison a working relationship and fatally undermine a client's rights. On the other hand, it is unrealistic to expect a lawyer to review daily developments with each client. Establish this balance up front with an understanding that adjustments are sometimes necessary.

Pin down your role before any potential settlement negotiations begin
Remember that the great majority of cases settle before trial. You should request advance notice of proposals before they are made on your behalf and of offers from the other side before any response is issued. Your attorney should be willing to respect your authority as the final decision-maker on any settlement. A client is in a position of comparative weakness if an attorney threatens to quit unless settlement terms are accepted on the eve of trial. Remember that your lawyer is the partner on your team who has unique expertise. Most of us have unrealistic expectations of what we deserve to achieve in a settlement. From a lawyer's standpoint, a client is being unreasonable if she rejects a settlement that is comparable to what she would receive if the case were won in court. If the whistleblower's primary motivation is to have his or her "day in court," the lawyer needs to know this at the outset.

Work out your financial options and obligations   Pursuing legal remedies can be a long and costly process. Although everyone would like to be able to hire a dream team of the best legal minds in the field, this may not be realistic. You must be aware of how much money you can afford to spend on this battle and how much a particular lawyer will cost you. Even if you expect to ultimately recover legal fees in court, be prepared for the possibility that you will not win the case or will have to settle for less monetary recovery than originally expected.

Discuss your attorney's fee structure up front and get a written contract explaining the terms in language you can understand. This contract should lay out the billing process, whether you will pay a retainer (a deposit against future fees and costs), when and how you will receive progress reports, and how conflicts with your lawyer will be resolved. Lawyers typically charge based on an hourly, a flat, or a contingency fee structure.

- *Hourly fee structure*   The advantage of the hourly rate is that you pay only for the time your attorney spends on your case. Possible problems include "over-lawyering" to run up bill, dragging the case out, and billing support staff time at the lawyer's hourly rate. To lessen these potential problems, you should compare bills to estimates, require your written consent to exceed a maximum amount, and offer to contribute your own time to complete minor tasks.

■ *Flat fee structure* The flat fee structure provides certainty in advance about the cost, and it may work out to be cheaper per hour than hourly billing. It's also good for *pro se* employees who need help with some issues. But it's not practical with lengthy proceedings whose duration is difficult to predict, and it's a financial disincentive to make extra effort. You should specify what is and is not covered in the fee.

■ *Contingency fee structure* The main advantage of the contingency fee is that you may not need to pay anything if you lose the case. This may be the only option for some employees. On the downside, there are considerable fees if you do win, and there's little financial incentive for sustained effort if settlement negotiations fail to produce easy resolution. You should ask several lawyers what your chances of success are and how much you might be awarded, determine the lawyer's percentage (calculated after deducting expenses from the court award), and specify in the retainer the minimum level of commitment the lawyer will make to ongoing efforts in the case.

Many lawyers will be quite flexible in fee arrangements that are customized for your resources. For example, if you cannot afford conventional representation, for drastically less money the lawyer may serve as your debate coach and editor while you represent yourself. Often this will be the case for early, informal stages of a lawsuit, with traditional representation deferred until the lawyer is indispensable for formal due process stages such as depositions or trial.

Remember that a retainer agreement is a contract Treat this agreement with as much respect as you would any other contract. It may be one of the most important contracts you ever sign. What is your attorney agreeing to do or not do? Read the terms carefully to make sure the scope of representation covers all critical issues and defendants and reflects any informal agreements reached on items listed above or from your own checklist. Consider getting a second opinion from a disinterested attorney. Remember that a retainer is usually drafted to protect *the lawyer,* not you, and may be rigged so that if anything goes wrong, the attorney can easily abandon the relationship without any messy carryover responsibilities. If you do not understand a term, ask the attorney to explain it and to replace the legalese with words you understand. If the attorney balks at this or is hostile to modifying any one-sided terms, think about hiring someone else.

Pointers for Working with Your Lawyer

After finding a good lawyer, maintaining a good working relationship that unites your values with your lawyer's expertise is the key to a successful outcome. Remember, your lawyer is working for you. Feel free to read and research the legal arguments so that you understand the basis for a decision. If necessary, get a second opinion. Be aware, however, that your attorney has only limited time to teach you about the legal process and will expect respect for professional judgment calls. Although you may be the boss, your attorney is the expert with the skills to lead you through largely unknown and potentially treacherous territory.

The high-stakes relationship between an attorney and a client requires regular tending. Here are a few suggestions for keeping it strong.

Pay your bills on time   Annoyance with a client for failing to keep up with expected payments is a major reason why lawyers reduce the time and the energy they put into a case. If there is a financial crisis, give your lawyer as much warning as possible and seek alternative arrangements.

Respect your attorney's time burdens and other responsibilities   View your lawyer as a human being who has a family and other clients and gets tired like everybody else. Attorneys understandably do not appreciate being seen only as instruments to bring their clients legal success and may become resentful if they feel that this is your only perception of them. Keep in mind that it is not to your advantage for your champion to resent you.

Do not cry wolf or demand instant attention for nonemergencies. When possible, put developments in writing instead of insisting on a phone call or a personal conference. Confirm periodically, however, that the lawyer has read, understood, and properly processed your written contributions.

Do not insist on dealing only with the lawyer running the case. Get to know any junior attorney, administrative assistants, and law clerks who are a part of your attorney's team. Work through them whenever necessary to relieve your lawyer from being an intermediary. They may be putting in a majority of the actual time invested in your case and may even be more familiar with some of the details.

Be a master of the facts   Your attorney should be able to count on you as the human encyclopedia of what happened. Be available to provide complete and reliable information about your case on request. Offer facts that can be verified on the spot through citation or documentation.

Inform your attorney of any initiatives that you wish to take   If you are compelled to advance your whistleblowing or secure additional advocacy partners, do not disclose information about your case without first consulting with your attorney. Your lawyer may have a plan to use this information strategically in court. In some instances, disclosure could violate a court order. You will make it much more difficult for your attorney to prosecute your case if you fail to discuss independent actions you are taking to advance it. This does not mean passively acquiescing to censorship by your lawyer—this is all about *your* choice whether and how to blow the whistle—but it must be an informed choice that does not blindside your lawyer.

Terminating the Attorney-Client Relationship

In most types of litigation, contracts with lawyers last for one stage of the process. This means that in the event of an appeal, most people will either renegotiate their agreement with their lawyer or find new counsel. If your attorney agrees, it is ideal to write an option into the contract for you to retain your attorney's services throughout multiple stages of proceedings, as it is advantageous to continue working with a lawyer that you are comfortable with and who knows your case well. The norm is to renegotiate after each stage of the process, however, so be prepared for the possibility that your attorney will not want to sign on for appeals up front.

Ideally, after your careful search for an attorney, you will not feel the need to terminate the relationship prematurely. As in any relationship, however, it is possible for things to sour. Your contract with your attorney should reflect this possibility. A typical termination clause will allow you to end the relationship at any time for any reason but will require you to pay all fees and costs incurred to date. The attorney is allowed to terminate the relationship if further proceedings would be frivolous, unreasonable, or groundless; if irreconcilable differences arise; or if you fail to perform your legal or financial obligations. In the case of a breach of contract, retainer agreements may specify arbitration or the law and the location of any court-based dispute. Consider whether arbitration is provided free of charge and whether the contract's jurisdiction is your state of residence.

Your contract's termination clause should include provisions that do not leave you vulnerable to waiving your rights. To illustrate, ensure an adequate transition to your next lawyer if your attorney does withdraw. This means having clauses that prevent your attorney from dropping the case or raising his fees within a certain time prior to the trial and guaranteeing that your attorney will pass on all relevant documents and information to your next lawyer. At the trial stage, once legal proceedings have commenced, rules of professional conduct typically require an attorney to seek court approval before withdrawing.

Like advocacy partners, lawyers are a valuable resource for navigating the rough terrain of a whistleblower claim. Due to the difficulty and the expense of obtaining counsel, it may be more practical to partner up with a public interest organization that has its own lawyers willing and able to assist or represent you. If you take that approach, however, remember that significant conflicts of interest are possible between you and the public interest group. Your retainer with the group's lawyer should clearly resolve where loyalties are in the event of a conflict, or you could face a bitter surprise.

CHAPTER 6

Whistleblowing and the Law

There are a number of statutory and common-law provisions aimed at safeguarding private-sector whistleblowers. Unfortunately, in addition to many lacking meaningful due process or adequate remedies, these protections are neither comprehensive nor well enforced by government agencies and the courts. What has evolved is a patchwork of specific employee legal protections covering environmental, health and safety, labor relations, and civil service issues, though recent legislative developments have consolidated whistleblower protections on the books for employees of publicly traded companies.

This chapter provides an introductory guide to your legal options, beginning with the Sarbanes-Oxley Act and other federal statutes with whistleblower provisions and concluding with state and common-law remedies. The chapter surveys the marketing gap for corporate free-speech rights, discerning what is advertised from what you get. It also contains practice tips, learned from the often-painful experiences of pioneer whistleblowers, so that you can get the most out of the rights you do have.

SOX and Federal Whistleblower Statutes: A Mirage of Protection

In the Sarbanes-Oxley law,[1] enacted after the 2002 Enron and MCI scandals, Senators Patrick Leahy (D-VT) and Charles Grassley (R-IA) attempted to replace 30 years of piecemeal corporate whistleblower protection with one comprehensive law for publicly traded companies that would protect some 42 million corporate employees. As described earlier, the goal was to ban retaliation against those like Sherron Watkins who challenge "cooking the books" and other concealed misconduct that threaten shareholder investment. The broad corporate free-speech law pioneered a new paradigm with unprecedented bite for whistleblowers: if the Department of Labor administrative process does not act within six months, whistleblowers are entitled to a fresh start in federal district court before a jury of their peers. Whistleblowers and their champions celebrated the groundbreaking new rights, which were on par with those against race, gender, and religious discrimination. Groups like the Government Accountability Project announced America's arrival in the promised land of corporate free speech.

For the past eight years, however, SOX's promised land has seemed like a mirage. Corporate whistleblowers have found themselves hamstrung by arbitrary barriers that were not in the law as passed by Congress. In the most comprehensive study of SOX whistleblower rights to date, Professor Richard Moberly identified the many "procedural and boundary hurdles" arising from DOL's "misapplication of Sarbanes-Oxley rights to the significant disadvantage of employees."[2] Regrettably, in practice the SOX "breakthrough" has been just one more in a long line of corporate whistleblower laws that routinely approve whatever retaliation is challenged.

Regardless, even paper rights can serve an effective role in a whistleblower strategy. They ensure that employers who retaliate do not get a free ride. Instead employers may have to spend years enduring the burdens of litigation before retaliation will stick. Filing a lawsuit provides the opportunity to negotiate and settle a case. Furthermore, some people do win, which sends a message of uncertainty to the industry about what they can continue to get away with.

Most encouragingly, the seed is taking root for a new model of jury trials to enforce corporate free-speech rights. The 2002 SOX law was riddled with generalities and implied or indirect rights because the reform commanded only a fragile congressional majority. But in 2005 Congress reaffirmed the mandate of jury trials for nuclear workers as part of the Energy Policy Act.[3] Since the November 2006 elections, Congress has intensified the pace of change, passing new laws for corporate ground transportation workers, defense contractors, some 20 million employees connected with the manufacture or sale of 15,000 retail products, and employees of any institution receiving stimulus funds. Healthcare and financial industry reform, the two major laws passed during the 110th Congress, both include whistleblower protection. The new laws all have best-practice whistleblower rights enforced by jury trials.[4] On December 21, 2010, the day before adjournment, Congress also enacted food safety reform legislation, which includes best-practice whistleblower rights enforced by jury trials for corporate workers challenging violations under the Food and Drug Administration's authority. President Obama signed the bill into law on January 4, 2011.[5]

In December 2007, House Education and Labor Committee leaders Lynn Woolsey (D-CA) and George Miller (D-CA) introduced H.R. 4047, the Private Sector Whistleblower Streamlining Act of 2007, to provide coverage for any corporate employee defending consumer rights, to create one consistent set of legal boundaries and rules, and to impose lessons that would directly correct many of the unanticipated problems in SOX's first five years. A law establishing comprehensive coverage with consistent rules for exercising freedom of speech on the job is a goal that every corporate whistleblower should support. Unfortunately, despite enactment of additional, increasingly strong piecemeal precedents, the Miller-Woolsey bill was not reintroduced in the next Congress. Until passage of a reform like it, corporate whistleblower law will remain dysfunctional.

Your Rights on Paper

For nearly 35 years, to strengthen enforcement Congress has included remedial, anti-retaliation witness protection clauses in 57 laws, of which 47 protect workers of corporations or contractors and 3 protect employees of government corporations. Twenty of the corporate laws are administered by the Department of Labor (see Tool E in the Whistleblower Toolkit).

The scope and the subject matter are in a state of flux. These laws traditionally were concerned with environmental protection or worker safety. In 1986 Congress included anti-retaliation rights for government contractors challenging fraud in federal contracts or related payments

such as Medicare.[6] Until SOX the whistleblower provisions found in each
law were generally restricted to employees challenging specific violations
laid out in that particular statute. SOX broadened the scope of protected
dissent to also cover fraud and the full range of Securities and Exchange
Commission regulatory authority. The new Dodd-Frank Wall Street
Reform and Consumer Protection Act of 2010 continues the expansive
trend, covering the full SEC and Commodity Futures Trading Commission jurisdictions.

As with the scope of protection, the ground rules are highly inconsistent for how you can enforce your free-speech rights. There are three
primary categories through the Department of Labor's administrative
law system:[7]

OSHA investigation   Primitive statutes such as those protecting whistleblowers against occupational safety hazards have no formal due process.
You can file a complaint for a government investigation, and if OSHA
agrees that your rights have been violated, it can seek justice on your
behalf by filing a lawsuit if its recommendations are rejected. If you are
turned down, you may appeal from OSHA's regional office to its national
office. But the latter cannot reverse the initial ruling; it can only send it
back to do over in what can become an indefinite closed loop. There is
no judicial review of an OSHA decision. The secretary of labor has unreviewable discretion to make a decision.[8]

OALJ/ARB administrative hearings   Most statutes before 2002 provide
due process rights but limit them to an initial investigation by OSHA
and an administrative hearing by its Office of Administrative Law Judges
(OALJ). If not satisfied with the results of the OSHA investigation, whistleblowers who proceed with an administrative hearing will then engage
in discovery, a process that involves requesting documents from the
other party, producing requested documents, and deposing or formally
interviewing under oath witnesses for both sides. According to DOL
regulations, the OALJ has broad discretion to limit examination of witnesses or documents in prehearing discovery[9] and may issue subpoenas
to force witnesses to appear. After discovery is complete, the administrative law judge (ALJ) presides over a full hearing with whatever witnesses

and evidence are necessary to reach a decision. DOL regulations permit administrative law judges or the Department of Labor's final decision-making body, the Administrative Review Board (ARB), to waive any provision in "special circumstances" or if good cause is shown.[10]

The ALJ issues a ruling at the conclusion of the hearing, but either party can appeal it to the DOL's Administrative Review Board within 30 business days. The ARB has authority to act on behalf of the secretary of labor and issue final decisions on SOX claims. If the ARB does not accept the case within 30 days, the decision of the ALJ becomes final. If the ARB accepts the case, the ALJ's decision is set aside pending ARB review, though any preliminary restraining orders that were issued remain in effect. The ARB does not hear new evidence but only reviews the evidence presented to the ALJ and decides whether the ruling was correct (i.e., supported by substantial evidence as to findings of fact and not arbitrary or capricious as to conclusions of law).[11] Under all these laws, you can challenge a final DOL ruling in appeals court.

Jury trials Sarbanes Oxley introduced jury trials to end the monopoly of administrative hearings, but this new due process right was not reliable due to loose statutory language. Congress learned its lessons, however, and the jury trials now are guaranteed by law. As a rule in statutes since 2006, your due process enforcement rights have included: an initial OSHA investigation for which interim relief is available; administrative due process hearing and appeal; de novo (starting from a clean slate) access to a jury trial in federal district court if there is no final DOL decision within a slightly longer 210-day time frame for post-SOX laws; modern legal burdens of proof as the ground rules for winning or losing at any level; disqualification of gag orders signed as a job prerequisite that would cancel statutory free-speech rights; disqualification of job prerequisite agreements for employer-controlled arbitrations as mandatory substitutes for trials or administrative hearings; and compensatory damages for whistleblowers who win their cases. Some laws, such as the Toxic Substances Control Act[12] and the 9/11 ground transportation whistleblower laws, also provide punitive damages, the latter with a $250,000 cap.[13]

The following list compares the nuts and bolts of a succession of whistleblower laws adjudicated through the DOL.

Occupational Safety and Health Act of 1970 § 11(c)

Who is covered?   Any employee who discloses an occupational health or safety violation

What counts as protected conduct?   Initiating an OSHA complaint or testifying in an OSHA proceeding

Statute of limitations   30 days

Burdens of proof[14]   *Mt. Healthy City Board of Ed. v. Doyle*

Access to court for jury trial?   No

Available remedies   Reinstatement and back pay

Toxic Substances Control Act of 1976 (TSCA)

Who is covered?   Any employee who discloses a violation of the TSCA

What counts as protected conduct?   Commencing, testifying, or assisting in any proceeding under the TSCA

Statute of limitations   30 days

Burdens of proof   *Mt. Healthy City Board of Ed. v. Doyle*

Access to court for jury trial?   No

Available remedies   Reinstatement, back pay, attorney's fees, and compensatory and exemplary damages

Clean Air Act of 1977 (CAA)

Who is covered?   Any employee who discloses a violation of the CAA

What counts as protected conduct?   Commencing, testifying, or assisting in a proceeding under the CAA or related plan

Statute of limitations   30 days

Burdens of proof   *Mt. Healthy City Board of Ed. v. Doyle*

Access to court for jury trial?   No

Available remedies   Reinstatement, back pay, attorney's fees, and compensatory damages

Aviation Investment and Reform Act of 2000 (AIR21)

Who is covered?   Any employee of an air carrier, subcontractor, or contractor

What counts as protected conduct?   Provide, file, or testify about any violation or any related provision or law

Statute of limitations   90 days
Burdens of proof   Whistleblower Protection Act
Access to court for jury trial?   No
Available remedies   Reinstatement, back pay, attorney's fees, and
    compensatory damages

Sarbanes-Oxley Act of 2002 § 806

Who is covered?   Any employee of a publicly traded company
What counts as protected conduct?   Disclose any violation of SEC
    rules or law relating to shareholders
Statute of limitations   180 days
Burdens of proof   Whistleblower Protection Act
Access to court for jury trial?   Yes, after an 180-day administrative
    exhaustion period
Available remedies   Reinstatement, back pay, attorney's fees, and
    special and compensatory damages

Energy Reorganization Act of 1974 § 5851 (amended 2005)

Who is covered?   Any employee of a licensee of the Nuclear
    Regulatory Commission, any employee of DOE or the
    NRC, and contractors
What counts as protected conduct?   Disclose a violation of the Energy
    Reorganization Act or Atomic Energy Act or refuse to
    assist in a violation
Statute of limitations   180 days
Burdens of proof   Whistleblower Protection Act
Access to court for jury trial?   Yes, after a 365-day administrative
    exhaustion period
Available remedies   Reinstatement, back pay, attorney's fees, and
    compensatory damages

Surface Transportation Assistance Act of 1982 (amended 2007)

Who is covered?   Any employee of a commercial motor carrier
What counts as protected conduct?   Disclose any violation of safety/
    security standard or refuse to operate vehicle
Statute of limitations   180 days
Burdens of proof   Whistleblower Protection Act

Access to court for jury trial?   Yes, after a 210-day administrative exhaustion period

Available remedies   Reinstatement, back pay, attorney's fees, and compensatory and punitive damages

Consumer Product Safety Improvement Act of 2008 (CPSIA)

Who is covered?   Any employee of a manufacturer, distributor, or retailer of a Consumer Product Safety Commission product

What counts as protected conduct?   Disclose any violation of any rule related to product safety or refuse to violate

Statute of limitations   180 days

Burdens of proof   Whistleblower Protection Act

Access to court for jury trial?   Yes, after a 210-day administrative exhaustion period or within 90 days of a final DOL administrative ruling, whether positive or negative

Available remedies   Reinstatement, back pay, attorney's fees, and compensatory and special damages

According to OSHA's Office of the Whistleblower Protection Program (OWPP), whistleblowing protected by section 11(c) of the Occupational Safety and Health Act produced the greatest number of complaints for the first half of fiscal 2009,[15] some 594 actions. The second most frequently used statute in the same time frame was the Surface Transportation Assistance Act, with 152 filings. SOX, AIR21, the Energy Reorganization Act, and the Consumer Product Safety Improvement Act saw 109, 46, 22, and 1 complaint, respectively. Environmental statutes such as the Toxic Substances Control Act and the Clean Air Act accounted for only 26 filings combined.[16] Those figures are consistent with current patterns. Although specifics vary from year to year, 60 to 65 percent of OSHA's docket comes from occupational safety whistleblowers under section 11(c).[17] More than 80 percent of OSHA's investigative docket consists of whistleblower cases from section 11(c), the Surface Transportation Assistance Act for truckers, and SOX.[18]

SOX on Paper

Sarbanes-Oxley is the pioneer of the new paradigm and the most widely used of the modern whistleblower laws. Its provisions are the best menu of your emerging rights. Its broad scope potentially overlaps with numerous other whistleblower laws such as environmental statutes. Consistent with equal employment opportunity laws, there is now a "use it or lose it" rule for the administrative process. If DOL does not issue a final decision within 180 days and the delays are not on your account, you can move your case to federal district court de novo—meaning starting with a clean slate—and let a jury decide the outcome.[19] This section offers a summary of additional SOX provisions *on paper*.

Who is covered   As written SOX applies to all employees of publicly traded companies and their officers, subsidiaries, contractors, subcontractors, or agents,[20] including a new role for attorneys, beyond their traditional role as mouthpieces for whoever is paying them.[21]

Protected conduct   The statute covers disclosures of alleged mail fraud, wire fraud, securities fraud, and violations of SEC regulations or of any law relating to fraud against shareholders. The latter requirement potentially creates protection for the full range of corporate misconduct. SEC rules require disclosure of any information that is "material,"[22] which in court has been defined as a "likelihood that the disclosure of the omitted fact would have been viewed by the reasonable investor as having significantly altered the total mix of information made available."[23] As a result, on paper SOX creates a broad free-speech safety net to blow the whistle on any concealed misconduct that risks significant consequences. The law should protect you for exposing cover-ups of activities that create serious legal liability, affect public confidence, or otherwise threaten stock values. Environmental lawlessness covered in other whistleblower statutes, product safety breakdowns, and corruption scandals are just a sampling of the wrongdoings employees theoretically have the right to challenge.

Reasonable belief   To qualify for protection, you must disclose information that assists the investigation of what you "reasonably believe" constitutes misconduct.[24] To have a "reasonable belief," you must pass two credibility tests. Subjectively, you must be acting in good faith, or have an "actual" belief. In the absence of conflicting proof, however, your good faith is presumed.[25] Objectively, whether your belief is reasonable depends on the knowledge available to a reasonable person in the same circumstances and with your training and experience. Although your conclusions can be mistaken, factually your disclosure must be specific and definite about what alleged misconduct violates the law. A general inquiry will not suffice. While you do not need to cite to section of the US Code or even say the words "SOX" or "fraud," you must disclose enough facts to prove each legal element for relevant misconduct.[26] This means common sense is not enough. Nor is it safe to disclose merely a piece of the legal puzzle proving fraud.

This issue also illustrates the mishmash of legal ground rules that can cancel your rights. In a 2009 decision, DOL's Administrative Review Board ruled that whistleblowers must cite to specific Department of Transportation regulations when they blow the whistle, or they do not have rights.[27] You'll need expert guidance as to whether your concerns satisfy the legal technicalities. Further, your protection can lapse. If you persist in whistleblowing after an employer has acted responsibly on your concerns, initially protected speech will lose that status.[28]

Protected audiences   The law explicitly shields disclosures to federal law enforcement, regulatory personnel, congressional or committee offices, and supervisors or others in the corporate chain of command. Unstated but consistent with all corporate whistleblower laws is the premise recognized by DOL precedents since 1980[29] that protecting disclosures to the government also sweeps in otherwise lawful communications with the media or public. While conceding that that may be true for other whistleblower laws, a recent federal district court opinion, however, flatly rejected that theory for SOX:

> Communications to the media are not protected by SOX. . . . Congress has made clear that while SOX was intended to protect whistleblowers, only certain types of whistleblowing would be afforded protection. Leaking documents to the media is not one of them.[30]

The decision's scarcely supported conclusion may be an aberration, but until the dust settles you cannot be sure if you are protected under SOX in these circumstances. At a minimum you should include the government as one of your audiences.[31] To be safe it may be necessary to channel disclosures to the media through legislative offices or committees.

Illegal retaliation   The law lists traditional reprisals like termination, suspension, and demotion but also bans actions that "threaten, harass, or in any other manner discriminate against the employee" because of lawful, protected activity.[32] The Supreme Court recently interpreted this to mean any act that "might have dissuaded a reasonable worker" from engaging in the protected conduct.[33]

Legal burdens of proof   This factor decides how high the bar is for an employee to win. SOX has modern burdens of proof from federal civil service law that are more favorable to employees than traditional DOL standards. You must show by a "preponderance of the evidence"—meaning more likely than not—that your protected activity was a "contributing factor" in the unfavorable personnel action, meaning the disclosure, "alone or in combination with other factors, tended to affect the decision in any way."[34] This is not an unfair test, and if you pass it you have established a prima facie case. But your employer can still win through an affirmative defense by proving with "clear and convincing evidence" that it would have taken the same action even if you had not engaged in the protected activity. Clear and convincing evidence is "evidence indicating that the thing to be proved is highly probable or reasonably certain."[35] In sum, to satisfy *your* legal burden you will need to demonstrate that more likely than not:[36]

- you made a protected communication;

- the employer knew of your disclosure;

- you suffered an unfavorable personnel action; and

- the protected activity was a "contributing factor" in the alleged discrimination.

Remedies   The SOX section for general and compensatory damages entitles prevailing employees to "all relief necessary to make the employee whole,"[37] including reinstatement with the seniority the employee would have had but for the retaliation, back pay with interest, and reasonable attorney's fees and other costs of litigation. Compensatory damages also include awards for emotional distress, pain and suffering, and loss of reputation.[38]

Criminal liability   SOX toughens the criminal penalties for retaliating against whistleblowers who disclose corporate violations of federal law provided the disclosure is to a law enforcement official. Corporations can be fined $500,000, and individuals can be fined $250,000 along with up to 10 years in prison,[39] although the prospects of criminal enforcement are dubious. A milder one-year prison penalty had been on the books for almost three decades, yet the Department of Justice never prosecuted a single case.

Supremacy of law   Amendments by Senator Robert Menendez (D-NJ) to the recent Dodd-Frank Wall Street Reform and Consumer Protection Act corrected two of SOX's Achilles' heels: vulnerability to gag orders and mandatory company arbitration, both of which are frequently made conditions of employment.[40] The former fix will be very beneficial if you are accused of stealing the company's intellectual property for bearing witness instead of joining a cover-up. The latter shields your independent administrative and jury trial due process rights from replacement by kangaroo courts, in which the arbitrator is selected and paid by your employer.

In sum, SOX adds court access and a wide range of other strengthened due process rights compared with whistleblower provisions tucked into various federal environmental, securities, or public health and safety statutes passed in the 1970s and 1980s.[41] Although many of the core statutes follow an analogous form, most have particular idiosyncrasies when it comes to which employees are protected; how soon they must file a complaint; what disclosures are protected; where the case may be brought; what legal burden of proof must be met; what, if any, interim relief is available; and what final relief is offered.

One technique SOX used to increase consistency was incorporating by reference the administrative procedures and the legal burdens of proof in the AIR21 legislation for airlines whistleblowers.[42] The 2010 health reform law took an analogous approach, incorporating the Consumer Product Safety Improvement Act's generic provisions.[43]

Your Rights in Reality

Unfortunately, there is too little common ground between what is advertised on paper and what you get in reality. In practice corporate whistleblower law is a patchwork of inconsistent protections. With scattered exceptions, if you file a lawsuit, you are sentencing yourself to an administrative process with short, unforgiving deadlines and a maze of bureaucratic procedures. Decisions are seldom issued in less than two to three years, and most statutes do not offer any chance for interim relief. If formal vindication is your goal, the odds are extremely long. At the end of the process, you likely will have spent years and five or six figures for results that predictably rubberstamp whatever retaliation you challenged. This section offers common questions about whistleblower rights in practice that we are asked at GAP and the painful answers we must give.

Who do the corporate whistleblower laws protect and for what kind of whistleblowing?

In any given industry, whistleblower laws protect potentially any employee or almost no one. The scattered forms of misconduct legally eligible for protected dissent are like a road with more potholes than pavement. Any corporation *may* violate environmental or occupational safety laws, so all employees have rights to challenge those particular types of misconduct. But for other potentially greater abuses of power, employees may have no rights. For other whistleblower laws, such as airlines safety, only industry employees are covered. No one can be sure without a lawyer to navigate.

For example, an employee at a meat-packing plant has best-practice free-speech rights supported by access to jury trials when challenging shareholder fraud; primitive administrative due process rights for challenging the release of fecally contaminated water into a river; and no rights against retaliation under federal law when challenging fecally contaminated meat and poultry that violates food safety laws and shows up on our families' dinner tables.

If I speak out, when will I become a legally recognized whistleblower?

You may not have rights until you communicate with the government, which means you are proceeding at your own risk when trying to work within the corporate system. It used to be that challenging corporate misconduct internally triggered rights because this was deemed an "essential preliminary step" for responsible disclosures to the government. While the minority, some decisions have disqualified protection for internal disclosures, pushing employees to contact the government behind their employer's back lest they waive their rights.

Am I protected for refusing to violate the law?

It depends. You are protected under occupational safety statutes and most recent laws but not under SOX and most whistleblower laws prior to 2007. Unlike the Whistleblower Protection Act for government workers and an increasing number of state laws, most DOL-administered laws protect you only for making noise. Recent laws such as those in the Energy Policy Act (nuclear), 9/11 ground transportation (trains, buses, trucks, and regional mass transit), consumer products, health reform, and financial regulatory reform reverse that trend. But under the pioneer statutes, if you try to walk the talk, you are walking the plank.

How long do I have to act on my rights?

It ranges from 30 to 90 days in most early DOL-administered statutes, and 180 days in newer laws for nuclear, ground transportation, defense contractor, and retail product safety whistleblowers. In theory the law could provide flexibility through a doctrine called "equitable tolling," which allows you to meet a deadline if you asserted your rights on time but merely in the wrong forum. In practice this does not always pan out. In one case DOL extended the deadline to a year, but in the instance of Henry Immanuel the case was thrown out even though he initially asserted his rights less than two weeks after being fired.

The Right Time but the Wrong Place

Henry Immanuel's ordeal is illustrative of the surreal problems whistle-blowers face with filing timely complaints. Immanuel, an employee of an organic market, was fired for refusing to throw four 5-gallon buckets of industrial cleaner into an on-site trash dumpster. Within 15 days he filed a reprisal complaint with the Maryland Occupational Safety and Health (MOSH) agency. After six months MOSH informed him that it was the wrong agency to handle the dispute. Immanuel then began contacting government offices to find out where he was supposed to assert his rights. Despite a series of false leads and dead ends, he found out about OSHA and immediately filed a complaint. Seventy-three days had passed since he had been fired, 43 days over the normal 30-day deadline. According to DOL it was too late and there were no excuses. Without explanation the ARB disregarded a series of prior rulings extending deadlines up to one year due to similar circumstances, and Immanuel was left with no recourse.[44]

How long will this case take?

On paper most statutes give the Department of Labor 90 days for a decision. In reality expect to be twisting in the wind for at least two to three years. Six years is not uncommon. One Department of Energy employee who was vindicated for blowing the whistle on radioactive releases at nuclear weapons facilities waited 14 years while victories on the merits kept getting jettisoned by technicalities. Note that it took DOL four and a half years to tell Mr. Immanuel that he was too late to keep his rights by filing 43 days after the 30-day deadline.

Can I get any interim relief while I'm waiting?

Again it depends on which generation of whistleblower law. In nine recent DOL-administered laws—AIR21, the Energy Policy Act, SOX, three ground transportation statutes in the 9/11 law, CPSIA, and the health reform and Dodd-Frank financial regulatory reform laws—you can get a ruling for preliminary reinstatement.

What do I have to prove to win? What tests will I have to pass?

As with your other rights, it depends on which generation of law. Most are governed by antiquated burdens of proof from 1974. To establish a basic prima facie case, an employee must prove that protected activity is the "primary, motivating factor." Then the burden of proof shifts, but the employer can still prevail by proving with a preponderance of the evidence that it would have taken the same action for independent reasons.[45] Under all DOL-administered statutes enacted since 1992, the more modern standards of the Whistleblower Protection Act apply.[46] As discussed above, the employee has to prove only that the protected activity was a "contributing [or relevant] factor" for a prima facie case, and the employer must prove its independent justification with "clear and convincing" evidence.

Will I be able to get my day in court?

A few statutes, such as banking reforms passed in response to the 1990s savings-and-loan scandal, allow employees to go straight to court on a retaliation claim but do not provide for jury trials. For the laws passed since SOX, you can take your case to a federal court if DOL (or a relevant Office of Inspector General [OIG] when inspectors general conduct first-stage investigations) misses the deadline for taking administrative action. Under SOX this deadline is 180 days. Defense contractor employees, ground transportation workers, and consumer products, medical, and financial workers can go to court if there is no final ruling within 210 days. For claims under the Energy Reorganization Act, the waiting period is 365 days.

Under all the other DOL-administered statutes, you are a prisoner of DOL's administrative law system until it reaches a final decision after two to three years, if you are lucky. To appeal this decision, most DOL-administered laws provide limited review in US courts of appeals, but not all. In the case of mine safety, an autonomous "external" commission substitutes for court review. In occupational safety retaliation cases, review is entirely within OSHA—and secret. For all practical purposes, your rights are none of your business.

If I go to court, will a jury decide whether my rights were violated?

It's complicated, and does not happen often. The answer depends on which law and when you acted on your rights. After the first seven cases seeking court access under SOX, only two whistleblowers have made it to a jury trial, with one victory and one defeat.[47] No nuclear whistleblowers have yet had cases decided by a jury under the Energy Policy Act 2005 amendments. Five judges dismissed the cases summarily before they could reach a jury.[48] Four courts rejected jury trials despite clear congressional intent because of drafting technicalities in the law[49] prior to the addition of clarifying language for SOX in the Dodd-Frank bill that explicitly establishes the right.

When it's over, will I understand why I won or lost?

It depends on which institution made the decision. Although there are impressive exceptions, a frequent practice at OSHA and OIG offices has been to *not* supply a meaningful answer, with only sporadic comments about why any given conclusion was reached. Sometimes at OSHA the "rulings" have been personal diatribes, such as accusing the whistleblower of being a coward for speaking to the government and suggesting punishment beyond termination, such as loss of professional credentials.

The bottom line: What are my chances of winning?

If there is no realistic chance of success, the law is a trap that reinforces legal wrongs, not rights. Unfortunately, that has been the case with DOL-administered corporate whistleblower laws. The percentage of whistleblowers who win formal victories, compared with those who file complaints, ranged from 2.9 percent for nuclear workers from 2003 through 2007 under the Energy Reorganization Act, to 9.8 percent for airlines whistleblowers from 2000 through 2007 under the AIR21 law.

Professor Richard Moberly conducted the first comprehensive study of SOX. Looking at more than 700 administrative decisions, he analyzed its track record in its first three years. In 2007 he reported a 3.6 percent win rate at the OSHA level, 6.5 percent with administrative law judges, and not a single case where the ARB ordered retaliation to stop.[50] Similarly, OSHA went from 2005 to 2007 without backing a single SOX whistleblower, despite receiving 150 to 250 retaliation complaints annually under that law. In 2010 former SOX whistleblower David Welch, whose career has since graduated to teaching his ethical lessons learned to college students, released a study reporting 27,298 claims under all whistleblower statutes between 1994 and 2008. For that broader context, OSHA found merit in 3.2 percent. Under SOX, however, the figure was a pathetic 1.4 percent, or 18 whistleblower victories out of 1,242 investigations after the law's 2002 passage.[51]

To put your odds in perspective, out of some 1,500 complaints filed by whistleblowers under SOX since its passage, through September 2010 only one employee in 2009 finally prevailed at the DOL's Administrative Review Board,[52] one in a jury trial,[53] and one in a "bench" trial where a federal district court judge decided the case without a jury.[54]

The SOX track record is consistent with the fate of section 11(c) occupational safety whistleblowers, who account for more than 60 percent of OSHA's total docket. In 14 years the Department of Labor, which must file suit to enforce investigative findings under section 11(c), has done so only 32 times. To put your almost night-marish odds in perspective, consider fiscal 2009—a comparatively good year for 11(c) whistleblowers: out of 1,280 complaints, OSHA investigators recommended litigation for corrective action in 15. But the Office of the Solicitor, which has the final word on whether to go to court, followed through only four times, or 0.31 percent.[55]

This pathetic track record would not be so significant if OSHA were merely a nonenforceable dry run for testing your rights before your day in court. But for the overwhelming majority of whistle-blowers, this is all they have. It is OSHA or nothing. By law occupa-tional safety whistleblowers have no control of their cases.

Financial reality means that those are the same facts of life for most other whistleblowers, despite formal access to due process. Few can afford to finance a lawsuit when they are unemployed and facing years of blacklisting. In fiscal 2007, out of 1,078 non-11(c) cases investigated by OSHA, only 207 were appealed for a hearing by DOL's Office of Administrative Law Judges, or less than 20 percent. In proportion to all 1,864 cases OSHA closed that year, it had the final word for nearly 90 percent.[56]

Further, if you do not exercise administrative appeal rights against an OSHA determination, it can be binding for all other contexts. In 2010 the California Supreme Court held that under those circumstances the OSHA decision precluded a common-law public policy exception jury trial lawsuit in state court.[57]

The sometimes-toxic silver lining has been settlements, which without any rational basis OSHA claims are legal complaints where it found merit in the employee's case. OSHA reports that on its watch 21 percent of whistleblower cases settle; the Government Accountability Office corrected this figure to 19 percent based on faulty records.[58] Moberly reported that a significant number of SOX complainants settle their cases—11.6 percent at the OSHA level and 18.3 percent with ALJs.[59] Even so, with such a remote chance of winning, whistleblowers negotiate their settlements from a position of weakness.

While there are dramatic exceptions, the average settlements at the Department of Labor tend to be paltry compared with loss of job and likely blacklisting. During one period in 2007, for example, settlements under all statutes averaged slightly more than $55,000, ranging from $6,000 for Surface Transportation Act cases covering truck and cross-country-bus safety to $170,000 in SOX cases.[60] Further, the price of this token compensation is frequently professional exile. One-third of settlements include banishment clauses, where the employee is barred from working for the same company or even within the industry.[61]

The Whistleblowing Saga at Wal-Mart

Wal-Mart's vice chairman, Thomas Coughlin, was defrauding the retail behemoth out of hundreds of thousands of dollars. An employee cast suspicion on the executive by reporting information about Coughlin's questionable use of gift cards. This triggered an internal investigation. During the course of that investigation, Jared Bowen, a Wal-Mart vice president, came forward with additional information used to condemn the vice chairman for his fraudulent activities, which consisted of reporting false information on third-party invoices and company expense reports.

Although Coughlin was asked to resign, Bowen's employment with the company was terminated. The former vice president filed a claim with the Department of Labor under Sarbanes-Oxley, alleging that his termination was retaliation in response to his coming forward during the investigation.

Wal-Mart maintains that Bowen was fired because he too was involved in the same misconduct Coughlin had committed. Meanwhile the worker who first reported the fraud remains a Wal-Mart employee in good standing.

What Went Wrong: OSHA

Part of the reason for what went wrong is a management breakdown at the Department of Labor. DOL's corporate whistleblower system has become dysfunctional. The Office of Administrative Law Judges, whose hearings are the "day in court" for most whistleblowers, is respected and generally has produced a balanced track record of decisions. The two Achilles' heels traditionally have been that the beginning and the end of the process—the Occupational Safety and Health Administration and the Administrative Review Board—neutralize OALJ's credible track record.

To begin it is important to pin down what the cause of the problems is *not:* OSHA's national Office of the Whistleblower Protection Program. Like the Office of Administrative Law Judges, OWPP has earned respect and maintained legitimacy. It has compiled an outstanding resource library of research for everything covered by DOL-administered whistleblower laws;[62] developed even-handed policies for their enforcement; and regularly participates in public education events. Unfortunately, the national office has only token authority to enforce its policies and is shamelessly starved of resources. OWPP traditionally has operated with a staff of two to four employees to oversee a legal system handling some 2,000 cases annually, including appellate review of regional decisions on section 11(c) cases. While not the cause of the problem, OWPP also is not equipped with the authority or resources to act as a solution.

So what is the matter? The causes are no mystery. First, as an anti-retaliation vehicle to protect dissent against corporate misconduct generally, the whistleblower program is a bureaucratic stepchild at OSHA. The resource discrimination is crude against whistleblower investigations compared with OSHA's primary mission of direct safety oversight. Second, for the past two decades the agency has earned a well-deserved, widely perceived reputation for being dysfunctional. To put frustrations at OSHA in perspective, one of the catalysts for this book was requests from whistleblowers for help tracking down their cases when

OSHA loses them. Third, the whistleblower program is captive to OSHA's generic feudal management structure of regional control. As one whistleblower from inside OSHA put it, "Each region is its own fiefdom that can do what it wants." For all practical purposes, the OWPP is background noise. Fourth, OSHA's political leadership and career officials high on the bureaucratic food chain traditionally have, and continue to engage in, determined denial that anything serious is wrong.

For years, through testimony and briefings of OSHA political appointees, GAP has reiterated the track record of failure summarized as follows.

Anti-leadership Incumbents have demonstrated their antipathy for the program through repeated efforts to privatize whistleblower investigations. While those efforts have failed to date, the attempts have exposed bias.

Vacuum of credible data OSHA's incumbent leadership can dismiss any criticisms as anecdotal because it repeatedly has rejected Government Accountability Office and congressional calls for a national audit. This foundation of ignorance has been essential for OSHA's leadership to maintain plausible deniability. As a matter of public policy, however, it is inexcusable.

Mediations When the Wage and Hour Division conducted whistleblower investigations, the attempt to seek constructive resolution was the highest priority for initial processing of a whistleblower complaint. These initiatives were very effective, and in the course of calling negotiating bluffs the Wage and Hour "street" mediators were able to discern animus and retaliation. Since OSHA has taken control, this constructive, useful contribution has virtually vanished. It partly explains OSHA's low settlement rate compared with other settings where attempts at mediation are institutionalized as a top priority in every lawsuit.

Schizophrenic merit rates Merit rates are the track record for the bottom line—whether or not OSHA finds retaliation. Unfortunately, the law has drastically different meanings, depending where an alleged violation occurs. Rates between regions range almost 300 percent including settlements, from 14 percent in some regions to 41 percent in others for the same statute. The national office, which can review regional rulings, has remanded cases at a 50 percent rate for some statutes over sustained periods—setting the standard for arbitrary chaos within the administrative law system. Unfortunately, the national office has authority to issue only advisory remands. As a result, when it rejects an initial decision due to error, as a rule the only impact is to cause delays while waiting for the region to reaffirm its initial judgment. Amazingly, OSHA has responded by proposing to eliminate national office reviews. Instead the agency has been considering a pilot program in which employees can appeal only to the same region for review regardless of whether its ruling was wrong. That is a formula to institutionalize the current disgrace.

Schizophrenic translations of statutory language   The contradictory merit rates reflect inconsistent translations of the law. The regions do not speak the same statutory language. To illustrate, regions have contradictory interpretations on:

- whether duty speech to carry out job assignments is covered by anti-retaliation laws;

- which type of corporate fraud an employee can challenge as protected conduct;

- whether an employee must be the first to disclose alleged corporate misconduct or is protected as a supporting witness;

- the standards for protected speech;

- whether employees working in extraterritorial settings have any anti-retaliation rights;

- how to define the legal burdens of proof; and

- relevance of circumstantial evidence.

These issues are the core factors in whether a whistleblower law is an effective, metal shield that gives employees a fighting chance to survive or a cardboard shield that guarantees whistleblowers finish themselves off professionally by acting on their rights.

Processing time Again, consistency is not a part of the current program. Average processing times range from 77 days to more than 300, depending on the region.

Inconsistent due process procedures Some regions share an employer's response; others only paraphrase it for the whistleblower. Some regions interview the complainant; others consistently refuse. None do it consistently. Nineteen to 68 percent of whistleblowers have at least one face-to-face interview before their cases are closed, depending on the region.[63] Some regions pressure employers to provide documentary evidence recommended by the whistleblower, whereas others refuse or give up in the face of anything beyond voluntary cooperation. Some regions enforce the specific standards of 29 C.F.R. § 70.26 for an employer's claim that documents are confidential and should be kept off the public record. Others accept any confidentiality claim at face value. Some OSHA investigators permit company employees to be interviewed in private. Others permit corporate counsel to observe the entire interview, which can be extremely intimidating.

These inconsistencies are not mere legal technicalities. They can thoroughly rig the rules so that seeking justice through OSHA is unrealistic. It means that employees would be better off *not* acting on their rights rather than spend time and money for a predictable rubber stamp of whatever harassment they challenge.

Inadequate resources The field staff faces an impossible challenge to properly process whistleblower cases. Their caseloads are five to six times the maximum for adequate time for one investigator to respond professionally, and often they do not have such basic support as laptop computers, printers, administrative help, and frequently even supervision.

Lack of training The lack of investigator training is a key cause of all the problems listed previously, and responsibility falls squarely with incumbent OSHA management. Although OSHA conducts introductory training courses with qualified instructors from the national office, the program merely scratches the surface compared with the in-depth instruction on direct occupational safety issues. A serious commitment to training is the necessary base for a respected national program.

Civility breakdown   Due to resource limitations, whistleblowers frequently do not ever talk with an investigator face to face. When they do, some wish they hadn't. While most OSHA investigators are committed to employee rights and dedicated to finding the truth, there are glaring exceptions. GAP receives complaints of some investigators yelling at whistleblowers, threatening them, and engaging in crude taunts. There are two possible explanations for the cause of these aberrations: they reflect regional managers' impatience with and disrespect of whistleblower investigations, or there is impunity for hostile behavior toward whistleblowers. Accountability is a prerequisite for professionalism.[64]

The frustrations have been particularly acute for whistleblowers challenging occupational safety violations under section 11(c), for whom it literally is OSHA or nothing. April 2010 congressional testimony by Lynn Rhinehart, general counsel for the American Federation of Labor and Congress of Industrial Organizations (AFL-CIO), highlighted the experience of Roger Wood (also a GAP client), who worked as an electrician at a chemical weapons disposal plant, with working conditions "probably as dangerous as any undertaken in the world."[65] Wood disclosed two serious safety violations that resulted in citations and was then ordered to work in a toxic area without safety equipment. When he refused, he was fired. This was one of the rare cases in which OSHA backed the whistleblower and recommended prosecution. But after five years of internal review, DOL's Office of the Solicitor declined, and five years later his judicial appeal was rejected in deference to the secretary of labor's unreviewable authority.[66]

Unfortunately, new Obama administration political appointees have dismissed these concerns as isolated anecdotes, despite briefings by GAP and others. While many of these reported problems came from whistleblowers *within* OSHA, we decided to check further through a website survey of practitioners and employees who filed complaints. Out of 47 respondents, the following survey results, while not purported to be scientific, indicate that the complaints reflect a pattern rather than isolated anecdotal aberrations:

■ Two agreed that OSHA made a good-faith effort to resolve their case through settlement.

■ Fifteen agreed that OSHA regions enforce the law consistently.

- Twelve were told by the OSHA investigator that to be protected they must be the first to disclose particular misconduct.

- Nineteen were informed that the OSHA investigator would not consider evidence of other retaliation for context if it occurred outside the statute of limitations for their case (meaning more than six months previously for most statutes).

- Eleven were told that protection is limited to written whistle-blowing disclosures and that they were not covered for oral communications.

- Nine were accurately informed how the federal Whistleblower Protection Act legal burdens of proof would control whether they won or lost.

- Thirty-three reported that it took OSHA more than a year to decide their cases.

- Thirty-one received a copy of a paraphrased summary of the employer's defense so that they could respond.

- Thirteen received an opportunity to respond to the statements of witnesses.

- Five reported that the OSHA investigator consistently returned telephone calls in a timely manner.

- Four reported that the OSHA investigator sought and obtained documents recommended by the complainant.

- As partial explanation, 20 reported that OSHA accepted the employer's claim of privilege or confidentiality at face value when refusing to supply relevant evidence.

- Only one respondent was satisfied that OSHA's decision credited and applied the evidence presented for investigation.

- By contrast, 31 stated that the OSHA decision accepted the employer's explanations at face value, without recognizing or resolving contrary evidence.

- Twenty-three felt that the OSHA investigator had not acted consistently with normal standards of courtesy and integrity.[67]

The GAP survey also is consistent with two recent in-depth government reports. In August 2010 the Government Accountability Office reported to Congress about whether OSHA was honoring corrective action commitments after a 2009 GAO audit found that its whistleblower program was deficient in the following areas:

- tracking for whistleblower cases, including judgment calls whether to open an investigation;

- accurate data on case processing, necessary for national OWPP oversight;

- consistent regional audit criteria;

- independent audits of the regions;

- circumvention of the national OWPP on audit results and corrective action updates;

- interim corrective action milestones to measure compliance; and

- minimum standards for equipment and software.[68]

The 2010 GAO report found that OSHA had failed to act on its commitments except with respect to starting work on a case-tracking system.[69] GAO's key conceptual conclusions concisely summarize both cause and effect:

- "OSHA has done little to ensure that investigators have the necessary training and equipment to do their jobs, and that it lacks sufficient internal controls to ensure that the whistleblower program operates as intended."[70]

- "Without further action, whistleblowers will continue to have little assurance that a complaint filed in one region would have the same outcome if it were filed in another.

- "Serious questions remain about whether the whistleblower program is appropriately structured or that the national office has sufficient control mechanisms to ensure the quality and consistency of investigations.

- "Without improved accountability for program resources, it may be difficult for OSHA to demonstrate that it is using the resources as Congress intended.

- "Further, absent goals specifically related to the whistleblower program, OSHA will continue to lack the ability to gauge program performance."[71]

- "For over 20 years, we have repeatedly found that OSHA lacks sufficient internal controls to ensure that standards for investigating whistleblower complaints are consistently followed.

- "Little progress has been made in implementing our recommendations and significant internal control problems remain."[72]

Among the report's most telling specific insights are findings concerning the following indicators of institutionalized dysfunction.

Training and equipment   Only 60 percent of investigators have taken or registered for the second of two "mandatory" training courses, and supervisors in two regions have not received any whistleblower training at all. Some regions do not send investigators to training courses, citing no need. Training curricula have not even been developed for the new whistleblower statutes like SOX that require knowledge of highly technical fields such as securities law. The agency still does not have minimum computer and equipment standards and has not committed to develop them.[73]

Staffing   Since 2000 OSHA has received major new responsibilities to protect whistleblowers under seven new laws, including SOX, for more than 40 million employees of corporations that trade stock, and, under the Consumer Product Safety Improvement Act, some 20 million workers involved in retail manufacturing and commerce. But the number of investigators to handle this new load has "remained relatively flat" (63 in 2000 and 80 in 2010).[74]

Feudal structure   The regions operate autonomously in regard to how they process and investigate cases, allocate resources, and supervise investigators. The Office of the Whistleblower Protection Program lacks access to accurate data necessary even to monitor national policies. With respect to its appellate review of regional 11(c) rulings, OSHA is experimenting with a pilot program to eliminate it entirely. Three regions now rule on appeals of their own decisions.[75]

Fiscal accountability   OSHA received funds for 25 new whistleblower investigators in fiscal 2010, but it cannot account for the spending carried out in a nontransparent manner nor can it demonstrate that the newly hired staff is working on whistleblower cases.[76]

Bottom line: commitment to its whistleblower protection mission   In practice OSHA performance standards do not include effectiveness in achieving its anti-retaliation mission. GAO reported, "Timeliness is the only performance measure OSHA tracks for the program. . . ."[77] Whistleblower groups have vocally protested that OSHA's strategic mission does not even include whistleblower protection on its agenda. GAO recommended that OSHA "incorporate strategic goals specifically for the whistleblower program into Labor's strategic plan."[78]

On September 20, 2010, OSHA was flunked again, this time by the DOL's Office of Inspector General.[79] The OIG report examined 1,200 cases in 2009 and 2010. Its findings include the following:

- Eighty percent of whistleblower investigations flunked one or more standards in OSHA's own *Whistleblower Investigations Manual.*

- OSHA found merit for only 2 percent of retaliation complaints.

- OSHA issued final rulings without conducting any face-to-face interviews in nearly half its "investigations" (46 percent).

- Only 21 percent of cases settled prior to a ruling. Of those, only 3 percent of employees went back to work and only 13 percent received financial compensation.

- There is no written guidance to conduct investigations under new corporate whistleblower statutes. (Congress has passed four new DOL-administered laws since 2006 and overhauled three that were passed earlier.)

- There are no subject matter experts available to help with investigations of technical issues raised by corporate whistleblowers surrounding railroad safety, mass transit safety, consumer product safety, medical care, and financial markets.

- No training is required for supervisors, and none in the four audited regions had completed the two courses required for investigators.

- While investigators can properly handle 6 to 8 open investigations at a time, they are being assigned up to 35.

- OSHA claims to have hired only 16 of 25 new investigators already paid for by Congress, and even those are not reserved as full-time employees.

- There is inconsistent regional enforcement of national laws, with two out of four audited regions not disclosing the methodology for their internal audits. The other two relied on self-audit checklists, which covered as few as two of the eight elements in the *Whistleblower Investigations Manual*.

- The national OWPP cannot regularly review regional performances because the regions control performance reviews of themselves and bypass OWPP by sending the results directly to the same deputy assistant secretaries who have been denying any problems.

- All regional performance standards exclusively evaluated timeliness, with none checking the quality of the investigations.

- The *Whistleblower Investigations Manual* has not been updated since August 2003, and there is no final written guidance for the seven laws enacted or modified since. Investigators have made do with a draft from the national OWPP since 2007, but three more laws have been enacted or modified since.

- Previous OIG reports found that OSHA policies and procedures did not cover eight of the statutes on its watch, even before recent legislation.

- OSHA's case management system is an ineffective, unreliable source of data for reports or monitoring.[80]

What Went Wrong: ARB

After an administrative hearing, the Administrative Review Board has the final word on behalf of the secretary of labor. Unfortunately, until the current presidential administration, the ARB has traditionally been the legal system's least competent venue for appellate review. The members are political appointees selected by the secretary for two-year terms— effectively minor league patronage appointments without enough time to accumulate expertise even if they were qualified. Until the Obama administration, some tended to view their jobs as part-time, even liv- ing in their home states except to fly in for meetings, where they fre- quently would tell career employees how to rule without first reading the staff's memoranda analyzing the record and the law. While the Office of Administrative Law Judges is well respected, realistically it cannot over- come the legitimacy breakdown that surrounds it.

The Administrative Review Board regularly kept secret both the evi- dence and the arguments supporting its conclusions. With its reasoning cloaked in secrecy, the Department of Labor throws out prior rulings and doctrines at will. As discussed earlier, decisions stopped consistently pro- tecting job duties as "essential preliminary steps" to a government disclo- sure, reversing more than two decades of case law without explanation. This means workers like auditors, safety inspectors, and truck drivers risk waiving their whistleblower rights when issuing the types of reports or notices that are necessary for quality control.

The ARB traditionally has had a blind spot for congressional lan- guage. For example, it has functionally erased the common catchall pro- vision providing protection for any action to assist the government in carrying out the purposes of the relevant statute. Rulings on the Surface Transportation Assistance Act truck safety law are illustrative. In one case, the ARB disregarded a driver's refusal to drive while impaired due to sleep deprivation—a specifically protected activity in that statute. Instead it created a loophole with the explanation that the employee should not have been hired in the first place.[81]

Despite unqualified statutory language banning any discrimination on the basis of legally protected activity, discrimination no longer counts until there is a victim. For example, companies can issue retaliatory warning letters at will, even though it means the person can be fired for the next offense. Although that might help demonstrate retaliatory intentions behind the later action, the warning letter will not support a lawsuit despite serving as the first strike leading up to termination.[82]

The early fate of the SOX whistleblower law demonstrates how a clear congressional mandate can be eliminated through hostile judicial activism, generally at the administrative law level. The key problem is that whistleblowers do not have access to the law. A gauntlet of procedural roadblocks and shrunken boundaries, almost none intended by Congress, kicks the cases out before anti-retaliation rights can be considered on their merits. While employers won 93.5 percent of ALJ decisions, only 24.1 percent of outcomes were based on whether retaliation occurred.[83] The rest were screened out by the procedural or boundary firewalls. If your case reaches a hearing on retaliation grounds, you have a fair chance of winning. Professor Moberly's study found that 55.6 percent of whistleblowers succeeded in that context.[84]

The precedents are evolving rapidly and are split in many instances. Sarbanes-Oxley, however, was drastically stunted in early test cases and then regularly rewritten. Rulings such as the following illustrate how the Department of Labor, with initial complicity of the courts, largely undermined SOX's promise to allow juries to determine justice for whistleblowers challenging significant corporate misconduct.

- Despite explicit statutory language and SEC definitions, subsidiaries were ignoring the scope of liability in the underlying law— securities regulations.[85] In truth subsidiaries of publicly traded corporations are inextricably connected to the financial makeup of their parent companies. Unless these subsidiary employees are protected under SOX provisions, large-scale fraud might go unreported and undetected, resulting in significant harm to investors. Congress explicitly closed this loophole by statute in the 2010 Dodd-Frank law.

- The generally accepted accounting principles (GAAP) is a framework of guidelines widely used for proper financial bookkeeping and relied upon by the Securities and Exchange Commission. To reverse an ALJ's favorable ruling in the pioneer *Welch* case, the ARB held that challenging the failure to honor it is not a protected activity unless the specific GAAP standard that was violated also mirrors an SEC rule.[86]

■ In some instances SOX's broad antifraud mandate has been narrowed to protect disclosures of only shareholder fraud despite specific statutory language that encompasses *wire, mail, and banking fraud;* violations of "any Federal law *relating to* fraud against the shareholders"; and violations of any SEC rules, including failure to disclose misconduct that could materially threaten the shareholder's interest.[87] (emphasis added)

■ One earlier hostile activist court interpretation reflected the ARB's limitations, holding that you are not protected when disclosing mere illegality. The government must also have caught the wrongdoing and taken action to punish the misconduct; and the government penalty must have a direct and specific impact on shareholders' stock value. There is no protection for challenging any misconduct with "speculative" punitive consequences. So much for the freedom to warn.[88] Fortunately, that precedent is no longer the final word. As a 2009 ruling explained, "Requiring an employee to essentially prove the existence of fraud before suggesting the need for an investigation would hardly be consistent with Congress's goal of encouraging disclosure."[89]

■ The legislative text of SOX requires proving only discriminatory action, not any specific motivation. Foreshadowing the fate of SOX, the Department of Labor has flouted Congress's prerogative and rewritten regulations for non-SOX statutes to require proof of "retaliation," which entails specific evidence of animus or hostility toward you because of the whistleblowing.[90]

■ Rather than grant a whistleblower his day in court when DOL fails to issue a decision within 180 days, DOL has issued SOX regulations suggesting that courts send the case back to DOL with an order to issue a decision.[91] Again, judicial precedent subsequently erased the loophole,[92] and it no longer is DOL policy.

These examples illustrate loopholes carved into the law. While there are conflicting rulings and the law is evolving, the lowest common denominators cast doubt and uncertainty on your rights. To be sure, SOX remains a pioneering statute in its legislative mandate. It creates a back door into federal court for those times when the politicized administrative law system becomes a black hole. Yet in formal rights, SOX's meaning is unstable; and in tangible results, it remains a paper tiger. It may be useful as a part of a legal campaign, but you are doomed if you come to depend solely on these legal rights.

The Pyrrhic Victories of David Welch

In 1999 David Welch became chief financial officer for the Bank of Floyd. Floyd is a small agricultural town in central Virginia. Less than 500 people call it home. The Bank of Floyd runs a handful of branches in the state and, at the time Welch began working there, local residents owned almost all of the bank's stock, and its board of directors consisted mostly of local farmers. This fact did not distract Welch from his responsibilities as CFO. He approached his new position with tenacity and soon noticed a trend that suggested insider trading.

According to Welch, the bank's president, Leon Moore, and other officers frequently purchased bank stock shortly before making public announcements that would send the stock price up. In addition to having suspicions of insider trading, Welch discovered that entries to the bank's accounting books were being prepared to make profits seem larger than they truly were. In one instance the bank had written off loans equaling $195,000 because they did not expect them to be repaid. When the loans ended up being repaid, however, Moore instructed the internal auditor to prepare journal entries recording the repayments as income. At other times, when earnings were better than expected, some of Moore's expenses, such as meals, education, travel, and entertainment, were recorded in one year (although those expenses had not actually occurred) and then reversed during the following year. The result of the expense reversals was an inflated net income.

In October 2001 Welch approached Moore with his suspicions of insider trading. When Welch did not get answers, he notified the Securities and Exchange Commission. Three months later Welch wrote a memo to Moore, comparing the fraudulent activities within the Bank of Floyd to those that went on at Enron. When SOX went into effect later that year, Welch expressed to Moore and others at the bank that he would not certify the accuracy of any financial documents he believed to be deliberately misleading. After suspending Welch without notice, bank officials requested a meeting with him to discuss his allegations. After Welch requested that he be allowed to consult his attorney during the requested meeting (either by phone or outside the meeting room), bank officials claimed that Welch refused to meet because he could not bring his own lawyer. The board of directors fired him for insubordination.

Welch filed a SOX claim with OSHA. After losing with OSHA, the administrative law judge ruled in Welch's favor, making him the first employee to win under the new law. The ALJ ordered Welch's reinstatement with back pay. The bank refused to comply, however, and appealed the decision to the Administrative Review Board, arguing that "SOX was never intended to protect employees from a dispute with management, but instead was enacted to root out corruption in big companies that employ a lot of people." A four-year string of appeals ensued.

In July 2007 the ARB abruptly reinterpreted the law and held that Welch was not a whistleblower. In a blockbuster decision, the ARB ruled that: despite statutory language there was no protection for disclosures of wire fraud; despite statutory language requiring only a reasonable belief of a material threat to shareholders, an employee must disclose an actual violation resulting in actual harm to qualify as a whistleblower; and despite contrary statutory language, what the SEC characterizes as violations of its rules on generally accepted accounting principles and internal controls do not qualify for protected whistleblowing.

On August 5, 2008, the Fourth Circuit Court of Appeals issued a ruling that made a caricature of Welch's rights while restoring some rationality to interpretations of SOX. On the positive side, the court rejected DOL holdings that a whistleblower must cite specific violations of a law for a protected disclosure—or that he even be right. Mistaken allegations that are factually specific deserve protection if reasonably believed. Further, it restored the rights of juries to rule on whether an employee qualifies for protection by having a genuine, actual belief—the subjective dimension of the reasonable-belief test. It held that Welch's disclosure of misclassifying assets deserved protection even if the false statements did not affect the company's bottom line.

Amazingly, the court ruled against Welch anyway. Its rationale? His lawyers had not filed legal briefs early enough in the lawsuit demonstrating the link between misconduct and relevant SEC laws, so the Department of Labor could ignore whether there was one and render Welch's rights irrelevant.

Even while he was winning, Welch struggled to find employment. He sold his family farm, earned a doctorate in accounting, and moved to Ohio, where in 2007 he secured a position on the accounting faculty of Franklin University. His insight after exercising his rights? When you're in deep trouble, keep your mouth shut and your eyes straight ahead.[93]

The Times Are They a-Changin'?

The Obama administration's arrival brought high expectations that times are, indeed, a-changin'. What have been the results through 2010? A review of the two bookends for corporate whistleblower frustration— OSHA and the Administrative Review Board—reveal a positive but mixed track record.

With respect to the ARB, the answer is a resounding hooray. Labor Secretary Hilda Solis has appointed four new members to the five-member board. Together they have the most experience, subject matter expertise, and demonstrated commitments to the board's mission of any members in its history.[94] Although two of the new board members did not start participating in decisions until September, a case-by-case review of ARB decisions demonstrates that the streamlined new majority's impact already has been dramatic. For the six-month period from March through August 2010, whistleblowers had a 6-to-10 (37.5 percent) win/loss record for decisions on the merits (cases not disposed on timeliness or other procedural grounds). That was almost twice the prospects for success compared with 2009's 8-to-33 (19.75 percent) win/loss track record.

At OSHA, however, there are only glimmers of hope. On the positive side, OSHA's new leadership team headed by Assistant Secretary of Labor for Occupational Safety and Health Dr. David Michaels has given unabashed support for legislative reform to strengthen whistleblower rights, including a best-practice infrastructure for section 11(c) occupational safety whistleblower cases.[95] Dr. Michaels has been a visible figure in the whistleblower rights community, regularly sponsoring and attending town halls and conferences.

But the same team has been lukewarm to fixing its own infrastructure, making only generalized commitments and minor repairs while digging in against structural change that would alter the agency's identity or internal balance of power. This is reflected by the agency's response to the GAO and OIG recommendations. In generalities OSHA pledged cooperation to make improvements, but that is standard bureaucratic jargon and procedure. More significantly, OSHA has not agreed to impose professional-quality independent audits on regional operations; provide resources and enforcement teeth for the national OWPP to enforce agency policy; impose fiscal controls to ensure that funds appropriated for the whistleblower program are spent on it; institute minimum laptop and equipment standards for investigators; or even to develop a strategic plan for the whistleblower program.

Instead the agency pledges reform through a "top to bottom" management review. While conscientiously staffed, the review lacks credibility because it was designed by the same career staff above the OWPP that was responsible for adverse GAO and OIG findings and not surprisingly excludes review of management actions above the OWPP. It derisively has been labeled the "topless to bottom" review, and the results are widely anticipated to scapegoat the national OWPP for regional failures beyond its control.

There *are* signs of change in the field. After a rare preliminary victory in a 2008 case, a UPS employee won a $254,000 settlement under the trucking whistleblower law.[96] In a 2009 case, OSHA ordered relief ranging from $541,000 to $1.6 million to each of nine air safety whistleblowers.[97] In March 2010 OSHA ordered reinstatement and some $1.6 million to a SOX whistleblower.[98] In one 2010 case, OSHA even refused to approve a settlement until receiving additional information to assess compliance with DOL policy on banishment clauses.[99]

So far, however, these instances of taking rights seriously are the rare anecdotal exceptions to overall patterns of neglect. While the cases demonstrate a fresh perspective by OSHA's regional administrators, results have not improved on the big picture. Both the GAO and the OIG assessments covered OSHA under the Obama administration. Dr. Welch's study revealed that in terms of win/loss records, while whistleblowers fared better overall at OSHA under the Obama administration compared with that of President George W. Bush (3.2 percent victories versus 2.4 percent), in SOX cases it deteriorated (1.4 percent to 1.0 percent). Dr. Welch explained that there may not have been time for new policies to take effect.[100] While that is reasonable, the administration must make those commitments and start honoring them. That change has not occurred to date. Whistleblowers hoping for a fair shot at justice through OSHA are waiting for Godot, unless OSHA's leadership extends its structural reform commitment from passing new laws to cleaning its own house.

An illustration of currently schizophrenic policy is the regulations for investigations of the new Consumer Product Safety Improvement Act and the new ground transportation whistleblower protection in the 9/11 law. On the positive side, the new regulations establish that:

- the statute of limitations for acting on rights does not begin to run after an employee becomes aware of an employment action;

- protected whistleblowing can be oral or written;

- the DOL will no longer fight access to court when there is not a final ruling within statutory time limits; and

- throughout its investigation OSHA will provide the complainant with responsive documents from the employer.[101]

When OSHA intends to order preliminary reinstatement, however, the employer will be notified of the ruling, get to see the file, meet with the investigator, and can file briefs to change OSHA's mind. The whistleblower will be disenfranchised from that whole process, including knowledge that it's occurring. In addition to being denied equal rebuttal opportunity, the whistleblower is denied access to evidence such as the witness statements in the investigative file. The latter is a major head start for the employer, who is now aware of the details of all witness testimony while the whistleblower remains in the dark.[102]

A particularly curious initiative reached the public record when the American Federation of Government Employees local union covering OSHA investigators protested that its collective bargaining agreement had been violated by plans to transfer OSHA's whistleblower function to the Office of Labor Management Standards (OLMS).[103] The OLMS mission has concentrated on investigating union corruption, and it was an attack agency against unions during the Bush administration. At a minimum it has a history of conflict with an employee rights institution that represents and supports many whistleblowers. That is a grating foundation for reform.

The government union's concern was well taken. A September 2010 DOL "thought piece" considered three options for the whistleblower program:

- transfer portions of it other than the 11(c) occupational safety docket to OLMS;

- make the program independent; or

- make it autonomous with its own budget within OSHA.

Most of the analysis centered on the benefits of further fragmenting whistleblower investigations by transferring some to OLMS—but not section 11(c) cases, which currently represent more than 60 percent of OSHA's whistleblower docket. The unidentified authors argued that both functions involve investigations and that OLMS has a better case-tracking system.

There do not appear to be any unique advantages. OSHA is an investigative agency as well, but its role is remedial investigations, not prosecutorial. Further OSHA needs to develop a functional case-tracking system for 11(c) cases even if other statutes were transferred.

The OLMS proposal is a high-risk gamble that could make a bad situation worse. Whistleblowers have long been frustrated with investigations by Offices of Inspectors General whose primary role is prosecutorial. They complain that OIG probes too often have targeted the victim, by searching for evidence of misconduct by whistleblowers more than evidence of retaliation by employers. The clash in overarching mission roots could make OLMS an even worse fit. This is a decision that should be made only after a full public record, including hearings to consider its impact. It will be a test of the current administration's transparency policies whether the dialogue on this change is conducted behind closed doors or with public participation.

To date, the jury is still out regarding whether the Obama administration is committed to change worth believing in for OSHA's whistleblower protection program. The success or failure of rights under DOL whistleblower laws rides on that outcome because for the overwhelming majority of unemployed whistleblowers an OSHA investigation is all they can afford.

Pointers for Filing a SOX Whistleblower Complaint

Many of the unhappy endings in SOX cases could have been avoided if whistleblowers knew how to navigate their legal maze of rights. Few lawyers have mastered the process. By sharing the lessons learned at the Government Accountability Project, we hope to prevent avoidable frustration. This section draws from the more comprehensive nuts-and-bolts guide in Tool A of the Whistleblower Toolkit, which summarizes the *Whistleblower Investigations Manual* used since 2003 by OSHA's Office of the Whistleblower Protection Program as well as interviews with OWPP staff.

These tips are organized chronologically, from getting started, to understanding OSHA, to packaging your rights, to making your case to OSHA, to finally getting to court.

Get a lawyer as quickly as possible   This applies even for the initial, informal stage of an OSHA investigation. The terrain is saturated with legal traps, and a mistake at the OSHA stage cannot always be cured in the later due process phase. Further, the initial OSHA stage may be the best chance for a settlement, which will benefit from a skilled professional to negotiate the best terms.

Research the law governing misconduct   Before you disclose your evidence, research the law governing the misconduct on which you are blowing the whistle so that you can tailor your disclosure to relevant legal requirements. At a minimum your whistleblowing will not qualify for protection unless your accusation "definitely and specifically" conforms to the legal requirements for proving that misconduct. For trucking and cross-country bus safety, you will have to cite to specific government regulations. If you don't do your homework first and apply the lessons when you speak out, the truth and the significance of your disclosure may not protect you.

Beware of time limits   Be mindful of the time limits in your statute and give yourself ample margin for error. Keep in mind that they run from the date you learn of the alleged discrimination, not when it takes effect.[104] Settlement negotiations will not toll or suspend the time limits even if the employer waives them.[105] It is irrelevant if you raised your reprisal allegations in another forum or even if government officials misled you.[106] In Professor Moberly's study, 33.8 percent of employee losses were due to missing the statute of limitations.[107]

File your complaint with the regional office   OSHA's national Office of the Whistleblower Protection Program sets policy and reviews outcomes, but the cases are investigated and decided by regional OSHA offices. Learn the procedures of the region where you file and seek to learn how it interprets the law, such as its interpretations for protected conduct. There are enormous variations among the regional offices in how they conduct business.

Be reasonable in your expectations   Be sensitive that OSHA's whistleblower program is hopelessly understaffed. The regional offices have a staff of 80, including 10 managers and no administrative support, to conduct the first stage processing for 17 whistleblower statutes. Many SOX investigators do not have laptop computers. Some have been trained only in antiquated, hostile legal standards, although they must interpret laws with modernized burdens of proof more favorable to employees. No additional resources were granted for handling the new flood of SOX complaints—around 250 per year, or 13 percent of the agency's expanded caseload. The headquarters OWPP staff of four reviews nearly 2,000 cases annually and handles a steady stream of inquiries.[108] These all are unrealistic workloads.

Take the informal stage seriously   Although OSHA's findings are not binding in later administrative or court proceedings, ALJs and judges refer to them regularly. Their "first impression" is significant.

Allege all the legal elements to prevail   In your initial complaint, allege all the legal elements to prevail, or else OSHA will not investigate. In some contexts it is a good strategy to hold back, but here that would be fatal. By statute you must present a referenced script for victory; otherwise OSHA will rule against you without further investigation.[109] Even if all the elements are covered, also list all the possible acts of alleged discrimination in your initial complaint. Otherwise the investigator may not consider them if submitted subsequently. First impressions on paper are all important in this setting.

List all the individual defendants   List all the individual defendants in your lawsuit before the OSHA investigation is over. It may be too late to add them later when you seek a hearing.[110] Further, the specter of broader personal liability creates a greater incentive within the employer's ranks to settle the case.

Allege retaliation for disclosing the full scope of eligible violations   In your complaint, if applicable, allege retaliation for disclosing violations of the SOX requirements for independent auditors and adequate internal controls for financial records. These are in SOX sections 202 and 404, respectively. Citing these specific provisions avoids limiting your whistle-blowing solely to shareholder fraud.

Allege retaliation for disclosing wire fraud   For the same reason, also charge retaliation for disclosing wire fraud if a telephone or fax has been used. This again helps prevent your case from being restricted to share-holder fraud issues.

Explain how the misconduct proves how each law is violated   In your complaint and in any relevant legal arguments, explain why you believe the specific alleged misconduct in your disclosure proves how each par-ticular law is violated. It does not matter how obvious the connection seems. David Welch ultimately lost his case for failing to spell it out in the early stages.

Mention the lack of a hotline   If relevant, reinforce your complaint by attacking the company's failure to construct a professionally credible hot-line. This is its own SOX requirement and can help demonstrate disre-gard for your anti-retaliation rights as well.

Demonstrate that your employer "should have known"   In your initial complaint, demonstrate that at a minimum whoever retaliated "should have known" of your whistleblowing. It is your burden to prove that your employer had "knowledge" of your whistleblowing activities. Otherwise, how could the company retaliate against you for them? While it may seem surreal after all the internal hostility, in many cases the officials who actually fire you will claim blissful ignorance of your dissent. OSHA's whistleblower regulations require you to prove only "constructive knowledge"—that the employer "should have known" of your protected conduct.[111] From the start take advantage of this resource against plausible deniability if there is any room for doubt.

Now it's time to start making your case to OSHA.

Develop a relationship with the investigator   At the informal stage, your rights will be handled in a more personal and idiosyncratic manner than later before an administrative law judge. Respect what the OSHA investigators are coping with. It is not realistic to expect that they will dig beneath the surface or take initiatives beyond reviewing what is submitted. You must be sensitive to the investigator's workload, know and meticulously respect the region's procedures, and spell out your evidence.

Press hard for an initial interview   Although an interview is not a formal entitlement, it is hard for OSHA to refuse because the employer has an explicit right to meet with the investigator in your case.[112] This may be your only chance to establish credibility and earn the investigator's trust.

Persistently build the record in a responsible way   Get the investigator's e-mail address so that you can update the record of evidence. Transfer it in well-organized files limited to significant factual material. Skip the background. Do not bombard the investigator with a constant stream of updates. Instead supplement the record every other week to show trends in evidence unless there is a major development.

Insist on your right to know and rebut the employer's defense   Until last year you did not have the right to know the employer's response to your complaint. Now you are entitled, but you may not get it unless you are assertive. Make sure the investigator confirms that there are no opposing arguments you have not had an opportunity to read and rebut.

Do not expect the investigator to negotiate a settlement For decades the Department of Labor played a significant role in mediating settlements during the informal stages of whistleblower complaints. The OSHA personnel for SOX and other recent laws, however, are investigators whose primary role is fact finding. Although they will cooperate with settlement efforts, that is not their responsibility.[113]

Beware of banishment clauses and gag orders In any settlement be aware of department policy on banishment clauses and gag orders, to deflect pressure for those restraints. Both are common demands in exchange for voluntary resolution of your case and compensation. But they are subject to review and if unreasonable can result in disapproval of the settlement under DOL policy.[114] Gag orders have been declared void and unenforceable under nearly all the recent whistleblower laws. If you know your rights, you can disarm heavy-handed negotiating tactics by informing the employer that the issue is a waste of time because gag demands are illegal and an unreasonable banishment clause could risk the settlement's approval.

Pursue victory on at least one or two elements of the retaliation claim Even if you lose at the OSHA level, this will put you on higher ground in negotiating a settlement before seeking a hearing.

The next step is getting to court.

Give notification Notify the official presiding over your DOL case 15 days before moving it to federal district court. This is necessary to prevent the transfer from being rejected on procedural grounds.[115]

SOX Eligibility Criteria

All of the following must have occurred for a federal court to have jurisdiction over a SOX claim:

- ☐ The employee filed a complaint with OSHA within 90 days of the alleged employer misconduct;

- ☐ If OSHA's preliminary order was in favor of the employer, the employee appealed that order;

- ☐ At least 180 days elapsed since the filing of the complaint;

☐ The secretary of labor, as represented by the Administrative Review Board, did not issue a final decision on that complaint;

☐ The lack of a final decision within 180 days was not due to bad faith on the employee's part; and

☐ The employee gave 15 days' notice to the administrative law judge or the ARB and the other party before filing in federal district court.

Seek damages   In your initial complaint, state that to be "made whole" you must receive specific "damages" for all the losses caused by whistleblower discrimination. Specifically list and seek monetary compensation for items like loss of reputation, emotional distress, lowered credit rating, medical bills, and any other direct or indirect impact of the unlawful reprisal.

Bundle your legal rights   For example, when you go to court on a SOX case, add a "public policy exception state tort claim" to your lawsuit. Public policy exception cases are common-law wrongful discharge tort lawsuits available in most states; they are discussed more fully later in this chapter. Their common feature is a right to a jury trial because they are by definition "actions at law" seeking money damages. Punitive damages are generally available, increasing the value of statutory whistleblower cases commonly limited to "make whole" remedies. Similarly, you can bundle federal and state *qui tam* False Claims lawsuits.

Do as much discovery as possible   On balance, complete as much discovery as you can at the administrative level before moving a case to court. Although an ALJ is much less sympathetic than a jury, the administrative level is much less expensive than the same procedures in federal court. Finish as much of that work as possible before going to court. What you learn also may help spark a settlement that obviates the need for a trial.

Be prepared to accept reinstatement   Finally, if you do win at any level, be prepared to return to your job. Refusing to go back, even if only for a brief transition period before you find another job or resign, can cause you to lose back pay.[116]

False Claims Act

Unlike the 90-day statute of limitations under Sarbanes-Oxley, early judicial precedents based on the Federal False Claims Act allow lawsuits to be filed up to six years after the adverse employment action was taken[117]—the same as to file a *qui tam* lawsuit challenging the fraud.

Section 4 of the 1986 amendments provides that "Any employee who is discharged, demoted, suspended, threatened, harassed, or in any other manner discriminated against . . . by his or her employer because of lawful acts done by the employee . . . in furtherance of an action under this section" is entitled to "all relief necessary to make the employee whole."[118] This "make whole" relief provision is similar to that of SOX and can include reinstatement with the seniority status the employee would have had but for the discrimination, *double* back pay plus interest, and compensation for any "special damages," including litigation costs and reasonable attorney's fees.[119]

An employee may bring an action in US federal district court to obtain this relief. The availability of federal district court as a venue and the possibility of double back pay as a remedy can make this act attractive for employees to whom it applies. Dodd-Frank amendments to the False Claims Act clarified that its statute of limitations for retaliation claims is three years.[120]

Early in the False Claims Act's history, whistleblowers had hardly any success, but recent history has been more satisfactory. As of September 2005, the Taxpayers Against Fraud website reported that claimants had settled or won more than 1,000 retaliation cases and lost more than 2,750.[121] There are signs of increasing judicial hostility in administering the False Claims Act. One disturbing trend has been the courts' rejection of employees' warnings of illegality as protected activity. To qualify for protection, the employee must make an explicit accusation of defrauding the government, identifying specific legal violations.[122]

State Statutory Protections

The common-law rule is that at-will employees, meaning all employees who do not work under contract for a definite term, may be fired at any time for any reason or no reason. Recognizing that punishing employees who identify illegal public health and safety hazards is often contrary to the public interest, however, 18 states have enacted whistleblower protection laws that provide an exception to this employment-at-will doctrine.[123] With exceptions, state whistleblower statutes are the legal system's lowest common denominator for whistleblower rights.

State law may include or exclude particular classes of employees. Statutes may also cover only disclosures of particular kinds of wrongdoing. The law may vary greatly from state to state; and even where statutory language is very similar, it is the way the courts *apply* these laws that makes some jurisdictions preferable to others. On the other hand, there can be pleasant surprises. Consulting a seasoned practitioner is a useful supplement to your own statutory research.

The District of Columbia has the nation's strongest state or municipal whistleblower law, mirroring the federal Whistleblower Protection Act's favorable legal burdens of proof but going even further through provision for jury trials and remedies that include discipline for those found guilty of illegal retaliation. Although primarily for government employees, it also extends to whistleblowers working for contractors.[124] In 2010 the law was strengthened to add protection against gag orders and retaliatory investigations, to expand the statute of limitations from one to three years, to overcome judicial precedents that have weakened the federal law, and even to expand protection to government contractor companies retaliated against by the government for challenging misconduct.[125]

California, New Jersey, and Florida have particularly strong state whistleblower protection statutes that cover private as well as public employees.[126] These laws do not overlap completely as they have somewhat different statutory protections and procedures. Although it is unlikely that an individual will have a choice as to which of these laws, if any, to seek protection under, we briefly present them here to demonstrate some of the stronger whistleblower provisions available under state law.

California's corporate whistleblower protection law provides that employers may not make or enforce any rule or policy that would discourage employees from disclosing information of noncompliance with a law, rule, or regulation to a government or law enforcement agency.[127]

The employee must show only that his or her protected conduct was a factor that contributed to the retaliatory action.[128] The employer then must prove by "clear and convincing evidence" that it would have taken the adverse action irrespective of the protected activity.[129] This law provides not only for the same remedies as most whistleblower laws but also for up to $10,000 in punitive damages per violation.[130] The state attorney general's office also maintains a hotline for whistleblowers and refers callers to the most appropriate government authority.[131] California also has a law that protects government employees who expose fraud, waste, or other illegal behavior.[132]

New Jersey's Conscientious Employee Protection Act prohibits "retaliatory actions" against any employee who has a "reasonable basis for objecting to a co-employee's activity, policy, or practice."[133] A retaliatory action is defined as the discharge, suspension, or demotion of an employee, or other adverse employment action taken against an employee in the terms and conditions of employment.[134] An employee need only prove by a preponderance of the evidence that he or she engaged in protected conduct and was subject to subsequent retaliation and that there was a causal connection between the conduct and the retaliation.[135] On the downside New Jersey whistleblower law does not provide for jury trials.[136]

Florida has separate whistleblower acts for the public and private sectors. Under the latter, private employers are prohibited from retaliating against an employee who has engaged in any of three activities.[137] First, employers cannot retaliate against an employee who, under oath and in writing, discloses or intends to disclose an illegal employment activity, policy, or practice.[138] This prohibition on retaliatory action applies only, however, if the employee has first notified his employer in writing about the wrongful conduct and given the employer a reasonable time to correct the situation.[139] Second, employers cannot retaliate against an employee who provided information to, or testified before, any appropriate governmental agency, person, or entity investigating the employer's alleged violations.[140] Third, employers cannot retaliate against employees who refuse to participate in any activity, policy, or practice that is illegal.[141]

Common-Law Protections

Even in the absence of state statutory protections, many common-law, or judicially created, remedies exist. In 44 states and the District of Columbia, courts recognize that the disclosure of a wide variety of violations falls within the public policy exception to the employment-at-will doctrine.[142] Various courts have found that reporting improper accounting, mismanagement of property, or fraud; actions that violate public welfare, consumer, or employee protection laws; activities that violate commercial, trade restraint, or environmental protection laws; and misconduct relating to transactions with governmental entities fall under the public policy exception.[143] Although the specifics vary by jurisdiction, employees filing common-law actions must prove that they were fired in retaliation for engaging in a protected activity and that their discharge was in violation of a clear public policy.[144] This is usually the case when the alleged misconduct is itself of serious concern to the public.[145]

Not all employees who are fired after disclosing misconduct by their employers have a case at common law, and those boundaries vary arbitrarily. Generally, the misconduct must be a violation of the Constitution or a specific state or federal law.[146] Violating a code of ethics or a set of guidelines is often insufficient.[147] The reason for this is that enforcing a professional or private code of conduct is not necessarily as strongly in the public interest as enforcing state and federal laws.

In some cases even an employee who reports illegal activity and is discharged as a result cannot bring a common-law suit. An employee who is not obliged to go looking for illegality but does so anyway may or may not be eligible to file a suit at common law, depending on the jurisdiction.[148]

An employee must also disclose illegal conduct in a "reasonable" way and to an appropriate person. "Reasonable" disclosures must have at least a substantial chance of bringing the misconduct to light in such a way that it can be corrected.[149] In some jurisdictions, filing a claim under a state whistleblower statute precludes pursuing a common-law action such as a tort or contract lawsuit, but in others the two claims can be made simultaneously.[150] It is always possible to file both federal and state claims.[151]

The Senate Judiciary Committee's passage of Sarbanes-Oxley stemmed from the need to reform corporate whistleblower rights due to the "patchwork and vagaries" of a diverse set of state and federal laws.[152] These include dozens of federal environmental and regulatory statutes, the False Claims Act, state legislation, and common law of varying strength and scope. SOX is a pioneering reform because it systematically extends corporate freedom of speech in principle, solidifies modern legal burdens of proof, and creates the right to seek justice from a jury. But to date it has helped few whistleblowers actually achieve justice.

In practice, initially the scope of SOX was drastically shrunk until it was not effective in consolidating corporate whistleblower rights. Access to jury trials proved elusive, and other institutions from OSHA to the courts have engaged in systematic, hostile activism against the congressional mandate. The law is in flux from these growing pains, but they remain a sobering reminder of the limitations of even the most ambitious whistleblower laws. Remember that your legal rights are a resource, not a solution. Use them as a part of your survival strategy, but do not depend on them.

Most importantly, do not be passive about settling for your rights as they currently exist. There are many major steps before corporate freedom of speech becomes a reality, starting with leadership by corporate executives. But a milestone would be a system of legal rights that are a resource for corporate whistleblowers rather than a threat. We explore whistleblower reform in chapter 7.

CHAPTER 7

Corporate Whistleblower Reform

A fundamental premise of this book is that you cannot always count on the law to help you get away with committing the truth. As a result, one of our primary goals has been to provide corporate employees with information and guidance to successfully blow the whistle in the absence of full legal rights. Ideally, corporations would provide their employees with a voluntary disclosure system that genuinely aims to uncover and correct internal problems and then thanks the whistleblower. Until the day corporations are willing to make this commitment voluntarily, however, legal support is needed.

Fortunately, the law is in transition, with Congress enacting a series of promising piecemeal measures. A comprehensive law standardizing the free-speech rights of corporate whistleblowers is on the horizon. This is the moment to codify lessons learned over more than three decades of haphazard federal legislation.

The Principles of Reform

The principles of reform are no mystery—but resistance to the necessary systematic changes is powerful. These principles lock in the public's right to know and the employee's right to bear witness against corporate wrongdoing. The question of how to transform these principles into meaningful legislative reforms is a political and strategic issue. GAP's analysis of best practices in existing whistleblower laws identifies 20 criteria for standardized legislative reform, which can be found as Tool G in the Whistleblower Toolkit, along with references to precedents in current law.

The primary legislative goal for corporate whistleblower protection is to consolidate the current hodgepodge of inconsistent, hit-or-miss rights with a standardized law covering all corporate employees. Having one consolidated national corporate whistleblower law incorporating these piecemeal precedents would be a win-win from every perspective. Currently, neither management nor employees can be sure what the boundaries of free-speech rights are without a lawyer to guide them through the maze of some three dozen different, overlapping laws and their various ground rules. All will benefit if they know where they stand.

By allowing whistleblowers to serve as an organization's own early-warning signal, a national corporate whistleblower law will also help companies fight internal fraud, which is a significant drain on corporate resources. Even more significantly, it will provide corporate leaders with the knowledge necessary for effective leadership—if they choose to listen to the messengers. One tangible benefit for whistleblowers will be more immediate: You will have a fair chance to defend yourself when asserting your rights against retaliation. More intrinsically, you will have the legal right to freedom of speech when you act as a public citizen on the job.

Citizen Enforcement Act

Another possible avenue of legislative reform is through a "Citizen Enforcement Act" such as modeled in Tool I of the Whistleblower Toolkit. This would expand the private attorney general model of the False Claims Act to cover not just fraud but violations of any law. The goal would be to give citizens standing to help enforce the law against corporate wrongdoing. In its most modest version, a citizen could obtain injunctive relief against an imminent threat and take the case to a jury of peers to decide whether the law has been violated. The most effective approach would permit actual and punitive damages against individual and institutional wrongdoers. This would provide a market incentive for commercial law firms to defend the public rather than wealthy institutions. A Citizen Enforcement Act could be adopted at the national, state, or local level for both public- and private-sector employees.

Corporate Policies and Guidelines

A genuine corporate commitment and policy to protect whistleblowers can help companies address internal problems early and effectively, long before they erupt into scandal and bankruptcy. It is such an essential part of any risk management strategy that some insurance companies are offering corporate clients who go this route 1 to 2 percent off their general liability premiums.[1] The lesson from corporate fraud studies discussed earlier is that an internal whistleblower system promotes a corporate culture of responsibility and accountability. This boosts efficiency and productivity, not to mention shareholder and employee confidence. If that is not reason enough for the boardroom, consider that the US Sentencing Commission allows courts to hold a company liable for the misconduct of its officers or employees if it fails to implement a sufficiently rigorous whistleblower system.[2]

Past experience suggests that there are two primary reasons why employees first consider but then decide against disclosing illegal conduct. The first reason is that they do not expect the disclosure to bring about an end to the illegal or harmful conduct. The second is that they fear retaliation. In GAP's experience active commitment and competent leadership by an organization's CEO is a prerequisite to building trust with employees and encouraging them to risk coming forward. This suggests to management and labor alike that a whistleblower program is a business priority rather than merely a formality for legal compliance. In many cases making whistleblowers feel and be safe working within the organization will require a cultural sea change.

To be sure, although Sarbanes-Oxley mandates an internal whistleblower system for publicly traded companies, the Securities and Exchange Commission and Congress have declined to specify what procedures this entails. Until there is further clarification, companies will enjoy a great deal of discretion. Some freedom to tailor a system to the company's particular characteristics is no doubt beneficial. A variety of promising approaches have been suggested, including a third-party, web-based complaint-handling system that maintains a confidential database and triggers investigations by an outside attorney.[3] Former SEC Enforcement Director Stephen M. Cutler "urged companies to appoint a permanent ombudsman or business practices officer to receive and investigate complaints."[4]

Corporate Whistleblower's Bill of Rights and Responsibilities

The following Corporate Whistleblower's Bill of Rights and Responsibilities encompasses legislative best practices. It applies them as a model corporate whistleblower policy.

1. *A broad freedom-of-speech mandate.* All individuals who perform services for a corporation have the right to lawfully disclose information that they reasonably believe is evidence of illegality or other misconduct that undermines the interests of corporate shareholders. These rights extend to all disclosures of misconduct, without unnecessary restrictions on form, context, audience, or connection with job duties. Employees who are about to make a disclosure or are perceived to be whistleblowers are protected as well.

2. *Loyalty to the law.* An employee has a right to refuse to violate the law, including the corporate charter, without undue coercion or discipline.

3. *Protection from retaliation.* A company has a duty not to tolerate or engage in any form of discrimination or harassment against good-faith whistleblowers. This duty includes providing appropriate and timely relief to ameliorate the consequences of actual or threatened reprisals and holding accountable those who retaliate.

4. *Fair procedures.* An employee has a right to fair and objective procedures for investigating and resolving complaints, disputes, and allegations of retaliation—procedures that do not require him or her to waive other legal rights to participate. To ensure objectivity and expedited proceedings, employees should have the option to enforce their rights through binding arbitration based on mutual strike (consensus) selection of arbitrators and a sharing of arbitration costs.

5. *Confidentiality.* A whistleblower has a right to privacy and confidentiality when making a disclosure. That right extends beyond personal information to any identifying information. It includes knowledge

of any limits on confidentiality and the right to reasonable advance notice if confidentiality must be breached.

6. *Investigation.* A whistleblower has a right to a full investigation if there is reasonable evidence of wrongdoing. A company should first conduct an initial evaluation of the complaint to determine its seriousness and urgency so that corporate resources can be best prioritized. The investigation should examine the complaint, the facts, and all relevant witnesses and material evidence to determine whether any misconduct, violation of law, or breach of ethics or company policy did in fact occur. This should be laid out in a report and provided to those with the authority to take corrective action. During the investigation, an employee has a right to remain apprised of the progress of the investigation and any preliminary findings.

7. *Enfranchisement.* A company has a duty to elicit, retain, and fully and objectively evaluate all concerns raised by whistleblowers. Whistleblowers have unique knowledge that is needed to evaluate the misconduct in question. Consequently, a competent investigation should keep a well-preserved record and provide whistleblowers with multiple opportunities to not only access it but also respond and contribute to it.

8. *Corrective action.* The bottom line is that a company must correct confirmed misconduct that prompted the whistleblowing. It also has a duty toward the employee whose disclosures enabled the corrective action. Whistleblowers whose allegations are substantiated have a right to corporate recognition if they consent to it. If they have suffered retaliation, they have the right to be made whole through compensation for any direct or indirect consequences of the retaliation.

9. *Accountability.* A company has the duty to impose its strictest zero-tolerance policies and mandatory progressive penalties on those found responsible for retaliation. Adequate discipline may also include reporting them to the appropriate regulatory authorities. A company has a duty to stay in contact with the whistleblower after the investigation is complete to ensure that no retaliation or further wrongdoing occurs.

10. *Notice.* Employees, alongside shareholders, consumers, and other stakeholders, have a right to know about their rights, what whistleblower complaint systems are at their disposal, and how to use them. A company has a duty to disseminate this information broadly through annual reports, employment contracts, workplace posters, employee handbooks, and special training sessions. Managers should be made aware of this bill of rights and trained in dealing with whistleblowers appropriately.

Every right carries with it a corresponding responsibility. In this context, the Corporate Whistleblower's Bill of Rights and Responsibilities also obligates employees to:

- respect the confidentiality of sensitive information such as trade secrets, patent information, and other intellectual property;

- raise concerns in good faith and with a reasonable belief;

- exhaust available corporate channels unless they have a reasonable suspicion of bad faith or conflict of interest;

- facilitate the expeditious resolution of cases by good-faith participation in investigations; and

- avoid false statements and unlawful behavior.

Alternative Dispute Resolution

Alternative dispute resolution (ADR) is a counterweight to more-traditional adversarial methods and provides an effective win-win resource for resolving whistleblower complaints. The expense and the limits of adversarial models in addressing whistleblower disputes are obvious. Even when whistleblowers "win" their case, it is seldom realistic for them to go back to work for an employer they just defeated in court. At a minimum hard feelings remain. Employers who lose in litigation may engage in continued albeit subtle harassment efforts to make an example of victorious whistleblowers. To keep dissent from spreading, many employers strive to demonstrate that even whistleblowers who win in court will inevitably lose when they return to their jobs.

Types of Alternative Dispute Resolution

Mediation   Mediation is a form of ADR in which an impartial third-party facilitator assists the disputing parties in reaching a consensual agreement. Because this agreement is voluntary, it tends to have greater buy-in and compliance than something imposed from the outside. Despite strong results among parties who are open to dialogue, mediation is less effective where there is a lack of good faith or an imbalance of power. Under these circumstances binding arbitration may be more appropriate.

Binding arbitration   Arbitration is a hybrid form of ADR that combines traits of both mediation and traditional litigation. In arbitration, parties choose to refer their dispute to one or more arbitrators and agree to be bound by their decision. The arbitrators may conduct a formal hearing with witnesses, testimony, evidence, and legal arguments but have the discretion to simplify the process as they see fit. Arbitrators may base their decision-making on actual statutory and case law or on personal judgments about what is a fair and equitable outcome.

Arbitration can be a low-cost, streamlined alternative to conventional litigation. Through binding arbitration clauses in employment and collective bargaining contracts, it long has been used to resolve labor disputes, including whistleblower reprisals against government employees in federal unions.

Be careful, however, as arbitration has legitimacy only when two factors are present:

- mutual strike selection to ensure a consensus on who will be the arbitrator; and

- sharing in the cost of compensating the arbitrator so that there is no conflict of interest.

Corporations often require employees to waive statutory rights, such as a day in court before a jury, for an arbitration decided by someone the company has hired. Recent whistleblower laws preclude enforceability of those clauses.

Advantages of ADR   Alternative dispute resolution can provide a constructive approach to making a difference. These methods can be applied to resolving a whistleblower's allegations of wrongdoing against the public, not merely to the subsequent retaliation. ADR could be used in isolation or as an alternative to litigation under new model laws such as the Citizen Enforcement Act. The goal would be to replace the win-lose dynamic of litigation with more constructive approaches to long-term problem-solving. Commercial ADR programs can reduce some of the delay, expense, inefficiency, and hostility associated with litigation. A survey by the Center for Public Resources found that its 652 reporting companies saved more than $300,000 each on average by implementing ADR programs. A similar survey indicated that 80 percent of business executives and lawyers found that mediation helped preserve business relationships.[5]

The Hanford Concerns Council

A promising mediation experiment is the Hanford Concerns Council at the nation's nuclear waste facility in Richland, Washington. It was created in response to dozens of filed whistleblower claims. The council originally grew out of recommendations from a study conducted by the University of Washington.[6] Both prior antagonists—government contractors and the interested groups that had represented whistleblowers and their concerns—agreed to adopt the proposal calling for a unique independent body. The Department of Energy field offices at Hanford support the function and encourage contractor involvement. Its goal is the full, fair, and final resolution of whistleblower cases, ideally at an early enough stage to solve the underlying problem and avoid or promptly redress any retaliation.[7]

To achieve this goal, the contractor at Hanford has agreed to implement any of the independent council's advisory recommendations that are supported by consensus of the council. These are developed among the council members, who consist of three management representatives from each participating contractor company (three companies at present), four public interest representatives, and four independent representatives, one of whom is the chair of the council. The council operates with a full-time mediator/administrator who plays a key role both in daily interactions with employees and corporate staff and in the management and the mediation of the cases themselves.[8]

Unique features of the council include that it is independent of the contractors and the DOE but also knowledgeable about the site and attached to its daily work. This is because the membership includes senior contractor officials as well as interest group representatives who are knowledgeable about the site. To ensure independence each case is meticulously assessed de novo, regardless of what investigations have already been done. Also, in contrast to the usual approaches, the council develops comprehensive and nuanced recommendations to address any underlying safety issues it finds, as well as any allegations of retaliation, issues related to workplace relationships and culture, and other individual impacts. The council's charter, which defines its authorities, allows each case to be assessed and resolved in accordance with its specific characteristics.[9] In most instances the council is able to reintegrate the employee back into the workforce, sometimes in a different position, and the site thereby keeps an experienced person in the workforce.[10]

Increasingly, underlying problems are solved as they are uncovered during the council assessment. Open dialogue in the council process often helps the contractor improve the implementation of safety systems. The council operates under state statutes governing mediation and must maintain significant confidentiality in operation and communication. In only about 5 percent of cases received does the council reach a conclusion that includes the employee's departure. The membership structure allows frank feedback to both company and employee about how to avoid similar problems in the future as well as about the conflict's causes. The focus is on the future and problem solving, not on fixing blame. This stands in stark contrast to the typical results of litigated cases or formal cases filed. It should be noted that most cases at the site are handled through the contractor employee concerns programs and other channels, which have greatly expanded and improved since the council began in 1994. The council continues to receive the cases that seem to be the most polarized and difficult to resolve, of which there are a number each year.

The Hanford Concerns Council is in its second iteration at Hanford. The original version, called the Hanford Joint Council, began under Westinghouse as the general contractor for most site functions.[11] It later

involved different companies, as the work was divided among more contractors, but these successor contractors were not a part of the initial
agreement, nor was the agreement reviewed when they came on-site.
Partly for this reason, some of these companies were not cooperative
with the system, and the resignation of several of the companies led to
its abandonment. After a two-year hiatus, the current council came into
existence in July 2005, along with the initial hiring of CH2M Hill, one of
the companies that acknowledged its value and favored its retention.[12]
All the contractors that have since joined, some succeeding CH2M Hill,
have had an opportunity to review the council arrangements and reach
an agreement to participate. The DOE field offices have an ex-officio representative, which has further strengthened the council's ability to both
assess cases and implement case resolutions.[13]

Corporate, interest group, and government participants strongly
agree that both councils have been extremely effective at addressing
whistleblowers' concerns and alleged retaliation as well as specific and
sitewide cultural issues that work against the free disclosure of safety,
health, and environmental problems at the site.[14] The original Joint Council, after nine years of operation, resolved more than 50 cases.[15] Since its
restart in 2005, it has addressed approximately 20 cases. Approximately
70 cases were referred to other processes or otherwise considered outside
of council jurisdiction as defined in the charter.

As an ADR tool, the Hanford Concerns Council has been a great
success. Though the council was specifically tailored to the situation at
Hanford, the model may be adapted to other corporate programs after
careful assessment of the different ruling circumstances. Its main ingre-
dients include a neutral staff, knowledgeable contractor and advocacy
members, and a charter that guarantees independence while complying
with mission, law, and regulation.[16]

In a sense, the council creates a supplemental conflict resolution and
implementing mechanism that allows whistleblower protection statutes
and regulations to actually deliver. It has tools to provide interim stabili-
zation until the case is assessed and resolved, which keep the issues and
the conflict from escalating and keep the parties from further errors and
accusations. It can also help an employee and a company find a mutually satisfactory resolution that complies with all regulatory reporting

obligations and creates benefit for the mission, the individual, the government, and the taxpayers. Average costs of council resolutions are a minuscule proportion of what similar cases by noncooperating companies have cost when pursued to litigation, even when settled. Moreover, council cases create minimal diversion from the work and the mission of the site.[17]

As the Hanford example suggests, the possibilities for addressing and realizing the principles identified above are numerous. They can be pursued by concerned citizens at the local, state, and national levels. Even at the international level, the precedents for whistleblower protection exist. Enforcement mechanisms to protect against violations of human rights and child labor standards have been adopted as elements of domestic trade legislation; similar provisions could be incorporated for whistleblower protection and the freedom to dissent in the workplace. These principles can and should be built into domestic legislation and international trade or human rights conventions alike in the effort to increase accountability and protect ethical action on the job.

Conclusion

Our warnings and advice in this handbook are drawn from the lessons learned by individuals who told the truth and often paid a bitter price. The good news is that the lessons can be learned. Whistleblowing does not have to be synonymous with professional suicide. Despite high personal risk, whistleblowers can and do make a difference. Many not only survive their whistleblowing experience but thrive professionally afterward. In many instances, they have prevented disasters from occurring by acting as modern-day Paul Reveres issuing badly needed public warnings.

We hope that your eyes are wide open to the full range of risks that come with the territory. If we have scared you away from blowing the whistle, perhaps you were not ready. If you are still determined to go ahead, we hope that this handbook will empower you to commit the truth in a smart way and thereby do the right thing for the public while protecting your career and personal life. Good luck!

Whistleblower Toolkit

Filing a Sarbanes-Oxley Whistleblower Complaint

Introduction

The Sarbanes-Oxley Act of 2002 resulted from the congressional response to problems highlighted in the corporate failures of Enron and World-Com.[1] Trust and confidence in financial markets were eroded by the daily news of accounting irregularities and possible fraudulent acts occurring at major corporations around the country.[2] The legislation sought to establish a framework to deal with conflicts of interest that undermined the integrity of the capital markets. The act is applicable to public companies only.[3]

To secure the integrity of the capital markets, Congress determined that meaningful protections must be provided for whistleblowers.[4] Congress attempted to "protect the 'corporate whistleblower' from being punished for having the moral courage to break the corporate code of silence."[5] As Senator Patrick Leahy acknowledged during the debate regarding the act, "When sophisticated corporations set up complex fraud schemes, corporate insiders are often the only ones who can disclose what happened and why."[6]

Whistleblowers from publicly traded companies may access the protections provided in the statute in the event that they suffer retaliation or discrimination for reporting violations of the act.

This tool attempts to demystify how SOX is supposed to operate, based on OSHA's generic manual for its investigators and the Department of Labor's regulations.

Sarbanes-Oxley Act Whistleblower Protection in Plain English

SOX provides whistleblower protection for employees of publicly traded companies. No officer, employee, contractor, subcontractor, or other agent of a publicly traded company may fire, demote, suspend, threaten, harass, or in any other way discriminate against an employee with respect to job, job duties, or benefits because the employee has lawfully provided information either directly or indirectly or assisted in an investigation regarding any conduct which the employee believes to constitute mail, wire, bank, or securities fraud; any violation of rules or regulations of the Securities and Exchange Commission; or any federal law concerning fraud against shareholders to a federal regulatory or law enforcement agency, a member of Congress or a congressional committee, or a person with supervisory authority over the employee or another person with authority within the organization. The law further protects those who file, testify, participate, or assist in a proceeding that will be filed or has been filed regarding any of the previously mentioned violations with the knowledge of the employer.[7] (This is not to imply that the employee must seek consent of the employer, but the employer must be aware that the employee has raised concerns.)

Anyone who feels they have been either discharged or discriminated against by anyone in violation of the above may file a complaint with the secretary of labor. One must file a claim no later than 180 days after the date on which the violation occurs.[8] If the secretary of labor has not issued a final decision on the individual's complaint within 180 days of the filing, absent any bad faith of the complaining party, the complainant may file an action for de novo review in federal court in the appropriate district regardless of the amount in controversy.[9]

A complainant who prevails is entitled to all the relief necessary to adequately compensate the individual. The individual may be entitled to: compensatory damages or reinstatement with the same seniority he or she would have had absent the retaliation; back pay with interest; and compensation for damages that occurred because of the retaliation, such as litigation costs, expert witness fees, and reasonable attorney's fees. Complainants seeking protection under this law should be mindful that they may have additional rights, privileges, or remedies under other laws, both state and federal, as well as rights under a collective bargaining agreement where applicable, which they may wish to exercise.[10]

OSHA Complaint Process

Complaint

Where an employee feels that he (or she—gender-specific language is used herein for simplicity) has been discharged or suffered other discrimination as a result of participation in activities covered under SOX, he may file a complaint with Occupational Safety and Health Administration within 180 days after an alleged violation of the act occurs.[11] The statutory time period for filing a complaint begins when the adverse action takes place. It is important to take note that the date of the adverse action is the date that the employee receives notice of the action, not the date the action is implemented.

For example, if an employee receives notice that he will be terminated on July 1 but is given 90 days to resign instead, the date of the adverse action is July 1. If the action is a continuing one, the time period begins with the last act. If the last day of the time period falls on a weekend, federal holiday, or a date that the Department of Labor offices are closed, the next business day will count as the final day.

Some circumstances may extend the time eligible for filing: for example, if the employer has actively concealed or misled the employee about the adverse action or the grounds for the action; the employee suffered a debilitating illness or injury and was unable to file; a natural disaster caused conditions that would make it impossible for a reasonable person to communicate with the appropriate agency in a timely manner; or the employee filed a timely complaint with another agency that cannot grant relief. One should be aware, however, that such circumstances are rare and the DOL will conduct a thorough investigation to determine if a circumstance provides for the time period to be extended.[12]

The complaint should be filed with the OSHA area director responsible for enforcement in the geographical area where the employee resides or was employed. It can also be filed with any OSHA officer or employee.

A directory of OSHA offices nationwide is available at *http://www.osha .gov/html/oshdir.html*. The address of the national office is:

National Office
US Department of Labor
Occupational Safety and Health Administration (OSHA)
200 Constitution Avenue NW
Washington, DC 20210

Although the act does not specify how the writing may be delivered, the employee should be sure to get a receipt of the actual date of filing. It is recommended that the employee retain certified mail receipts or facsimile transmittal sheets proving the date the complaint was filed. On occasion complaints may be misplaced or lost, and it will be necessary to prove that the filing was timely or risk dismissal because the statute of limitations has expired. The date of the postmark, facsimile transmittal, or e-mail communication will be considered the date of filing. If filed by any other means, the complaint is considered filed when the complaint is received.[13]

SOX complaints are generally received by the area office but may be received at the regional or national office. Complaints are sometimes received by referral from other government agencies or Congress.[14]

Although no particular form is required, the complaint must be filed in writing. It should include a full statement of the acts and omissions, with pertinent dates, that are believed to constitute the violations.[15] The complaint should include the full name, address, and phone number of the person filing the complaint as well as the name, address, and phone number of the employer.[16] In addition the employee should furnish copies of all documents that are relevant to the claim. Some examples are notices of adverse employment actions, performance appraisals, compensation information, grievances that may have been filed, job specifications or descriptions, employee handbooks, and collective bargaining agreements.

The employee should also keep careful records of the medical costs related to the claim and other costs that result from the claim. The employee should be mindful that if he has been terminated or laid off, he is obligated to continue to seek work and keep records of his earnings during this period. They may be used where appropriate to compute back pay owed. Back-pay liability may also be affected by the employee's refusal of a bona fide offer of reinstatement.[17]

The employee should detail not only the adverse action but also the dates of such adverse action, with a summary of his experience. The summary should address the factors necessary to prove a prima facie case— namely that the employee has engaged in some protected activity and that the employer was aware of the employee's activity and took adverse action against the employee in response to the protected activity.[18]

If at all possible the complaint should address the statute that is applicable (e.g., Sarbanes–Oxley). If the employee states an incorrect statute or mistakenly identifies the statute, the receiving office will classify the complaint type. If applicable, the employee should also note that he has filed a complaint with another enforcement agency, such as the Securities and Exchange Commission.[19]

The complaint and any additional supplemental documentation must demonstrate a prima facie case, showing that the employee's protected behavior or conduct was a contributing factor in the unfavorable personnel action alleged in the complaint. While there may be an opportunity to supplement the initial filings to demonstrate a prima facie case, the employee should make every effort to satisfy this burden in the initial filing.

A prima facie case is had when the employee can show that:

- the employee engaged in protected activity or conduct;

- the employer knew or suspected that the employee engaged in the protected activity;

- the employee suffered an unfavorable personnel action; and

- the circumstances are sufficient to infer that the protected activity was a contributing factor to the unfavorable action.

If the complaint and the supplemental documentation do not demonstrate a prima facie case, the employee will be advised and no further investigation will be done.[20]

Even though an employee may be able to demonstrate a prima facie case, an investigation will not be conducted if the employer can show by clear and convincing evidence that it would have taken the same unfavorable personnel action in the absence of the employee's protected behavior or conduct.[21]

The decisions of the assistant secretary of labor for occupational safety and health ("assistant secretary") to dismiss a complaint without completing an investigation or OSHA's determination to proceed with an investigation are not subject to the review of the administrative law judge. Nor may the ALJ remand a complaint for completion of an investigation or for additional findings on the basis that a determination to dismiss was made in error.[22]

Pre-Investigative Stage

When OSHA receives a complaint, the basic information and the filing date are recorded by the receiving officer and immediately sent to a supervisor. If the complaint is received at the national office or from another government agency, it is usually forwarded to the regional administrator for documentation.[23]

Upon receipt of the complaint, it will be reviewed for jurisdictional requirements, timeliness, and whether a prima facie case is demonstrated. The office may contact you to get additional information.[24] At times the Department of Labor may send a questionnaire to get supplemental data.[25]

If the office finds that the case cannot proceed to the investigation phase, it will explain the reason why. A SOX complaint that is untimely or does not meet a prima facie analysis cannot be closed administratively. The officer will explain to the employee that an impediment exists and will allow the employee to decide if he wishes to withdraw the complaint.[26]

At any time before the filing of objections to findings or a preliminary order, an employee may withdraw the complaint by filing a written withdrawal. OSHA, through the assistant secretary of labor, will then determine whether to approve the withdrawal. If the withdrawal is approved, the employer will be notified.[27] If the employee does not withdraw the complaint, the case will be docketed and a written determination issued.[28]

After the initial screening phase is complete, the complaint will be docketed. At that time OSHA will formally notify both the employee and the employer in writing of receipt of the complaint and its intention to investigate.[29] OSHA, usually in the person of the OSHA supervisor, will notify the employer of the filing, the allegations, and the substance of evidence supporting the complaint. (Every effort is made to protect the identities of confidential informants.) The employer is notified of its rights.[30]

Simultaneously, the supervisor will request that the employer submit a written statement. The employer is also advised that it may designate an attorney or other representative.[31] Additionally, the employer will be advised that any evidence it may wish to submit to rebut the allegations in the complaint must be received within 20 days from receipt of the letter. The employer is also told that it may request a meeting during that 20-day period.[32] Another copy of the notice is mailed to the Securities and Exchange Commission.[33]

A case number is then assigned.[34] The case number identifies the region in which the case originates (from 0 to 10); the area office city number (according to the Worldwide Geographic Locator Codes); the fiscal year in which it was filed; and the serial number of the complaint for the area office and the fiscal year.[35]

The OSHA supervisor will send a letter to the employee, notifying him that the complaint has been reviewed and assigned a case number and an investigator; it will also include the investigator's name and contact information.[36]

Investigative Stage

An OSHA supervisor will assign the case to an investigator, although investigations that involve complex issues or unusual circumstances may be conducted by the supervisor or a team of investigators. Investigators will schedule investigations with the statutory time frames in mind. A SOX complaint has a time frame of 60 days.[37] Every effort is made to make a determination within 60 days; nevertheless there may be instances in which it is not possible to complete the determinations within the 60-day period.[38]

Generally, the investigator will make initial contact by phone. If the investigator finds that a prima facie case exists, she will proceed to a field investigation, during which personal interviews and evidentiary document collection are conducted. Site visits may be scheduled to interview witnesses. Some testimony and evidence may be obtained by telephone, by mail, or electronically.[39] If the investigator finds that the employee has filed a whistleblower charge with another government agency simultaneously, she may contact the other agency to get additional information and avoid duplicative investigative efforts.[40]

The investigator will, of course, wish to interview the employee and the employer in person and obtain signed statements. It is to the employee's advantage to identify as many witnesses as possible who may be able to support his allegations. The identification should include complete contact information and details of what the witnesses may have seen.[41]

Witnesses are allowed to have a personal representative or an attorney present during any interview.[42] If there is a collective bargaining agreement, appropriate union officials may be interviewed. Witnesses may request confidentiality.[43] Investigations will be conducted in a manner that protects those who provide information on a confidential basis.[44] Nevertheless their identities will be kept in confidence only as allowed by law; if they testify in a proceeding, their statements may be required disclosures. Their identities may also be disclosed to another federal agency where appropriate; the investigator will request that the other agency keep the information confidential.[45] Confidentiality cannot be extended to the employee, however.[46]

After the investigator has spoken with the employer and taken its evidence, the employee and, where appropriate, the witnesses will be contacted to resolve any discrepancies. Upon completion of the collection of all evidence, the investigator will evaluate the evidence and make conclusions as to whether reasonable cause exists to believe that the employer has discriminated against the employee.

After completing the field investigation and discussing the claim with the OSHA supervisor and the solicitor of labor, the investigator will conduct a closing conference with the employee either in person or by phone. The discussion will allow the employee to ask questions as necessary. At this time the investigator will give her recommended determinations as well as explain how the determination was reached and what actions may be taken. During the conference the investigator must instruct the employee of his rights to appeal or object and the time limit for filing. It should also be noted that the determination is subject to review by the solicitor of labor for the secretary.[47]

The investigator will write a final investigation report (FIR), which contains contact information for both the employee and the employer as well as contact information for their representatives, if designated. The FIR gives a brief account of the employee's allegations and the employer's defense. There will be a statement regarding the basis of coverage by the statute, a list of witnesses interviewed, and a list of potential witnesses not interviewed, complete with contact information and occupation. A narrative of the investigative findings must be included with exhibit references to evidentiary documentation.

The investigator will also give an analysis of the facts as they relate to the elements of a prima facie case. In cases in which the investigator recommends litigation, she will examine the strengths and the weaknesses of the case. Information regarding the closing conference, reasons for the findings, a description of the employee's reaction to the findings and whether he offered any new evidence or witnesses at the conference will also be included. If a recommendation of dismissal was given, notation is made that the employee was advised of appeal rights and objection procedures. If the case was settled, the FIR will contain an account of the settlement. Finally, the FIR will have the investigator's recommendations.[48]

After the investigator completes her investigation, the OSHA supervisor will review the file. If the recommendation is to approve a withdrawal, the supervisor will approve by signing the withdrawal form. (The employee may request a withdrawal of the complaint verbally, but it is recommended that the request be made in writing.) If the recommendation is for dismissal, the supervisor will prepare letters of dismissal to all parties, with information of the parties' right to object or appeal as required by law.[49]

If the supervisor determines that the claim warrants further investigation, the case will be returned for follow-up. The supervisor will forward the file to the regional administrator (or a delegate) to review the recommendations and the file and to sign the appropriate letter of determination. Copies of the determination and the complaint will be distributed to the Securities and Exchange Commission and the Office of Administrative Law Judges.[50]

Findings and Preliminary Orders

If the Department of Labor concludes that there is reasonable cause to believe that a violation has occurred, the assistant secretary of labor may issue a preliminary order for OSHA, providing relief to the employee. The preliminary order will include that relief necessary to make the employee whole, including: reinstatement with the seniority status the employee would enjoy had the violation not taken place; back pay with interest; and compensation for special damages resulting from the violation such as litigation costs, expert witness fees, and reasonable attorney's fees. If the employer can demonstrate that the employee is a security risk, reinstatement may not be appropriate.[51] Under such circumstances front pay may be available.

When it is determined that preliminary immediate reinstatement should be ordered, the OSHA supervisor will again contact the employer and provide the relevant evidence supporting the finding in favor of the employee. To ensure due process rights, the notification will describe the evidence relied upon to determine the violation, and copies of the relevant documents will be provided, including witness statements. Efforts will be made to keep the confidence of witnesses who requested confidentiality, but summaries of witness statements must include as much detail as possible. The employer is allowed to submit a written response, meet the investigator, and present rebuttal witnesses within 10 business days of receipt of OSHA's letter or at a later agreed-upon date.[52]

The findings and the preliminary order take effect 30 days after receipt by the employer unless an objection and a request for a hearing has been filed.[53] The assistant secretary may withdraw the findings or a preliminary order at any time before the expiration of the 30-day objection period, provided no objection has been filed, and substitute new findings or a new preliminary order. The date of the receipt of the substituted findings or preliminary order begins a new 30-day objection period.[54]

At any time before the findings or order becomes final, either the employer or the employee may withdraw their objections to the findings or order by filing a written withdrawal with the administrative law judge. The ALJ will decide whether to approve the withdrawal.[55]

Whether an objection is filed by any party to the preliminary reinstatement, any portion of a preliminary order requiring reinstatement is effective immediately upon receipt of the finding and the preliminary order. Enforcement may be had in the US district court in the appropriate jurisdiction.[56] Reinstatement is not stayed by the filing of an objection or request for a hearing.[57]

If no objection is filed regarding the findings or the preliminary order, the findings or preliminary order will become the final agency decision of the secretary of labor and is not subject to judicial review.[58]

Settlement

If the employee and the employer express the wish to explore settlement, the investigator will facilitate.[59] The parties may also use private alternative dispute resolution to aid them in settlement.[60] At any time after the filing of a complaint but before the findings and/or preliminary order are objected to or become a final order by operation of law, the case may be settled if the assistant secretary, the employee, and the employer agree to a settlement.[61]

Where possible 100 percent relief should be sought in settlement negotiations, although both parties are free to make concessions. An agreement may include provisions for reinstatement to the same or an equivalent job and restoration of seniority and benefits. The employer may offer front pay in lieu of reinstatement if the employee agrees. The agreement may include lost wages; deletion of warnings, reprimands, or negative references in the employee's personnel file; posting notices to employees about the settlement; other compensatory damages; and damages for pain and suffering.[62] Monetary damages may receive interest at the rate charged by the Internal Revenue Service for underpaid taxes. (This rate is computed by using the federal short-term rate established in the first month of each calendar quarter, plus three percentage points.)[63] Punitive damages may also be appropriate in cases where conduct was egregious.[64]

Any settlement agreement must be in writing. The employer must agree to comply with the statute and address the alleged retaliation. The agreement must specify the relief owed. The employer must also make a constructive effort to lessen any chilling effect. To ensure this, the employer may be asked to publicly post the agreement or notice. To avoid this, the employer may need to demonstrate why notice to other employees is not necessary.[65]

Settlement agreements made during the investigative stage must be reviewed by the secretary of labor. Under SOX any settlement made before the issuance of a final order must be submitted to an administrative law judge for approval even though the case has not been submitted to the OALJ.[66]

If the employer does not comply with the settlement agreement, the noncompliance may be treated as a new instance of retaliation and precipitate a new case.[67]

Objections and Request for Review

Any party may retain private counsel, represent themselves in a hearing, or be represented by a person other than an attorney.[68] The OALJ does not have the authority to appoint counsel or refer the parties to attorneys.[69] Witnesses may also choose counsel, self-representation, or personal representation. If a party chooses a personal representative, the representative must submit an application to the ALJ with the applicant's qualifications. After a hearing on the matter, the ALJ may deny the privilege of appearing to any person who is deemed not to possess the requisite qualifications to represent others, is lacking in character, has engaged in unethical or improper professional conduct, or has engaged in an act involving moral turpitude.[70]

Parties may waive their right to appear for argument and instead submit evidence for a written record on which the decision will be based. Such a waiver should be made in writing and filed with the chief administrative law judge or the ALJ hearing the case. When all parties waive appearance, the ALJ will make a record of the written documents submitted by the parties and pleadings and will make a decision accordingly.[71]

Office of Administrative Law Judges

The chief administrative law judge will, upon receipt of a timely objection, notify the parties of the date, time, and place of the hearing.[72] Sarbanes-Oxley requires that an expedited hearing be held. Hearings must be scheduled within 60 days from receipt of a request for hearing or order of reference. Decisions of the ALJ should be issued within 20 days after receipt of the transcript of any oral hearing or within 20 days after the filing of all documentary evidence if no oral hearing was conducted.[73]

Although the adjudication process is somewhat less formal than a court proceeding, the ALJ has all the powers necessary to conduct fair and impartial hearings. The ALJ may conduct formal hearings, administer oaths, and examine witnesses. Where necessary the ALJ may compel the production of documents and the appearance of witnesses in control of the parties as well as issue decisions and orders.[74] The ALJ may issue a default decision against any party failing without good cause to appear at a hearing.[75]

Persons participating in proceedings before the ALJ who disobey or resist any lawful order or process; misbehave during a hearing or obstruct a hearing; neglect to produce documents after an order; or refuse to appear, refuse to take the oath, or refuse examination may, where the statute allows, have such facts of their conduct certified to the federal district court having jurisdiction. The ALJ may request appropriate remedies.[76]

The ALJ has the authority to sanction parties just as any other judge. SOX provides that upon the determination by the secretary of labor that a complaint was filed frivolously or in bad faith, the employer may be awarded reasonable attorney's fees not to exceed $1,000 to be paid by the employee. The ALJ may award such at the request of the employer.[77]

Parties

Generally, the parties to the proceedings will be the employee and the employer. Other persons or organizations may participate as parties, however, if the ALJ determines that: the final decision could directly or adversely affect them or the class they represent; they will contribute materially to the disposition of the proceedings; and their interest is not adequately represented by the parties in the suit. Such additional persons or organizations must submit a petition to the ALJ within 15 days after they learn of or should have known of the proceedings. The petition must explain: their interest in the proceedings; how their participation as a party will contribute materially to the disposition of the proceedings;

who will appear for the petitioner; the issues the petitioner wishes to participate in; and whether the petitioner will present witnesses. They must also serve a copy on all parties. Other parties in the suit may object to the petitioner. The ALJ will determine if the petitioner may participate in the proceedings. If the ALJ denies the petitioner, the ALJ may treat the petition as a request to participate as amicus curiae.[78]

An amicus curiae brief can be filed only with the written consent of all the parties, by leave of the ALJ, or at the request of the ALJ. Neither consent nor leave is required when the brief is from an officer or agency of the United States, a state, a territory, or a commonwealth. The amicus curiae cannot participate in the hearing.[79]

Document Filing

Any documents that are filed with the ALJ must be served on all parties. In other words, the employee must send a copy of the document to all the named parties in the suit. Include on the document the case caption (e.g., *John Doe v. ABC Corporation*) the docket number, and a short title of the motion (e.g., Motion for Continuance). The signed documents should be mailed to the chief docket clerk or to the regional office to which the proceeding may have been transferred for a hearing. Remember that each document requires a proof of service stating when and how it was served to the other litigant(s).

When explicitly authorized one may also fax documents to the OALJ. Of course the fax should contain a cover sheet that identifies the sender, the number of pages sent, and the caption and the docket number of the case. Faxed documents should not exceed 12 pages inclusive of the cover sheet, the proof of service, and any and all accompanying exhibits. If prior permission has not been granted, one may file by fax and attach a statement of the circumstances that precipitated that the document be filed by fax. This does not ensure that the filing will be accepted, however.

It is extremely important to be cognizant of the time requirements. Time lines begin the day following the act or event.[80] Parties have 10 days after service of a motion or request in which to respond unless ordered otherwise by the ALJ.[81] If the last day of the time period is a Saturday, Sunday, or legal holiday observed by the federal government, the time period concludes on the next business day. When documents are filed by mail, five days are added to the time period.[82]

Adjudication Process

The ALJ may require that one or more of the parties file a prehearing statement explaining their position. A prehearing statement identifies the name of the party who is presenting it and generally: issues involved in the proceeding; stipulations; disputed facts; witnesses and exhibits (other than those that are privileged); a brief statement of applicable law; conclusions to be drawn; suggested time and location of hearing as well as an estimate of the time required for the party to present their case; and other such appropriate information that complies with the ALJ's request.[83]

The ALJ may order a prehearing conference at his or her discretion or upon a motion from a party. These conferences may be conducted by telephone unless otherwise required. Generally, prehearing conferences are used to discuss simplification of issues; the necessity of amendments to pleadings; evidentiary matters; limitation of witnesses; settlement issues; and identification of documents or matters of which official notice may be requested; or to expedite disposition of the proceedings. Such conferences are reported stenographically unless the ALJ directs otherwise. Usually, a written order is generated following the conference unless the ALJ decides the stenographer's report is sufficient or the conference happens within seven days of the hearing.[84]

After the conclusion of a hearing, the record will be closed unless the ALJ directs otherwise. (If the hearing was waived, the record closes at a date set by the ALJ.) Once the record is closed, no additional evidence may be accepted into the record unless one can demonstrate new material evidence that was unavailable prior to closing.[85]

After the case has been heard, the ALJ will issue a recommended decision and order. Within a reasonable time after the filing of the proposed findings of fact, conclusions of law, and order, or within 30 days of receipt of consent findings, the ALJ will make a decision. The decision will include findings of fact and conclusions of law with reasons regarding each material issue of fact or law presented.[86] The ALJ will order the appropriate remedy.[87]

A determination that a violation has occurred will be had when the employee has demonstrated that protected behavior or conduct was a contributing factor in the unfavorable personnel action alleged in the complaint. If the employer demonstrates through clear and convincing evidence that it would have taken the same unfavorable personnel action in the absence of any protected behavior, relief will not be ordered for the employee.[88]

An employee who prevails on his claim shall be entitled to all relief necessary to make the employee whole. This includes compensatory damages; reinstatement with the same seniority status the employee enjoyed prior to the discrimination; back pay with interest where appropriate; and compensation for any special damages sustained as a result of the discrimination. Special damages may be the cost of litigation, expert witness fees, and reasonable attorney's fees.[89]

The decision of the ALJ will become a final order unless the Administrative Review Board issues an order notifying the parties that the case has been accepted for review within 30 days of the filing of a petition. If a petition for review is accepted, the decision of the ALJ will be inoperative unless the board issues an order adopting the decision. A preliminary order of reinstatement will be effective while the ARB considers the case unless the ARB grants a motion to stay the order. The ARB will review the case under a substantial evidence standard.[90]

The ARB will issue a final decision within 120 days of the conclusion of a hearing, which is the conclusion of all proceedings before the ALJ (which is 10 business days after the date of the ALJ's decision unless a motion for reconsideration was filed with the ALJ in the interim). If the ARB concludes that the employer has violated the law, the final order will provide for all the relief necessary to make the employee whole, including reinstatement to his former position with the seniority status he would have enjoyed had there been no discrimination; back pay with interest; and compensation for any special damages sustained as a result of the discrimination. Special damages include litigation costs, expert witness fees, and reasonable attorney's fees. If the ARB finds that there has been no violation of the law, the complaint will be denied. The employer who prevails on an allegation that the complaint is frivolous or in bad faith may be awarded reasonable attorney's fees, although the fees may not exceed $1,000.[91]

Enforcement of Reinstatement Order

When a party fails to comply with a preliminary order of reinstatement or final order or the terms of a settlement agreement, the opposing party may file a civil action seeking enforcement of the order in the US district court for the district in which the violation occurred.[92]

Appeal

Within 60 days after the final order of the ARB has been issued, any person adversely affected or aggrieved by the order may file a petition for review of the order in the US court of appeals for the circuit in which the violation allegedly occurred or the circuit that the employee resided in on the day of the violation.[93]

Summary Decision

A party may file for a summary decision 20 or more days before the date of a hearing. The ALJ may set the matter for argument or ask the parties to submit briefs. A summary decision will be issued when the ALJ has determined that there is no genuine issue as to any material fact, so the case can be decided without a hearing on legal grounds alone.[94]

Settlement Judge Program

At any time the parties may ask to defer the hearing for a reasonable time to permit negotiation of a settlement. The parties may use a settlement judge to mediate.[95] There is no charge for the services of the settlement judge.[96] Settlement discussions are confidential, and no evidence of statements or conduct in the proceedings is admissible in the proceedings or subsequent administrative proceedings before the Department of Labor, unless agreed to by the parties. Any documents disclosed in the settlement process may not be used in litigation unless obtained through discovery. The settlement judge will not discuss the case with the ALJ or be called as a witness in the proceeding or subsequent proceedings before the DOL.[97]

Settlement negotiations shall not exceed 30 days from the appointment of the settlement judge. Nevertheless the settlement judge may request an extension of time from the ALJ. Upon a communication from either party that the party no longer wishes to participate, the negotiations will end.[98]

At any time after the filing of objections to OSHA's findings or order, the case may be settled if the participating parties agree to a settlement and the settlement is approved by the ALJ if the case is before the ALJ. An approved settlement is a final order and may be enforced as such.[99]

Administrative Review Board

Review

Either party may seek judicial review. To seek judicial review of a decision of the ALJ or in the case of a respondent's alleging that the complaint was frivolous or in bad faith, a written petition for review with the ARB must be made. The petition should specifically identify the findings, conclusions, or orders to which exception is taken. Any exception not raised will be deemed to have been waived. Either party has 10 business days from the date of the ALJ's decision in which to file a petition. A party seeking review must serve a petition on all parties in the litigation, the chief ALJ, the assistant secretary of OSHA, and the assistant secretary of the Division of Fair Labor Standards. The date of the postmark is considered to be the date of filing.[100] If the parties fail to do so, the ALJ's decision becomes final and is not reviewable.

Stays

Parties may request a stay of an order pending an appeal. One should be mindful, however, that the burden to receive a stay is rather high. To receive a stay, a party must show that: he is likely to prevail on appeal; irreparable injury will result if the stay is not granted; the stay will not cause substantial harm to the other litigants; and the stay will not interfere with the public interest. If the request for stay is denied, the party may appeal with the US court of appeals for the circuit in which the violation occurred.

Withdrawal

Anytime before the findings or order becomes final, a party may withdraw the objections to the findings or order by filing a written withdrawal with the Administrative Review Board. The ARB will decide whether to approve the withdrawal.[101]

Settlement

At any time after the filing of objections to OSHA's findings or order, the case may be settled if the participating parties agree to a settlement and the settlement is approved by the ARB if the case is before the ARB. An approved settlement is a final order and may be enforced as such.[102]

Appeal

An ARB decision may be appealed by any person adversely affected or by an aggrieved party within 60 days of a final decision to the US court of appeals for the circuit in which the violation occurred. Final orders of the ARB are not subject to judicial review in any criminal or other civil proceeding.[103]

Federal Court

If the secretary of labor has not issued a final decision within 180 days of the filing of the complaint and the delay has not been caused by the employee, the employee may wait for the decision of the secretary of labor or he may file suit in the US district court with jurisdiction over the matter. (The amount in controversy is not an issue in such cases as it is with traditional civil suits in federal courts.[104]) To do so the employee must file a notice of his intention to file such a complaint 15 days in advance of filing the complaint in federal court. The assistant secretary for OSHA and the associate solicitor of the Division of Fair Labor Standards should also be served with a copy of the notice.[105]

Frequently Asked Questions

When should I file my complaint?

A complaint now must be filed within 180 days, doubled from 90 before recent changes.

Where should I file my complaint?

A complaint can be filed at the OSHA area office. In states that do not have area offices, you should contact the OSHA regional office.

Can I keep my identity confidential?

No, the identity of the complainant will be revealed to the respondent (your employer). Under some circumstances, however, witnesses may keep their identities confidential.

Do I need an attorney to file a complaint?

No, you can represent yourself in all proceedings, or you may choose to have a personal representative who is not an attorney represent you. Although an attorney is not required, you should be mindful that without an attorney you may be at a disadvantage in more-complex proceedings.

If I change my mind, can I withdraw my complaint?

Yes, anytime before the findings or an order becomes final, a complaint may be withdrawn.

Is there a fee for the use of a settlement judge?

There is no fee for the settlement judge.

Can I return to work once I have a reinstatement order?

Reinstatement orders are applicable immediately upon receipt of the order. To enforce the order, however, additional steps may need to be taken.

How is front pay determined?

Numerous factors are considered when making a determination of a front-pay award. These factors include the discharged employee's duty to mitigate the damages, the availability of employment opportunities, the period within which the employee by reasonable efforts may be re-employed, the employee's work and life expectancy, and the utilization of discount tables to determine the current value of future damages.

What if my case does not meet the minimum amount required in federal court?

SOX cases may proceed to federal court regardless of the amount in controversy.

Appendix A: 18 U.S.C. § 1514 A

§ 1514 A. Civil action to protect against retaliation in fraud cases.

(a) Whistleblower protection for employees of publicly traded companies. No company with a class of securities registered under section 12 of the Securities Exchange Act of 1934 (15 U.S.C. 78l), or that is required to file reports under section 15(d) of the Securities Exchange Act of 1934 (15 U.S.C. 78o(d)), including any subsidiary or affiliate whose financial information is included in the consolidated financial statements of such company, or nationally recognized statistical rating organization (as defined in section 3(a) of the Securities Exchange Act of 1934 (15 U.S.C. 78c), or any officer, employee, contractor, subcontractor, or agent of such company, or nationally recognized statistical rating organization, may discharge, demote, suspend, threaten, harass, or in any other manner discriminate against an employee in the terms and conditions of employment because of any lawful act done by the employee—

(1) to provide information, cause information to be provided, or otherwise assist in an investigation regarding any conduct which the employee reasonably believes constitutes a violation of section 1341, 1343, 1344, or 1348 [18 USCS § 1341, 1343, 1344,

or 1348], any rule or regulation of the Securities and Exchange Commission, or any provision of Federal law relating to fraud against shareholders, when the information or assistance is provided to or the investigation is conducted by—

(A) a Federal regulatory or law enforcement agency;

(B) any Member of Congress or any committee of Congress; or

(C) a person with supervisory authority over the employee (or such other person working for the employer who has the authority to investigate, discover, or terminate misconduct); or

(2) to file, cause to be filed, testify, participate in, or otherwise assist in a proceeding filed or about to be filed (with any knowledge of the employer) relating to an alleged violation of section 1341, 1343, 1344, or 1348 [18 USCS § 1341, 1343, 1344, or 1348], any rule or regulation of the Securities and Exchange Commission, or any provision of Federal law relating to fraud against shareholders.

(b) Enforcement action.

(1) In general. A person who alleges discharge or other discrimination by any person in violation of subsection (a) may seek relief under subsection (c), by—

(A) filing a complaint with the Secretary of Labor; or

(B) if the Secretary has not issued a final decision within 180 days of the filing of the complaint and there is no showing that such delay is due to the bad faith of the claimant, bringing an action at law or equity for de novo review in the appropriate district court of the United States, which shall have jurisdiction over such an action without regard to the amount in controversy.

(2) Procedure.

(A) In general. An action under paragraph (1)(A) shall be governed under the rules and procedures set forth in section 42121(b) of title 49, United States Code.

(B) Exception. Notification made under section 42121(b)(1) of title 49, United States Code, shall be made to the person named in the complaint and to the employer.

(C) Burdens of proof. An action brought under paragraph (1) (B) shall be governed by the legal burdens of proof set forth in section 42121(b) of title 49, United States Code.

(D) Statute of limitations. An action under paragraph (1) shall be commenced not later than 180 days after the date on which the violation occurs, or after the date on which the employee became aware of the violation.

(E) Jury trial. A party to an action brought under paragraph (1) (B) shall be entitled to trial by jury.

(c) Remedies.

(1) In general. An employee prevailing in any action under subsection (b)(1) shall be entitled to all relief necessary to make the employee whole.

(2) Compensatory damages. Relief for any action under paragraph (1) shall include—

(A) reinstatement with the same seniority status that the employee would have had, but for the discrimination;

(B) the amount of back pay, with interest; and

(C) compensation for any special damages sustained as a result of the discrimination, including litigation costs, expert witness fees, and reasonable attorney fees.

(d) Rights retained by employee. Nothing in this section shall be deemed to diminish the rights, privileges, or remedies of any employee under any Federal or State law, or under any collective bargaining agreement.

(e) Nonenforceability of certain provisions waiving rights and remedies or requiring arbitration of disputes.

(1) Waiver of rights and remedies. The rights and remedies provided for in this section may not be waived by any agreement,

policy form, or condition of employment, including by a predispute abitration agreement.

(2) Predispute arbitration agreements. No predispute arbitration agreement shall be valid or enforceable, if the agreement requires arbitration of a dispute arising under this section.

Appendix B: Investigative Materials and Confidentiality

Investigative materials (such as notes, memos, work papers, records, and recordings received or prepared by the investigator) are included in the case file to support the findings of the investigation. Information and statements obtained from investigations are confidential except for those that may be released under the Freedom of Information Act or the Privacy Act and those that must be released for the purpose of due process. The region's document custodian will process any request for release of information in compliance with requisite laws and agency policy.[106]

After a case has been closed, much of the information in the file is available upon receipt of a FOIA request, a request from a federal agency or the ALJ, or through discovery procedures. A SOX case is closed once OSHA has completed its investigation and issued its determination letter, unless OSHA is participating in the proceeding before the ALJ or has recommended that OSHA participate as a party in the proceeding.[107]

Upon a FOIA request, the entire narrative report minus analysis and recommendation is generally disclosed. Included may be interviews of officials representing the employer as well as interviews of the employee and others who have not requested confidentiality after the redaction of passages that might be considered an invasion of privacy to a third party.[108]

Confidentiality

During the investigation the employer may identify materials it deems trade secrets or confidential or financial information. If the investigator finds no reason to question such identification and the disclosure officer agrees, the information will be labeled "confidential" and will not be released except in accordance with OSHA or similar statutory requirements.[109]

Sample FOIA Request Letter

Your address
Contact information
Date

Freedom of Information Office
Agency
Address [separate for each agency subunit where records may be located]

FOIA Request

Dear FOIA Officer,

Pursuant to the federal Freedom of Information Act, 5 U.S.C. § 552, I request access to the following records, as defined by the act: *[Here clearly describe what you want. Include the format the records may take (e-mails, audio files, documents) and identifying material, such as names, places, and the period of time about which you are inquiring. If you think it will help to explain what you are looking for, attach news clippings, reports, and other documents describing the subject of your research.]*

As a noncommercial requester of information, I am entitled to two hours of search time and copies of 100 pages for free. Provided they are reasonable, I agree to pay any additional processing fees for this request in an amount not to exceed $*[state dollar amount]*. Please notify me prior to your incurring any expenses in excess of that amount.

[Optional public interest fee waiver request] Please waive my applicable fees because release of the information is in the public interest. *[Argue why the request satisfies the six criteria laid out in chapter 3.]*

If my request is denied in whole or in part, I ask that you justify all deletions by reference to specific exemptions of the FOIA. I will also expect you to release all segregable portions of otherwise exempt material. I, of course, reserve the right to appeal your decision to withhold any information or to deny a waiver of fees.

I look forward to your reply within 20 business days, as the statute requires, and *[option to expedite the process]* would appreciate your communicating with me by telephone or e-mail, rather than by mail, if you have questions regarding this request.

Thank you for your assistance.

Very truly yours,

Your signature

T O O L C

Public Interest Organizations

In addition to the Government Accountability Project, the following public interest organizations may be of assistance to corporate whistleblowers.

Electronic Frontier Foundation (EFF)
454 Shotwell St.
San Francisco, CA 94110-1914
http://www.eff.org
information@eff.org
Tel: (415) 436-9333
Fax: (415) 436-9993

Founded in 1990, EFF confronts cutting-edge issues in free speech, privacy, and consumer rights by blending the expertise of lawyers, policy analysts, activists, and technologists.

Electronic Privacy Information Center (EPIC)
1718 Connecticut Ave. NW, Suite 200
Washington, DC 20009
http://epic.org
Tel: (202) 483-1140
Fax: (202) 483-1248

EPIC is a public interest research center in Washington, DC. It was established in 1994 to focus public attention on emerging civil liberties issues and to protect privacy, the First Amendment, and constitutional values.

Make It Safe Coalition
c/o Government Accountability Project
http://www.makeitsafecampaign.org
info@whistleblower.org
Tel: (202) 418-0034

This nonpartisan, transideological coalition of good government, taxpayer watchdog, transparency, consumer, professional, libertarian, and labor organizations is the umbrella for nearly all organized whistleblower rights advocacy in the United States. From 2007 to 2010, it has sponsored an annual May whistleblower conference in Washington, DC.

National Whistleblower Center (NWC)
3238 P St. NW
PO Box 3768
Washington, DC 20027
http://www.whistleblowers.org
contact@whistleblowers.org
Tel: (202) 342-1903
Fax: (202) 342-1904

The NWC has a small staff, but it actively participates in whistleblower rights coalitions and has an impressive website with excellent research. It is connected with the highly successful law firm of Kohn, Kohn & Colapinto, LLP, which has been particularly active with FBI whistleblowers.

Project on Government Oversight (POGO)
1100 G St. NW, Suite 900
Washington DC, 20005-3806
http://www.pogo.org
info@pogo.org
Tel: (202) 347-1122
Fax: (202) 347-1116

POGO conducts in-depth investigations of whistleblower disclosures and effectively airs the results in reports taken seriously by Congress and national media outlets. It helps find legal, political, and media champions to protect those with whom it works, and it has been an active leader in whistleblower rights campaigns for government employees and contractors.

Public Citizen
1600 20th St. NW
Washington, DC 20009
http://www.citizen.org
member@citizen.org
Tel: (202) 588-1000

Founded in 1971, Public Citizen is a national nonprofit consumer advocacy organization that fights for safer drugs and medical devices, cleaner and safer energy sources, a cleaner environment, fair trade, and a more open and democratic government. It also has been a cutting-edge leader in whistleblower rights legislative campaigns.

Taxpayers Against Fraud (TAF)
1220 19th St. NW, Suite 501
Washington, DC 20036
http://www.taf.org
Tel: (202) 296-4826 or (800) US-FALSE [800-873-2573]
Fax: (202) 296-4838

TAF is a nonprofit, public interest organization dedicated to combating fraud against the federal government through the promotion and the use of the *qui tam* provisions of the False Claims Act. Established in 1986, TAF serves to collect and evaluate evidence of fraud against the federal government and facilitate the filing of meritorious False Claims *qui tam* suits. TAF also works to advance public, legislative, and government support for *qui tam* measures.

Union of Concerned Scientists (UCS)
National Headquarters
2 Brattle Sq.
Cambridge, MA 02138-3780
http://www.ucsusa.org
Tel: (617) 547-5552
Fax: (617) 864-9405

UCS is the leading science-based nonprofit organization working for a healthy environment and a safer world. It combines independent scientific research and citizen action to develop innovative, practical solutions and to secure responsible changes in government policy, corporate practices, and consumer choices.

Although the following organizations deal primarily with public employees and government misconduct, they may be useful if the corporate wrongdoer is in a contract or regulatory relationship with a particular government agency.

American Civil Liberties Union (ACLU)
125 Broad St., 18th Floor
New York, NY 10004
http://www.aclu.org/contact-us
Tel: (212) 549-2500

Better Government Association (BGA)
11 E Adams St., Suite 608
Chicago, IL 60603
http://www.bettergov.org
info@bettergov.org
Tel: (312) 427-8330
Fax (312) 821-9038

Citizens against Government Waste (CAGW)
1301 Pennsylvania Ave. NW, Suite 1075
Washington, DC 20004
http://www.cagw.org
membership@cagw.org
Tel: (202) 467-5300
Fax: (202) 467-4253

OMB Watch
1742 Connecticut Ave. NW
Washington, DC 20009
http://www.ombwatch.org
Tel: (202) 234-8494
Fax: (202) 234-8584

OpenTheGovernment.org
1742 Connecticut Ave. NW, 3rd Floor
Washington, DC 20009
http://www.openthegovernment.org
info@openthegovernment.org
Tel: (202) 332-OPEN [6736]

Public Employees for Environmental Responsibility (PEER)
2000 P St. NW, Suite 240
Washington, DC 20036
http://www.peer.org
info@peer.org
Tel: (202) 265-7337
Fax: (202) 265-4192

The following whistleblower organizations operate outside the
United States.

Canadians for Accountability
532 Montreal Rd., Suite 221
Ottawa, ON, Canada K1K 4R4
http://www.canadians4accountability.org
info@canadians4accountability.org
Tel: (613) 304-8049
Fax: (613) 747-9317

Federal Accountability Initiative for Reform (FAIR)
82 Strathcona Ave.
Ottawa, ON, Canada K1S 1X6
http://fairwhistleblower.ca
david@fairwhistleblower.ca
Tel: (613) 567-1511

Integrity Line
Englischviertelstrasse 18
CH-8032 Zürich, Switzerland
www.integrityline.org
zora.ledergerber@integrityline.org
Tel: 041 76 339 41 18
Tel: 041 325 123 553

International Freedom of Expression eXchange (IFEX)
555 Richmond Street W, Suite 1101
PO Box 407
Toronto, ON, Canada M5V 3B1
http://www.ifex.org
ifex@ifex.org
Tel: (416) 515-9622
Fax: (416) 515-7879

Open Democracy Advice Centre (ODAC)
6 Spin Street
PO Box 1739
Cape Town, 8001, South Africa
http://www.opendemocracy.org.za
Tel: 027 21 4613096
Fax: 027 21 4613021

Public Concern at Work
3rd Floor, Bank Chambers
6–10 Borough High Street
London SE1 9QQ, United Kingdom
http://www.pcaw.co.uk
whistle@pcaw.co.uk
Tel: 020 7404 6609
Fax: 020 74038823

Whistleblower-Netzwerk e.V.
Allerseelenstrasse 1n
D-51105 Köln, Germany
http://www.whistleblower-net.de
Tel: 0221 1692194

Online Resources

The following is a brief list of sites on the World Wide Web that may be of assistance or interest to corporate whistleblowers.

A Citizen's Guide on Using the Freedom of Information Act and the Privacy Act of 1974 to Request Government Records

http://www.fas.org/sgp/foia/citizen.html

Cryptome: a secured online anonymous document disclosure forum

http://www.cryptome.org

Electronic Privacy Information Center's Online Guide to Practical Privacy Tools

http://epic.org/privacy/tools.html

POGO's Federal Contractor Misconduct Database

http://www.contractormisconduct.org

IBM Investor Relations: a guide to reading financial statements in annual reports

http://www.ibm.com/investor/help/guide/introduction.wss

Jobs with Justice: a US coalition for the rights of working people

http://www.jwj.org

LawMall: self-help publications for dealing with legal problems

http://www.lawmall.com/lm_pamph.html

The Motley Fool's guide to reading SEC filings and financial statements

http://www.fool.com/dripport/2000/dripport000106.htm

National Security Archive of government and contractor documents

http://www.gwu.edu/~nsarchiv

National Employment Lawyers Association

http://www.nela.org

New Grady Coalition

http://www.newgradycoalition.com

Qui Tam Information Center

http://www.quitam.com

US Department of Energy Hearings and Appeals: administrative whistleblower decisions

http://www.ohu.doe.gov

US Department of Labor: administrative whistleblower decisions

http://www.oalj.dol.gov

US General Services Administration Office of Inspector General FraudNet Hotline

http://www.gsa.gov/fraudnet

US Office of Special Counsel

http://www.osc.gov

US Securities and Exchange Commission: Electronic Data Gathering, Analysis, and Retrieval (EDGAR) system of corporate filings

http://www.sec.gov/edgar.shtml

US Environmental Protection Agency: information sources

http://www.epa.gov/epahome/resource.htm

US federal government online resource for recalls

http://www.recalls.gov

US Merit Systems Protection Board

http://www.mspb.gov

US Food and Drug Administration

http://www.fda.gov

WhistleblowerLaws.com: Whistleblower employee protection

http://www.whistleblowerlaws.com

WikiLeaks: a secured online anonymous document disclosure forum

http://wikileaks.org

Workplace Fairness: information about workplace rights and employment issues

http://www.workplacefairness.org

WorldwideWhistleblowers.com

http://worldwidewhistleblowers.com

Federal Statutes with Corporate Whistleblower Provisions

★ *Denotes laws restricted to government employees. Out of the 57 federal whistleblower statutes, 44 protect corporate employees, 7 are solely for government workers, 3 cover government corporations, and 3 are limited to government contractors.*

▶ *Denotes law enforced by the US Department of Labor.*

Age Discrimination in Employment Act, 29 U.S.C. § 623(d)

American Recovery and Reinvestment Act of 2009 (stimulus bill), Pub. L. 111-5 § 1553

Americans with Disabilities Act, 42 U.S.C. § 12203

★ Armed Forces, 10 U.S.C. § 1587 (civilian employee protection)

▶ Asbestos Hazard Emergency Response Act, 15 U.S.C. § 2651

Asbestos School Hazard Abatement, 20 U.S.C. § 4018

Asbestos School Hazard Detection and Control, 20 U.S.C. § 3608

★ Banking, 31 U.S.C. § 5328 (employee protection)

Banking, 12 U.S.C. § 1790(b) (credit unions)

Banking, 12 U.S.C. § 1831(j) (FDIC)

★ Civil Rights Act of 1871, 42 U.S.C. § 1983 (protection for constitutional rights of state and municipal government employees)

Civil Rights Act of 1871, 42 U.S.C. § 1985 (protection against conspiracy to obstruct justice or intimidate witnesses)

Civil Rights of Institutionalized Persons Act, 42 U.S.C. § 1997(d)

★ Civil Service Reform Act/Whistleblower Protection Act, 5 U.S.C. § 2302(b)(8)

▶ Clean Air Act, 42 U.S.C. § 7622

★ Coast Guard, 46 U.S.C. § 2114 (whistleblower protection)

▶ Commercial Motor Vehicle Safety Act/Surface Transportation Assistance Act, 49 U.S.C. § 31105

▶ Comprehensive Environmental Response, Compensation and Liability Act (CERCLA or Superfund), 42 U.S.C. § 9610

▶ Consumer Product Safety Improvement Act, 15 U.S.C. § 2087

Defense Contractors, 10 U.S.C. § 2409

Dodd-Frank Wall Street Reform and Consumer Protection Act, Pub. L. 111-203 §§ 748, 922 (bounties and associated anti-retaliation rights)

▶ Dodd-Frank Wall Street Reform and Consumer Protection Act, Pub. L. 111-203 § 1558 (anti-retaliation)

▶ Employment Retirement Income Security Act (ERISA), 29 U.S.C. §§ 1132(a), 1140

▶ Energy Reorganization Act/Energy Policy Act, 42 U.S.C. § 5851

Fair Labor Standards Act, 29 U.S.C. § 215(a)(3)

False Claims Act, 31 U.S.C. § 3730(h)

Family and Medical Leave Act, 29 U.S.C. § 2615(a), (b)

FBI whistleblower protection, 5 U.S.C. § 2303

▶ Federal Rail Safety Act, 49 U.S.C. § 20109

FDA Food Safety Modernization Act, Pub. L. 111-353 § 402 (employee protection)

★ Foreign Service Act of 1980, 22 U.S.C. § 3905

Government Contractors, 41 U.S.C. § 265

▶ International Safe Containers Act, 42 U.S.C. § 8057

▶ Job Training and Partnership Act/Workforce Investment Act, 29 U.S.C. § 2934(f)

★ Lloyd-LaFollette Act, 5 U.S.C. § 7211 (federal employees' right to petition Congress)

Longshore and Harbor Workers' Compensation Act, 33 U.S.C. § 948(a)

Major Fraud Act, 18 U.S.C. § 1031(h)

Migrant and Seasonal Agricultural Workers Protection Act, 29 U.S.C. §§ 1854–1855

★ Military Whistleblower Protection Act, 10 U.S.C. § 1034

Mine Health and Safety Act, 30 U.S.C. § 815(c)

National Labor Relations Act, 29 U.S.C. § 158(a)(4)

▶ National Transit Systems Security Act, 6 U.S.C. § 1142

▶ Occupational Safety and Health Act, 29 U.S.C. § 660(c)

▶ Patient Protection and Affordable Care Act, 29 U.S.C. § 218(c) and 42 U.S.C. § 300(gg-5)

▶ Pipeline Safety Act/Pipeline Safety Improvement Act, 49 U.S.C. § 60129

Racketeering Influenced and Corrupt Organizations Act (RICO), 38 U.S.C. §§ 1961–1968

▶ Safe Drinking Water Act, 42 U.S.C. § 300(j)-9(I)

▶ Sarbanes-Oxley Act, 18 U.S.C. § 1514(a)

Seaman's Protection Act, 46 U.S.C. § 2114

▶ Solid Waste Disposal Act, 42 U.S.C. § 6971

   Surface Mining Act, 30 U.S.C. § 1293 (employee protection)

   Title VII, 42 U.S.C. § 2000e-3(a) (anti-retaliation)

▶ Toxic Substances Control Act, 15 U.S.C. § 2622

★ Uniformed Services Employment and Reemployment Rights Act of 1994, 38 U.S.C. § 4311(b)

▶ Water Pollution Control Act, 33 U.S.C. § 1367

   Welfare and Pensions Disclosure Act, 29 U.S.C. § 1140

▶ Wendell H. Ford Aviation Investment and Reform Act for the 21st Century (AIR21), 49 U.S.C. § 42121

International Ombudsman Association Standards of Practice

Reprinted from http://www.ombudsassociation.org/standards/ IOA_Standards_of_Practice_Oct09.pdf

Preamble

The IOA Standards of Practice are based upon and derived from the ethical principles stated in the IOA Code of Ethics.

Each Ombudsman office should have an organizational Charter or Terms of Reference, approved by senior management, articulating the principles of the Ombudsman function in that organization and their consistency with the IOA Standards of Practice.

Standards of Practice

Independence

1.1 The Ombudsman Office and the Ombudsman are independent from other organizational entities.

1.2 The Ombudsman holds no other position within the organization which might compromise independence.

1.3 The Ombudsman exercises sole discretion over whether or how to act regarding an individual's concern, a trend, or concerns of multiple individuals over time. The Ombudsman may also initiate action on a concern identified through the Ombudsman's direct observation.

1.4 The Ombudsman has access to all information and all individuals in the organization, as permitted by law.

1.5 The Ombudsman has authority to select Ombudsman Office staff and manage Ombudsman Office budget and operations.

Neutrality and Impartiality

2.1 The Ombudsman is neutral, impartial, and unaligned.

2.2 The Ombudsman strives for impartiality, fairness, and objectivity in the treatment of people and the consideration of issues. The Ombudsman advocates for fair and equitably administered processes and does not advocate on behalf of any individual within the organization.

2.3 The Ombudsman is a designated neutral, reporting to the highest possible level of the organization and operating independently of ordinary line and staff structures. The Ombudsman should not report to nor be structurally affiliated with any compliance function of the organization.

2.4 The Ombudsman serves in no additional role within the organization which would compromise the Ombudsman's neutrality. The Ombudsman should not be aligned with any formal or informal associations within the organization in a way that might create actual or perceived conflicts of interest for the Ombudsman. The Ombudsman should have no personal interest or stake in, and incur no gain or loss from, the outcome of an issue.

2.5 The Ombudsman has a responsibility to consider the legitimate concerns and interests of all individuals affected by the matter under consideration.

2.6 The Ombudsman helps develop a range of responsible options to resolve problems and facilitate discussion to identify the best options.

Confidentiality

3.1 The Ombudsman holds all communications with those seeking assistance in strict confidence and takes all reasonable steps to safeguard confidentiality, including the following: The Ombudsman does not reveal, and must not be required to reveal, the identity of any individual contacting the Ombudsman Office, nor does the Ombudsman reveal information provided in confidence that could lead to the identification of any individual contacting the Ombudsman Office, without that individual's express permission, given in the course of informal discussions with the Ombudsman; the Ombudsman takes specific action related to an individual's issue only with the individual's express permission and only to the extent permitted, and even then at the sole discretion of the Ombudsman, unless such action can be taken in a way that safeguards the identity of the individual contacting the Ombudsman Office. The only exception to this privilege of confidentiality is where there appears to be imminent risk of serious harm, and where there is no other reasonable option. Whether this risk exists is a determination to be made by the Ombudsman.

3.2 Communications between the Ombudsman and others (made while the Ombudsman is serving in that capacity) are considered privileged. The privilege belongs to the Ombudsman and the Ombudsman Office, rather than to any party to an issue. Others cannot waive this privilege.

3.3 The Ombudsman does not testify in any formal process inside the organization and resists testifying in any formal process outside of the organization regarding a visitor's contact with the Ombudsman or confidential information communicated to the Ombudsman, even if given permission or requested to do so. The Ombudsman may, however, provide general, nonconfidential information about the Ombudsman Office or the Ombudsman profession.

3.4 If the Ombudsman pursues an issue systemically (e.g., provides feedback on trends, issues, policies, and practices) the Ombudsman does so in a way that safeguards the identity of individuals.

3.5 The Ombudsman keeps no records containing identifying information on behalf of the organization.

3.6 The Ombudsman maintains information (e.g., notes, phone messages, appointment calendars) in a secure location and manner, protected from inspection by others (including management), and has a consistent and standard practice for the destruction of such information.

3.7 The Ombudsman prepares any data and/or reports in a manner that protects confidentiality.

3.8 Communications made to the Ombudsman are not notice to the organization. The Ombudsman neither acts as agent for, nor accepts notice on behalf of, the organization and shall not serve in a position or role that is designated by the organization as a place to receive notice on behalf of the organization. However, the Ombudsman may refer individuals to the appropriate place where formal notice can be made.

Informality and Other Standards

4.1 The Ombudsman functions on an informal basis by such means as: listening, providing and receiving information, identifying and reframing issues, developing a range of responsible options, and—with permission and at Ombudsman discretion—engaging in informal third-party intervention. When possible, the Ombudsman helps people develop new ways to solve problems themselves.

4.2 The Ombudsman as an informal and off-the-record resource pursues resolution of concerns and looks into procedural irregularities and/or broader systemic problems when appropriate.

4.3 The Ombudsman does not make binding decisions, mandate policies, or formally adjudicate issues for the organization.

4.4 The Ombudsman supplements, but does not replace, any formal channels. Use of the Ombudsman Office is voluntary and is not a required step in any grievance process or organizational policy.

4.5 The Ombudsman does not participate in any formal investigative or adjudicative procedures. Formal investigations should be conducted by others. When a formal investigation is requested, the Ombudsman refers individuals to the appropriate offices or individual.

4.6 The Ombudsman identifies trends, issues, and concerns about policies and procedures, including potential future issues and concerns, without breaching confidentiality or anonymity, and provides recommendations for responsibly addressing them.

4.7 The Ombudsman acts in accordance with the IOA Code of Ethics and Standards of Practice, keeps professionally current by pursuing continuing education, and provides opportunities for staff to pursue professional training.

4.8 The Ombudsman endeavors to be worthy of the trust placed in the Ombudsman Office.

Source: www.ombudsassociation.org   Rev. 10/2009

International
Best Practices for
Whistleblower Policies

While whistleblower protection laws are increasingly popular, in many cases the rights have been largely symbolic and therefore counterproductive. Employees have risked retaliation, thinking they had genuine protection when in reality there was no realistic chance that they could maintain their careers. In those instances acting on rights contained in whistleblower laws has meant the near certainty that a legal forum would formally endorse the retaliation, leaving the careers of reprisal victims far more prejudiced than if no whistleblower protection law had been in place at all. The Government Accountability Project's review of the track records for these and prior laws over the past three decades has revealed numerous lessons learned, which have steadily been solved on the federal level through amendments to correct mistakes and close loopholes.

GAP labels such token laws as "cardboard shields" because anyone relying on them is sure to die professionally. We view genuine whistleblower laws as "metal shields," behind which an employee's career has a fighting chance. The following checklist of 20 requirements reflects GAP's 32 years of lessons learned. All the minimum concepts exist in various employee protection statutes currently on the books. This best-practice standard is based on a compilation of all national laws and intergovernmental organization policies such as those of the United Nations and the World Bank. It does not reference state or regional policies.

Scope of Coverage

The first cornerstone for any reform is that it is available. Loopholes that deny coverage when it is needed most, either for the public or the harassment victim, compromise whistleblower protection rules. Seamless coverage is essential so that accessible free-expression rights extend to any relevant witness, regardless of audience, misconduct, or context, to protect them against any harassment that could have a chilling effect.

Context for free-expression rights with no loopholes   Protected whistleblowing should cover *any* disclosure that would be accepted in a legal forum as evidence of significant misconduct or would assist in carrying out legitimate compliance functions. There can be no loopholes for form, context, or audience, unless release of the information is specifically prohibited by statute or would incur organizational liability for breach of legally enforceable confidentiality commitments. In that circumstance disclosures should still be protected if made to representatives of organizational leadership or to designated law enforcement or legislative offices. It is necessary to specify that disclosures in the course of job duties are protected because most retaliation is in response to "duty speech" by those whose institutional role is blowing the whistle as part of organizational checks and balances.

> United Nations whistleblower policy (U.N. policy), § 4; OAS Model Law (approved November 2000) to implement Inter-American Convention against Corruption (OAS Model Law), §§ 2(d)–(f); Asian Development Bank Audit Manual, § 810.200; Public Interest Disclosure Act of 1998 (PIDA), c. 23 (U.K.), amending the Employment Rights Act of 1996, c.18, § 43(G); Protected Disclosures Act of 2000 (PDA); Act No. 26, GG21453 of Aug. 7, 2000 (S. Afr.), § 7–8; Anti-Corruption Act of 2001 (ACA) (Korea; statute has no requirement for internal reporting); Ghana Whistleblower Act of 2005 (Ghana WPA), § 4; Japan Whistleblower Protection Act, Article 3; Whistleblower Protection Act of 1989 (WPA) (U.S. federal government), 5 U.S.C. § 2302(b)(8); Consumer Product Safety Improvement Act (CPSIA) (U.S. corporate retail products), 15 U.S.C. § 2087(a); Federal Rail Safety Act (FRSA) (U.S. rail workers) 49 U.S.C. § 20109(a); National Transportation Security Systems Act (NTSSA) (U.S. public transportation), 6 U.S.C. § 1142(a); Sarbanes-Oxley Act of 2002 (SOX) (U.S. publicly traded corporations), 18 U.S.C. § 1514(a); Surface Transportation Assistance Act

(STAA) (U.S. corporate trucking industry), 49 U.S.C. § 31105(a); American Recovery and Reinvestment Act of 2009 (ARRA), (U.S. Stimulus Law), P.L. 111-5 § 1553(a)

Subject matter for free-speech rights with no loopholes   Whistleblower rights should cover disclosures of any illegality, gross waste, mismanagement, abuse of authority, substantial and specific danger to public health or safety, and any other activity that undermines the institution's mission to its stakeholders as well as any other information that assists in honoring those duties.

> U.N. policy, § 2.1(a); OAS Model Law, Article 2(c); Inter-American Development Bank (IDB) Staff Rule 328 § 104; PIDA (U.K.); PDA, § 1(i) (S. Afr.); ACA (Korea), Article 2; Public Service Act (PSA), Antigua and Barbuda Freedom of Information Act, § 47; R.S.O., ch. 47, § 28.13 (1990) (Can.); Ghana WPA, § 1; Uganda Whistleblower Protection Act of 2010 (Uganda 2010 WPA), § 1; WPA (U.S. federal government), 5 U.S.C. § 2302(b)(8); FRSA (U.S. rail workers), 49 U.S.C. § 20109(a)(1); NTSSA (U.S. public transportation), 6 U.S.C. § 1142(a); STAA (U.S. corporate trucking industry), 49 U.S.C. § 31105(a)(1); ARRA (U.S. Stimulus Law); P.L. 111-5 § 1553(A)(1)-(5)

Right to refuse to violate the law   This provision is fundamental to stop faits accomplis and in some cases to prevent the need for whistleblowing. As a practical reality, however, in many organizations an individual who refuses to obey an order on the grounds that it is illegal must proceed at his or her own risk, assuming vulnerability to discipline if a court or other authority subsequently determines that the order would *not* have required illegality. Thus what is needed is a fair and expeditious means of reaching such a determination while protecting the individual who reasonably believes that she or he is being asked to violate the law from having to proceed with the action or from suffering retaliation while a determination is sought.

> OAS Model Law, Articles 2(c), (5); Inter-American Development Whistleblower Policy, § 28; WPA (U.S. federal government), 5 U.S.C. § 2302(b) (9); FRSA (U.S. rail workers), 49 U.S.C. § 20109(a)(2); NTSSA (U.S. public transportation), 6 U.S.C. § 1142(a)(2); CPSIA (U.S. corporate retail products), 15 U.S.C. § 2087(a)(4); STAA (U.S. corporate trucking industry), 49 U.S.C. § 31105(a)(1)(B)

Protection against spillover retaliation The law should cover all common scenarios that could have a chilling effect on the responsible exercise of free-expression rights. Representative scenarios include individuals who are perceived as whistleblowers (even if mistakenly) or as "assisting whistleblowers" (to guard against guilt by association) as well as individuals who are "about to" make a disclosure (to preclude preemptive strikes to circumvent statutory protection and to cover the essential preliminary steps to have a "reasonable belief" and qualify for protection as a responsible whistleblowing disclosure). These indirect contexts often can have the most significant potential for a chilling effect that locks in secrecy by keeping people silent and isolating those who do speak out. The most fundamental illustration is reprisal for exercising anti-retaliation rights.

> OAS Model Law, Articles 2(g), 5; World Bank Group Policy on Eradicating Harassment, Guidelines for Implementation (World Bank Harassment Guidelines), § 9.0 (Mar. 1, 2000); European Bank for Reconstruction and Development (EBRD), Grievance and Appeals Procedure (Employee Grievance Procedures), § 10.02 (2002); Asian Development Bank (ADB) Administrative Order No. 2.06: Administrative Review and Appeal (Administrative Review), § 10.1 (July 9, 1998), ADB Personnel Policy § 2.12; ACA (Korea), Article 31; Uganda 2010 WPA, § 1(d); WPA (U.S. federal government), 5 U.S.C. § 2302(b)(8) (case law) and § 2302(b)(9); Energy Policy Act of 2005 (U.S. Nuclear Regulatory Commission, Department of Energy and regulated corporations), 42 U.S.C. § 5851(a); FRSA (U.S. rail workers), 49 U.S.C. § 20109(a); NTSSA (U.S. public transportation), 6 U.S.C. § 1142(a); CPSIA (U.S. corporate retail products), 15 U.S.C. § 2087(a); STAA (U.S. corporate trucking industry), 49 U.S.C. § 31105(a)

No loopholes protection for all citizens with disclosures relevant to the public service mission Coverage for employment-related discrimination should extend to all relevant applicants and personnel who challenge betrayals of the organizational mission or public trust, regardless of formal status. In addition to conventional salaried employees, whistleblower policies should protect all who carry out activities relevant to the organization's mission. It should not matter whether they are full-time, part-time, temporary, permanent, expert consultants, contractors, employees seconded from another organization, or even volunteers. What matters is the contribution they can make by bearing witness. If harassment could create a chilling effect that undermines the organization's mission, the reprisal victim should have rights. This means the mandate must also cover those who apply for jobs, contracts, or other funding because blacklisting is a common tactic.

Most significantly, whistleblower protection should extend to those who participate in or are affected by the organization's activities. Overarching US whistleblower laws, particularly criminal statutes, protect all witnesses from harassment because it obstructs government proceedings.

> U.N. policy, § 8; OAS Model Law, § 2(b); Anti-Corruption Initiative for Asia-Pacific (Organization for Economic Cooperation and Development [OECD]), Pillar 3; Asian Development Bank Audit Manual, § 810.750; PIDA (U.K.), § 43 (K)(1)(b-d); ACA (Korea), Article 25; Whistleblower Protection Act of 2004 (Japan WPA), § 2; Ghana WPA, § 2; Uganda 2010 WPA, § 1(d); Foreign Operations Appropriations Act of 2005 (Foreign Operations Act) (U.S. MDB policy), § 1505(a)(11) (signed Nov. 14, 2005); False Claims Act (U.S. government contractors), 31 U.S.C. §§ 3730(h), 8-9; STAA (U.S. corporate trucking industry), 49 U.S.C. § 31105(j); ARRA (U.S. Stimulus Law) P.L. 111-5 § 1553(g)(2)-(4)

Reliable anonymity protection   To maximize the flow of information necessary for accountability, reliable protected channels must be available for those who choose to make confidential disclosures. As sponsors of whistleblower rights laws have recognized repeatedly, denying this option creates a severe chilling effect.

> U.N. policy, § 5.2; OAS Model Law, Articles 10(5), 20-22; Asian Development Bank Audit Manual, §§ 810.175, 820.915, 830.400, 830.500, 830.530; 2003 Office of Auditor General Anticorruption (OAGA) Annual Report, at 3, explained in letter from Peter Pedersen, ADB Auditor General to GAP (Nov. 12, 2003) (Pedersen letter) (available at GAP); PSA (Can.), §§ 28.17(1-3), 28.20(4), 28.24(2), 28.24(4); ACA (Korea), Articles 15 and 33(1); Uganda 2010 WPA, § 14; WPA (U.S. federal government), 5 U.S.C. §§ 1212(g), 1213(h); FRSA (U.S. rail workers), 49 U.S.C. § 20109(i); NTSSA (U.S. public transportation), 6 U.S.C. § 1142(h); STAA (U.S. corporate trucking industry), 49 U.S.C. § 31105(h)

Protection against unconventional harassment   The forms of harassment are limited only by the imagination. As a result, it is necessary to ban any discrimination taken because of protected activity whether active, such as termination, or passive, such as refusal to promote or provide training. Recommended, threatened, and attempted actions can have the same chilling effect as actual retaliation. The prohibition must cover recommendations as well as the official act of discrimination, to guard against managers who "don't want to know" why subordinates have targeted employees for an action. In nonemployment contexts it could include protection against harassment ranging from discipline to litigation.

> OAS Model Law, Article 2(g); World Bank Harassment Guidelines, § 1; ADB Audit Manual, §§ 810.750, 830.530; Pedersen letter; EBRD Employee Grievance Procedures, §§ 4.01, 6.01(a); IDB Staff Rule 323 §§ 102, 301, 2101-02; IDB Staff Rule 328 § 105; ACA (Korea), Article 33; Uganda 2010 WPA, §§ 1(d), 10, 11; WPA (U.S. federal government), 5 U.S.C. § 2302(b) (8) and associated case law precedents; FRSA (U.S. rail workers), 49 U.S.C. § 20109(a); NTSSA (U.S. public transportation), 6 U.S.C. § 1142(a); CPSIA (U.S. corporate retail products), 15 U.S.C. § 2087(a); SOX (U.S. publicly traded corporations), 18 U.S.C. § 1514(a); ARRA (U.S. Stimulus Law), P.L. 111-5 § 1553(a)

Shielding whistleblower rights from gag orders   Any whistleblower law or policy must include a ban on gag orders through an organization's rules, policies, or nondisclosure agreements that would otherwise override free-expression rights and impose prior restraint on speech.

> OAS Model Law, Article 6; PIDA (U.K.), § 43(J); PDA (S. Afr.), § 2(3)(a, b); Ghana WPA, § 31; Uganda 2010 WPA, § 13; WPA (U.S. federal government), 5 U.S.C. § 2302(b)(8); Transportation, Treasury, Omnibus Appropriations Act of 2009 (U.S.), § 716 (anti-gag statute) (passed annually since 1988); FRSA (U.S. rail workers), 49 U.S.C. § 20109(h); NTSSA (U.S. public transportation), 6 U.S.C. § 1142(g); STAA (U.S. corporate trucking industry), 49 U.S.C. § 31105(g); ARRA (U.S. Stimulus Law) P.L. 111-5 § 1553(d)(1)

Providing essential support services for paper rights   Whistleblowers are not protected by any law if they do not know it exists. Whistleblower rights, along with the duty to disclose illegality, must be posted prominently in any workplace. Similarly, legal indigence can leave a whistleblower's rights beyond reach. Access to legal assistance or services and to legal defense funding can make free-expression rights meaningful for those who are unemployed and blacklisted. An ombudsman with sufficient access to documents and institutional officials can neutralize resource handicaps and cut through draining conflicts to provide expeditious corrective action. The US Whistleblower Protection Act includes an Office of Special Counsel, which investigates retaliation complaints and may seek relief on the whistleblower's behalf. Informal resources should be risk-free for the whistleblower, without any discretion by relevant staff to act against the interests of individuals seeking help.

> OAS Model Law, Articles 9(11), 10(1)(5-8), 13, 29–30; World Bank Harassment Guidelines, § 3.0; Korean Independent Commission Against Corruption (Korea), First Annual Report (2002), at 139; WPA (U.S. federal government), 5 U.S.C. § 1212; Inspector General Act (U.S.), 5 U.S.C. app.; ARRA (U.S. Stimulus Law) P.L. 111-5 § 1553(b)

Forum

The setting to adjudicate a whistleblower's rights must be free from institutionalized conflict of interest and operate under due process rules that provide a fair day in court. The histories of administrative boards have been so unfavorable that so-called hearings in these settings have often been traps, both in perception and in reality.

Right to a genuine day in court   This criterion requires normal judicial due process rights—the same rights enjoyed by citizens generally who are aggrieved by illegality or abuse of power. The elements include timely decisions, a day in court with witnesses and the right to confront the accusers, objective and balanced rules of procedure, and reasonable deadlines. At a minimum, internal systems must be structured to provide autonomy and freedom from institutional conflicts of interest. This is particularly significant for the preliminary stages of informal or internal review, which are inherently compromised by conflict of interest, such as Office of Human Resources Management reviews of actions. Otherwise, instead of being remedial, those activities are vulnerable to becoming investigations of the whistleblower and the evidentiary base to attack the individual's case for any eventual day in a due process forum.

> U.N. policy, § 6.3; OAS Model Law, Articles 11, 14; Foreign Operations Act (U.S. MDB policy), § 1505(11); PIDA (U.K.), Articles 3, 5; PDA (S. Afr.), § 4(1); ACA (Korea), Article 33; Uganda 2010 WPA, §§ 9(3), (4); WPA (U.S. federal government), 5 U.S.C. §§ 1221, 7701-02; Defense Authorization

Act (U.S.) (defense contractors), 10 U.S.C. § 2409(c)(2); Energy Policy Act (U.S. government and corporate nuclear workers), 42 U.S.C. §§ 5851(b)(4), (c)-(f); FRSA (U.S. rail workers), 49 U.S.C. § 20109(c)(2)-(4); NTSSA (U.S. public transportation), 6 U.S.C. § 1142(c)(4)-(7); CPSIA (U.S. corporate retail products), 15 U.S.C. § 2087(b)(4)-(7); SOX (U.S. publicly traded corporations), 18 U.S.C. § 1514(b); STAA (U.S. corporate trucking industry), 49 U.S.C. § 31105 (c)-(e); ARRA (U.S. Stimulus Law) P.L. 111-5 § 1553(c) (3)-(5)

Option for alternative dispute resolution with an independent party of mutual consent   Third-party dispute resolution can be an expedited, less costly forum for whistleblowers. For example, labor/management arbitrations have been highly effective when the parties share costs and select the decision-maker by mutual consent through a "strike" process. It can provide an independent, fair resolution of whistleblower disputes while circumventing the issue of whether intergovernmental organizations waive their immunity from national legal systems. It is contemplated as a normal option to resolve retaliation cases in the model whistleblower law to implement the OAS Inter-American Convention against Corruption, as well as the US Whistleblower Protection Act.

OAS Model Law, Article 10(14); Foreign Operations Act (U.S. MDB policy), § 1505(a)(11); WPA (U.S. federal government), 5 U.S.C. § 7121

Rules to Prevail

The rules to prevail control the bottom line. They are the tests a whistleblower must pass to prove that illegal retaliation violated his or her rights—and win.

Realistic standards to prove a violation of rights   The US Whistleblower Protection Act of 1989 overhauled antiquated, unreasonable burdens of proof that had made it hopelessly unrealistic for whistleblowers to prevail when defending their rights. The test has been adopted within international law, within generic professional standards such as the OAS model law, and by individual organizations such as the World Bank.

This emerging global standard is that a whistleblower establishes a prima facie case of violation by establishing through a preponderance of the evidence that the protected conduct was a "contributing factor" in the challenged discrimination. The discrimination need not involve retaliation but occur only "because of" the whistleblowing. Once a prima facie case is made, the burden of proof shifts to the organization to demonstrate by clear and convincing evidence that it would have taken the same action for independent, legitimate reasons in the absence of protected activity.

Since the US government changed the burden of proof in its whistleblower laws, the rate of success on the merits has increased from 1 to 5 percent annually to 25 to 33 percent, which gives whistleblowers a fighting chance to successfully defend themselves. Many nations that adjudicate whistleblower disputes under labor laws have analogous presumptions and track records. There is no alternative, however, for the intergovernmental organization to commit to one of these proven formulas to determine the bottom line—tests the whistleblower must pass to win a ruling that his or her rights were violated.

> OAS Model Law, Articles 2(h), 7; World Bank, Department of Institutional Integrity Investigations Manual, § 7.4; Foreign Operations Act (U.S. MDB policy), § 1505(11); WPA (U.S. federal government), 5 U.S.C. §§ 1214(b)(2)(4), 1221(e); Energy Policy Act (U.S. government and corporate nuclear workers), 42 U.S.C. § 5851(b)(3); FRSA (U.S. rail workers), 49 U.S.C. 20109(c)(2)(A)(i); NTSSA (U.S. public transportation), 6 U.S.C. § 1142(c)(2)(B); CPSIA (U.S. corporate retail products), 15 U.S.C. § 2087 (b)(2)(B), (b)(4); SOX (U.S. publicly traded corporations), 18 U.S.C. § 1514(b)(2)(c); STAA (U.S. corporate trucking industry), 49 U.S.C. § 31105(b)(1); ARRA (U.S. Stimulus Law) P.L. 111-5 § 1553(c)(1)

Realistic time frame to act on rights   Although some laws require employees to act within 30 to 60 days or waive their rights, most whistleblowers are not even aware of their rights within that time frame. Six months is the minimum functional statute of limitations. One-year statutes of limitations are consistent with common-law rights and are preferable.

> World Bank, Appeals Committee Procedures, § 5, Administrative Tribunal Statute, Article II.2; EBRD Employee Grievance Procedures, §§ 2.03, 5.02; PIDA (U.K.), § 48.3; PDA (S. Afr.), § 4(1); WPA (U.S. federal government), 5 U.S.C. § 1214; False Claims Act (U.S. government contractors), 42 U.S.C.

§ 3730(h) and associated case law precedents; Energy Policy Act (U.S. government and corporate nuclear workers), 42 U.S.C. § 5851(b)(1); FRSA (U.S. railroad workers), 49 U.S.C. § 20109(d)(2)(A)(ii); NTSSA (U.S. public transportation), 6 U.S.C. § 1142(c)(1); CPSIA (U.S. corporate retail products), 15 U.S.C. § 2087(b)(1); STAA (U.S. corporate trucking industry), 49 U.S.C. § 31105(b)(1); ARRA (U.S. Stimulus Law) P.L. 111-5 § 1553(b)(1)

Relief for Whistleblowers Who Win

The twin bottom lines for a remedial statute's effectiveness are whether it achieves justice not only by adequately helping the victim obtain a net benefit but also by holding the wrongdoer accountable.

Compensation with "no loopholes"   If a whistleblower prevails, the relief must be comprehensive to cover all the direct, indirect, and future consequences of the reprisal. In some instances this means relocation or payment of medical bills for consequences of physical and mental harassment. In nonemployment contexts, it could require relocation, identity protection, or withdrawal of litigation against the individual.

OAS Model Law, Articles 10(10), 16-17; Foreign Operations Act (U.S. MDB policy), § 1505(11); ACA (Korea), Article 33; PIDA (U.K.), § 4; WPA (U.S. federal government), 5 U.S.C. § 1221(g)(1); False Claims Act (U.S. government contractors), 31 U.S.C. § 3730(h); Defense Authorization Act (U.S.) (defense contractors), 10 U.S.C. § 2409(c)(2); Energy Policy Act (U.S. government and corporate nuclear workers), 42 U.S.C. § 5851(b)(2)(B); FRSA (U.S. rail workers), 49 U.S.C. § 20109(e); NTSSA (U.S. public transportation), 6 U.S.C. § 1142(c)(3)(B), (d); CPSIA (U.S. corporate retail products), 15 U.S.C. § 2087(b)(3)(B), (b)(4); STAA (U.S. corporate trucking industry), 49 U.S.C. § 31105(b)(3)(B); ARRA (U.S. Stimulus Law) P.L. 111-5 § 1553(b)(2)(A), (B), (b)(3)

Interim relief   Relief should be awarded during the interim for employees who prevail. Anti-reprisal systems that appear streamlined on paper commonly drag out for years in practice. Ultimate victory may merely be an academic vindication for unemployed, blacklisted whistleblowers who go bankrupt while waiting to win. Injunctive or interim relief must occur after a preliminary determination. Even after winning a hearing or trial, an unemployed whistleblower could go bankrupt while waiting for the completion of an appeals process that frequently takes years.

> U.N. policy, § 5.6; OAS Model Law, Articles 9(12), 10(1), 24; PIDA (U.K.), § 9; WPA (U.S. federal government), 5 U.S.C. §§ 1214(b)(1), 1221(c); CPSIA (U.S. corporate retail products), 15 U.S.C. § 2087(b)(1); SOX (U.S. publicly traded corporations), 5 U.S.C. § 1214(b)(1)

Coverage for attorney's fees   Attorney's fees and associated litigation costs should be available for all who substantially prevail. Whistleblowers otherwise couldn't afford to assert their rights. The fees should be awarded if the whistleblower obtains the relief sought, regardless of whether it is directly from the legal order issued in the litigation. Otherwise, organizations can and have unilaterally surrendered outside the scope of the forum and avoided fees by declaring that the whistleblower's lawsuit was irrelevant to the result. Affected individuals can be ruined by that type of victory because attorney's fees often reach sums that exceed the whistleblower's annual salary.

> OAS Model Law, Article 16; EBRD Employee Grievance Procedures, § 9.06; WPA (U.S. federal government), 5 U.S.C. § 1221(g)(2-3); False Claims Act (U.S. government contractors), 31 U.S.C § 3730(h); Energy Policy Act (U.S. government and corporate nuclear workers), 42 U.S.C. § 5851(b)(2)(B)(ii); FRSA (U.S. rail workers), 49 U.S.C. § 20109(e); NTSSA (U.S. public transportation) 6 U.S.C. § 1142(d)(2)(C); CPSIA (U.S. corporate retail products), 15 U.S.C. §§ 2087(b)(3)(B), (b)(4)(C); SOX (U.S. publicly traded corporations), 18 U.S.C. § 1514(c)(2)(C); STAA (U.S. corporate trucking industry), 49 U.S.C. §§ 31105(b)(3)(A)(iii), (B); ARRA (U.S. Stimulus Law), P.L. 111-5 §§ 1553(b)(2)(C), (b)(3)

Transfer option   It is unrealistic to expect a whistleblower to go back to work for a boss whom he or she has just defeated in a lawsuit. For any realistic chance at a fresh start, whistleblowers who prevail must have the ability to transfer. This option prevents repetitive reprisals that cancel the impact of newly created institutional rights.

> U.N. policy, § 6.1; OAS Model Law, Article 10(7); EBRD Employee Grievance Procedures, § 9.04; ADB Audit Manual, § 810.750; PDA (S. Afr.), § 4(3); ACA (Korea), Article 33; WPA (U.S. federal government), 5 U.S.C. § 3352

Personal accountability for reprisals   To deter repetitive violations, those responsible for whistleblower reprisal must be held accountable. Otherwise, managers have nothing to lose by doing the dirty work of harassment. The worst that will happen is they won't get away with it, and they may well be rewarded for trying. The most effective option to prevent retaliation is personal liability for punitive damages by those found responsible for violations. Another option is to allow whistleblowers to counterclaim for disciplinary action, including termination. In selective scenarios such as obstruction of justice, some nations, including Hungary and the United States, impose potential criminal liability for whistleblower retaliation.

> U.N. policy, § 7; OAS Model Law, § 18; EBRD, Procedures for Reporting and Investigating Suspect Misconduct, § 6.01(a); Staff Handbook, ch. 8.5.6; ACA (Korea), Article 32(8); Hungary, Criminal Code Article 257, "Persecution of a Conveyor of an Announcement of Public Concern"; Public Interest Disclosure Act, No. 108, § 32; Uganda 2010 WPA, § 16; WPA (U.S. federal government), 5 U.S.C. § 1215; FRSA (U.S. rail workers), 49 U.S.C. § 20109(e)(3); NTSSA (U.S. public transportation), 6 U.S.C. § 1142(d)(3); CPSIA (U.S. corporate retail products), 15 U.S.C. §§ 2087(b)(3)(B), (b)(4)(C); SOX (U.S. publicly traded corporations), 18 U.S.C. § 1513(e); STAA (U.S. corporate trucking industry), 49 U.S.C. § 31105(b)(3)(C)

Making a Difference

Whistleblowers risk retaliation if they think that challenging abuse of power or any other misconduct that betrays the public trust will make a difference. Numerous studies have confirmed this motivation. This is also the bottom line for affected institutions and the public: positive results. Otherwise, the point of a reprisal dispute is limited to whether injustice occurred on a personal level. Legislatures unanimously pass whistleblower laws to make a difference for society.

Credible corrective action process   Whether through hotlines, ombudsmen, compliance officers, or other mechanisms, the point of whistleblowing through an internal system is to give managers an opportunity to clean house, before matters deteriorate into a public scandal or law enforcement action. In addition to a good-faith investigation, two additional elements are necessary for legitimacy.

First, the whistleblower who raised the issues should be enfranchised to review and comment on the charges that merited an investigation and to report whether there has been a good-faith resolution. As a rule the whistleblower, rather than investigators or finders of fact, is the most knowledgeable, concerned witness in the process. Whistleblowers' evaluation comments have in fact led to significant improvements and changed conclusions in the US Whistleblower Protection Act. Whistleblowers should not be silenced in the final stage of official resolution of the alleged misconduct they risked their careers to challenge.

Second, transparency should be mandatory. Secret reforms are an oxymoron. As a result, unless the whistleblower elects to maintain anonymity, both the final report and the whistleblower's comments should be a matter of public record, posted on the organization's website. The most significant reform is to enfranchise whistleblowers and citizens to "walk the talk" by filing formal actions against illegality exposed by their disclosures. In government statutes, these types of suits are known as private attorney general, or *qui tam,* actions (see the following section).

> OAS Model Law, Articles 10(13), 27-28; ACA (Korea), Articles 30, 36; PSA (Can.), § 28.14(1) (1990); Japan WPA, § 9 (2004); Uganda 2010 WPA, § 18; WPA (U.S. federal government), 5 U.S.C. § 1213; Inspector General Act of 1978 (U.S. federal government), 5 U.S.C. app.; False Claims Act, 31 U.S.C. § 3729 (government contractors); FRSA (U.S. rail workers), 49 U.S.C. § 20109(j); NTSSA (U.S. public transportation), 6 U.S.C. § 1142(i); STAA (U.S. corporate trucking industry), 49 U.S.C. § 31105(i)

Private attorney general option: Citizen Enforcement Act   Even more significant is enfranchising whistleblowers and citizens to file suit in court against illegality exposed by their disclosures. These types of suits are known as private attorney general, or *qui tam,* actions, in reference to the Latin phrase for "he who sues on behalf of himself as well as the king." These statutes can provide both litigation costs (including attorney's and expert witness fees) and a portion of money recovered for the government to the citizen whistleblowers who file them, a premise that merges "doing well" with "doing good"—a rare marriage of the public interest and self-interest.

In the United States, this approach has been tested in the Federal False Claims Act for whistleblower suits challenging fraud in government contracts. It is the nation's most-effective whistleblower law in history for making a difference, increasing civil fraud recoveries in government contracts from $27 million annually in 1985 to more than $20 billion since, including more than $1 billion annually since 2000.

Another tool that is vital in cases of continuing violations is the power to obtain from a court or an objective body an order that will halt the violations or require specific corrective actions. The obvious analogy for intergovernmental organizations is the ability to file for proceedings at independent review mechanisms or inspection panels—the same as for an outside citizen personally aggrieved by institutional misconduct.

False Claims Act, 31 U.S.C. § 3730 (U.S. government contractors)

Model Whistleblower Hotline Policy

Since the 2002 passage of the Sarbanes-Oxley Act for corporate accountability, all corporations that are publicly traded in the United States must have whistleblower "hotlines" to the audit committee for each board of directors. This requirement has institutionalized a common practice for decades at government agencies and companies. It has also created a dynamic, growing cottage industry in the United States for what traditionally was a scattered phenomenon with widely varying standards of quality.

Historically, there has been little credible evidence that hotlines are an effective vehicle through which whistleblowers could challenge corruption or other abuses of power sustained by secrecy. This model policy is drawn from the accumulated best practices of the past seven years since SOX reform created a growth market.

Hotline Requirements

Individuals are invited to make disclosures of information that evidence illegality, gross waste, mismanagement, abuse of authority, substantial and specific danger to public health or safety, and any other action that could create significant liability or other risks to the health of the corporation.

The hotline shall be operated 24 hours a day, seven days a week.

Operators designated to receive calls for the hotline shall be certified, based on possession of academic credentials and completion of additional training that represents best practices for this purpose.

The hotline shall be accredited by a recognized national accrediting organization.

The hotline shall be operated in a manner consistent with the following best practices.

Independence from conflicts of interest   The hotline shall report directly to the agency head, the board of directors of a corporation, or the chief executive officer if no board exists, and may be subjected to discipline only by the board or the CEO if no board exists.

Access through multiple communication sources   Access shall include confidential telephone reporting, e-mail, personal interview, and confidential mail deposit or similar mechanism.

Protection from retaliation   The hotline shall be subject to all federal statutory and agency protections for citizens and employees, prohibiting retaliation for reporting illegal or unethical conduct or behavior.

Confidentiality   The hotline shall comply with federal and agency or department rules providing for the confidentiality of disclosures made to hotline officials and employees. The hotline shall adopt procedures, including secure firewalls and the encryption of e-mail, and employ technology and equipment that reasonably ensure the confidentiality of disclosures that are received or maintained by the hotline.

Enfranchisement   The hotline shall be operated in a manner that encourages employee and citizen participation. This includes the opportunity to supplement and comment on responses to the disclosures. It also includes an on-the-record assessment that evaluates the effectiveness of hotline resolution for the employee's concerns and that supports the contribution of additional information promoting evaluation of the initial employee disclosures.

Transparency   The hotline shall issue an annual report on its effectiveness in terms of overall numbers of complaints or reports received and their disposition, including moneys recovered in a manner consistent with the protection of confidentiality of the covered employee. The annual report shall include findings and resolution for each case, along with the employee's evaluation comments, which shall be maintained in a publicly available file also posted on the Internet, with necessary deletions for properly classified information or information whose disclosure is specifically prohibited by statute.

Model Citizen Enforcement Act

Whereas:

Citizens have been frustrated that they have not been empowered with meaningful control of their lives through expensive, cumbersome government regulatory agencies; and

Whereas:

The public interest requires that it be illegal to discriminate against government or private employees who make disclosures responsibly challenging violations of law because they are invaluable to law enforcement, to the public's right to know, and to prevent or minimize the consequences of institutional misconduct.

Therefore Be It Resolved:

Section 1: Jurisdiction and procedure Any citizen may challenge violations of law through a jury trial under the procedures available in the False Claims Act (31 U.S.C. § 3729 *et seq.*) unless the parties mutually consent to alternative dispute resolution procedures such as mediation or arbitration.

Section 2: Relief A jury may award injunctive relief to stop ongoing illegality, as well as actual or exemplary damages, as it deems appropriate.

Section 3: Employee Protection

(A) *In general* No employee or other person may be harassed, prosecuted, held liable, or discriminated against in any way because that person (1) has made or is about to make disclosures not prohibited by law or executive order; commenced, caused to be commenced, or is about to commence a proceeding; testified or is about to testify at a proceeding; assisted or participated in or is about to assist or participate in, in any manner, such a proceeding or in any other action to carry out the purposes, functions, or responsibilities of this Act; or (2) is refusing to violate or assist in the violation of this Act.

(B) *Procedures* Cases of alleged discrimination shall be governed by the procedures of the Federal False Claims Act (31 U.S.C. § 3730(h)), unless the parties mutually consent to alternative dispute resolution procedures such as mediation or arbitration.

(C) *Burdens of proof* The legal burdens of proof with respect to prohibited discrimination under subsection (A) shall be governed by the applicable provisions of the Whistleblower Protection Act of 1989 (5 U.S.C. §§ 1214, 1221).

Section 4: Conflicts No funds may be spent to implement or enforce any nondisclosure policy, form, or agreement without explicit provision that, in the event of a conflict, any restrictions on protected activity are superseded by this Act.

Acknowledgments

W e extend a hearty thank-you to everyone that made this book possible. We are grateful to former interns Richard Ewenstein, Erik Kojola, Kristina Lederer, Mark Merdinger, Micha Reisner, Yohannes Sium, Alejandro Soto-Vigil, Shelia Thorpe, and the University of the District of Columbia's Government Accountability Project law clinic for tireless research into the charted and uncharted territories of whistleblower law and its implementation. In particular, Ms. Thorpe authored Tool A in this book's Whistleblower Toolkit—the how-to guide for filing a Sarbanes-Oxley Whistleblower Complaint.

Thanks also to former and current staff at GAP, particularly Dylan Blaylock, Mary Brumder, Tom Carpenter, Louis Clark, Kasey Dunton, Jeff Gulley, Thad Guyer, Adam Miles, Joanne Royce, and Shelly Walden for their insight and editing assistance. While we are the authors, this book primarily reflects lessons learned from whistleblowers served by the entire GAP community. Similarly, outside attorneys Reuben Guttman, Alan Kabat, Debbie Katz, Ann Lugbill, David Marshall, and Cyrus Mehri deserve kind praise for the insights and the research that they shared, and especially Jason Zuckerman, who did volunteer legal research contributions beyond the call of duty.

Groundbreaking research with encyclopedic thoroughness by Professor C. Fred Alford, Richard Moberly, Robert Vaughn, and Dr. David Welch supplied the factual basis to generalize from individual whistleblowers' frustrations. We are grateful to Executive Director Mark Cohen for unqualified support (that included finding a publisher!) and to the Governmental Accountability Project Board of Directors, as well as the supporting foundations and individual donors that make GAP tick.

More broadly, our appreciation extends to our sister organizations: the Project on Government Oversight and Public Employees for

Environmental Responsibility. Alongside the champions of whistle-blower rights, countless citizen organizations have helped whistleblowers make a difference and get away with "committing the truth."

We also wish to acknowledge the tremendous support of the Nathan Cummings Foundation, the Rockefeller Family Fund, the C. S. Fund, the Fund for Constitutional Government, the Open Society Foundation, and two anonymous angels without whom this achievement would not have been possible.

We are also indebted to the people at Berrett-Koehler for giving us the opportunity to share our lessons learned and for their patience and graciousness in trying to enforce deadlines with a whistleblower M*A*S*H unit.

Most importantly, we salute the collective soul for this book: all the whistleblowers whose experiences directly or indirectly shaped the lessons learned and expressed here. They have been the inspiration for all our work.

Finally, special thanks to Shanna Devine, Tom's daughter and partner at GAP, who not only flawlessly does whatever is necessary for this book or otherwise to help whistleblowers, but is the improved version of Tom's soul.

Notes

Introduction: Whistleblowing in Corporate America

1. *The Forbes 2000,* FORBES (2006), http://www.forbes.com/lists/2006/18/06f2000_ The-Forbes-2000_Rank.html.

2. *Financial Collapse of Enron (Part 3): Hearing Before the H. Subcommittee on Oversight and Investigations of the Committee on Energy and Commerce,* 107th Congress (2002) (Statement of Sherron Watkins, Enron Employee).

3. Gretchen Morgenson, *Finance Chief Tried in Vain to Raise Cash for WorldCom,* NEW YORK TIMES, July 10, 2002, http://www.nytimes.com/2002/07/10/business/ finance-chief-tried-in-vain-to-raise-cash-for-worldcom.html.

4. Patricia Horn, *Whistle-Blower Tells of High Price of Truth: Cynthia Cooper Helped Expose Massive Fraud at WorldCom. It Cost Her Money, Health and Privacy,* PHILADELPHIA INQUIRER, Oct. 26, 2005, at E8.

5. Richard Lacayo and Amanda Ripley, *Persons of the Year: Sherron Watkins of Enron, Coleen Rowley of the FBI and Cynthia Cooper of WorldCom,* TIME, Dec. 30, 2002, http://www.time.com/time/subscriber/personoftheyear/2002/poyintro.html.

6. Andrew Clark, *Lehman Whistleblower Lost His Job Weeks after Raising Alarm,* GUARDIAN, March 16, 2010, http://www.guardian.co.uk/business/2010/mar/16/ lehman-whistleblower-auditors-matthew-lee.

7. 5 U.S.C. § 2302.

8. Joanna Gualtieri, *When the Whistle Blows,* CA MAGAZINE, Aug. 2004, http:// www.camagazine.com/index.cfm/ci_id/22181/la_id/1.htm.

9. Democracy Corps Frequency Questionnaire, Greenberg Quinlan Rosner (Feb. 2007) at 14–15.

10. Ethics Resource Center, *Reporting: Who's Telling You What You Need to Know, Who Isn't, and What You Can Do About It* (2010), at 15.

11. *Id.* at 1.

12. PricewaterhouseCoopers and Martin Luther University Economy and Crime Research Center, *Economic Crime: People, Culture and Controls: The 4th Biennial Global Economic Crime Survey* (2007), http://www.pwc.com/en_GX/gx/economic-crime-survey/pdf/pwc_2007gecs.pdf.

13. *Id.* at 8.

14. *Id.* at 10.

15. Society of Certified Fraud Examiners, *2008 Report to the Nation on Occupational Fraud and Abuse* (2008), at 4, 30.

Chapter 1: Deciding to Blow the Whistle

1. Professor C. Fred Alford, University of Maryland, Keynote Address to the AK Rice Leadership Institute (Oct. 8, 2010), at 4 ("Alford Speech").

2. Gene Emory, *Money Not Major Incentive for Whistle-Blowers—Study*, REUTERS, May 12, 2012, http://www.reuters.com/article/idUSN1221530120100512.

3. *Id.*

4. David J. Graham, *Testimony of David J. Graham MD, MPH* (Nov. 18, 2004), http://www.consumersunion.org/pub/campaignprescriptionforchange/001651.html.

5. *Dr. David Graham's Full Story*, Government Accountability Project (2004), http://whistleblower.org/program-areas/public-health/vioxxdavid-graham/dr-david-grahams-full-story.

6. Chuck Grassley, *Floor Statement of U.S. Senator Chuck Grassley of Iowa: One-Year Anniversary of the Committee's Hearing on the FDA and Vioxx*, US Senate Committee on Finance, 109th Congress (Nov. 17, 2005).

7. Press Release, Government Accountability Project, House Hearing Focuses on GAP Clients (Feb. 12, 2007), http://whistleblower.org/press/press-release-archive/2007/881-house-hearing-on-drug-safety-highlights-gap-clients.

8. Press Release, Government Accountability Project, GAP Client Exposes Flawed Procedure in Procter & Gamble Drug Study (Feb. 22, 2006), http://www.whistleblower.org/press/press-release-archive/2006/882-gap-client-exposes-flawed-procedure-in-procter-a-gamble-drug-study.

9. *Saving Our Pets: GAP Client Blows Whistle on Dangerous Dog Drug*, BRIDGING THE GAP, Government Accountability Project (Washington, DC, Spring 2006), at 3, http://whistleblower.org/storage/documents/NewsletterSpring2006.pdf.

10. *Spotlight: A Conversation with GAP President Louis Clark,* Bridging the GAP, Government Accountability Project (Washington, DC, Spring/Summer 2004), at 4, http://whistleblower.org/storage/documents/NewsletterSS2004.pdf.

11. Tarek F. Maassarani, *Redacting the Science of Climate Change: An Investigative and Synthesis Report,* Government Accountability Project (March 2007).

12. Justin Rood and Avni Patel, *Domestic Spying Worries May Tip House Vote,* ABC News, March 12, 2008, http://abcnews.go.com/Blotter/story?id=4439900 &page=1.

13. Tom Devine, *Courage without Martyrdom: The Whistleblower Survival Guide,* Government Accountability Project (1997), at 5.

14. *Id.* at 6.

15. *Id.* at 7.

16. Andy Pasztor, *US Investigates Charges Starrett Defrauded Clients,* Wall St. Journal, Sept. 12, 2002.

17. *Id.* at 2.

18. Devine, *supra* note 13, at 6.

19. *"Singled Out by US Customs: Atlanta Investigative News Team Wins the Peabody Award for 'The Cathy Harris Story,'"* http://www.thecathyharrisstory.com.

20. Department of Homeland Security Office of the Inspector General, *Review of Alleged Actions by Transportation Security Administration to Discipline Federal Air Marshals for Talking to the Press, Congress, or the Public* (Office of Audits) (2004), http://www.dhs.gov/xoig/assets/mgmtrpts/OIG-05-01_Nov04.pdf.

21. Examples of this corruption included using leaks of classified documents as political patronage; granting overpriced "sweetheart" contracts to unqualified political supporters; overrunning costs 10-fold to obtain research already available for an anti-corruption law enforcement training conference; and using the government's visa power to bring highly suspect Russian women to work for DOJ management, such as one who had been previously arrested for prostitution during a dinner with a top DOJ official in Moscow. The whistleblower, Martin E. Andersen, was so effective that the US Office of Special Counsel gave him its Public Servant Award.

22. Ray Locker, *Study: Lack of MRAPs Cost Marine Lives,* USA Today, Feb. 15, 2008, http://www.usatoday.com/news/washington/2008-02-15-mraps_N.htm.

23. *See* Karen L. Soeken and Donald R. Soeken, *A Survey of Whistleblowers: Their Stressors and Coping Strategies* (unpublished manuscript 1987); and Philip H. Jos et al., *In Praise of Difficult People: A Portrait of the Committed Whistleblower,* 49 Public Administration Review, 554 (Nov.–Dec. 1989).

24. Alford Speech, *supra* note 1, at 16.

25. Joyce Rothschild and Terance D. Miethe, *Whistle-Blower Disclosures and Management Retaliation: The Battle to Control Information About Organizational Corruption*, 26 WORK AND OCCUPATIONS, 107, 121 (Feb. 1999), http://wox.sagepub.com/content/26/1/107.short?rss=1&ssource=mfc.

Chapter 2: The Red Flags

1. Tom Devine, *Courage without Martyrdom: The Whistleblower Survival Guide,* Government Accountability Project (1997), at 39.

2. Watergate Hearings, "Responsiveness Program," Book 19, 9006. *See also* Gebhardt et al., *Blueprint for Civil Service Reform,* Fund for Constitutional Government (1976).

3. Devine, *supra* note 1, at 28.

4. *Id.* at 33.

5. Case Acceptance Proposal: Government Accountability Project (March 27, 2003), at 6–7.

6. *Id.* at 9, 10.

7. Memorandum Opinion and Order. Upon request, the full citation has been omitted here to protect the whistleblower's identity.

8. *Id.*

9. *Id.*

10. Testimony of Jeffrey Wigand Before the Chancery Court of Jackson County, Mississippi, Pascagoula, Mississippi (Nov. 29, 1995) in the *In re* Mike Moore, Attorney General *ex rel.,* State of Mississippi Tobacco Litigation, http://www.tobacco.neu.edu/litigation/hotdocs/wigand_depo.htm ("Testimony of Jeffrey Wigand").

11. *Id.*

12. Written Examination of Jeffrey Wigand, PhD, US District Court for the District of Columbia, *USA v. Phillip Morris,* at 30.

13. Testimony of Jeffrey Wigand, *supra* note 10.

14. Michael Janofsky, *For a Trial Lacking in Drama, a Star Witness, of Sorts,* NEW YORK TIMES, Feb. 1, 2005, at National Desk 16.

15. Marie Brenner, *Jeffrey Wigand: The Man Who Knew Too Much,* VANITY FAIR, May 1996, http://www.vanityfair.com/magazine/archive/1996/05/wigand199605.

16. *Id.*

17. Summary of the Attorneys General Master Tobacco Settlement Agreement, prepared by Joy Johnson Wilson, Director, Assembly on Federal Issues Health Committee (March 1999), http://www.ncsl.org/statefed/tmsasumm.htm#Summary.

18. Testimony of Jeffrey Wigand, *supra* note 10.

19. Suein L. Hwang and Milo Geyelin, *Getting Personal: Brown & Williamson Has 500-Page Dossier Attacking Chief Critic—Court Files, Private Letters, Even a Suspicious Flood Are Fodder for Sleuths—Ivana Trump's Private Eye*, WALL STREET JOURNAL, Feb. 1, 1996, http://www.jeffreywigand.com/wallstreetjournal.php.

20. Brenner, *supra* note 15.

21. David Enrich, *Jeffrey Wigand*, US NEWS AND WORLD REPORT, Aug. 12, 2001), http://www.usnews.com/usnews/culture/articles/010820/archive_038242.htm.

22. The author was on the telephone with Dr. Murtagh from the hospital after he was stricken. *See also* Murtagh v. Emory, No. 1:09-CV-0752-HTW (N.D. Ga.).

23. *Inez Austin—Protecting the Public Safety at the Hanford Nuclear Reservation,* Online Ethics Center for Engineering and Research, Case Western Reserve University (Oct. 16, 2005), http://www.onlineethics.org/Topics/ProfPractice/Exemplars/BehavingWell/austinindex.aspx ("*Inez Austin*").

24. First Amendment Complaint for Damages and Demand for a Jury Trial. In the Superior Court of the State of Washington for Benton County. Scott Brundridge v. Fluor Daniel, No. 99-2-01250-7, at 3-4, http://www.whistleblower.org/storage/documents/Pipefitter_first_amended_complaint.pdf.

25. Letter from Tom Carpenter of GAP to the Hon. Samuel Bodman, Re: Hanford Pipefitters Retaliation and Jury Verdi (Sept. 23, 2005), http://www.whistleblower.org/storage/documents/Bodman.pdf.

26. Letter from Richard S. Terrill, Fluor Regional Administrator, to Rhonnie L. Smith, President and General Manager Fluor Daniel Northwest, Re: Fluor Daniel Northwest, Inc., Walli, Killen, Nicacio, O'Leary, and Stull (May 6, 1999), http://www.whistleblower.org/storage/documents/oshapipe.doc.

27. *See* Brundridge v. Fluor Daniel, 99-2-01250-7.

28. Shannon Dininny, *Workers Get $4.7 Million in Hanford Trial*, ASSOCIATED PRESS, Sept. 2, 2005, http://www.highbeam.com/doc/1P1-112772120.html.

29. Eric Nalder and Elouise Schumacher, *Hanford Whistle-Blower—Breaking the Code—Citing Harassment, An Employee Stands Firm: "If it Costs Me My Job, This One Was Worth Saying No To,"* SEATTLE TIMES, Dec. 2, 1990, http://community.seattletimes.nwsource.com/archive/?date=19901202&slug=1107269.

30. *Id.*

31. Keith Schneider, *Inquiry Finds Illegal Surveillance of Workers in Nuclear Plants,* NEW YORK TIMES (July 31, 1991), http://www.nytimes.com/1991/08/01/us/inquiry-finds-illegal-surveillance-of-workers-in-nuclear-plants.html.

32. *Inez Austin, supra* note 23.

33. *Id.*

34. *Id.*

35. *Id.*

36. Professor C. Fred Alford, University of Maryland, Keynote Address to the AK Rice Leadership Institute (Oct. 8, 2010), at 11.

37. Richard Dunn, *A Whistleblower Feels the RTC's Long Arm,* HARPERS, Nov. 1994, at 20, http://dev.harpers.org/archive/1994/11/0001847.

38. Letter from Dr. David Welch to Dr. David Michaels, Assistant Secretary of Labor, summarizing attached study (May 7, 2010), at 2 n.1.

39. Matthew L. Wald, *Questions Raised About the Safety of Navy Reactors,* NEW YORK TIMES, Jan. 1, 1991, http://www.nytimes.com/1991/01/01/us/questions-raised-about-the-safety-of-navy-reactors.html.

40. *Appeals Court Kicks Union Out of Suit,* TIMES UNION (Albany, NY), Aug. 21, 1990, at B4.

41. Phil Brown, *Free-Speech Suit Against GE Dismissed,* TIMES UNION (Albany, NY), March 20, 1990, http://www.highbeam.com/doc/1G1-156189926.html.

42. Jenny Jones, *Challenger Engineer Boisjoly Tells Story Behind Disaster at Lecture Series Finale,* MADISON COURIER (Madison, WI), Feb. 18, 2005, http://madison courier.com/main.asp?SectionID=4&SubSectionID=253&ArticleID=22475 &TM=54076.17.

43. Roger M. Boisjoly, *Ethical Decisions—Morton Thiokol and the Space Shuttle Challenger Disaster,* Online Ethics Center for Engineering and Research, Case Western Reserve University, http://www.onlineethics.org/cms/7050.aspx.

44. Jones, *supra* note 42.

45. *Id.*

46. Devine, *supra* note 1, at 42.

47. Fred Bruning, *Challenger: The Shuttle Disaster; 7 Killed in Flight, Stunning a Nation,* NEWSDAY (Melville, NY), Jan. 29, 1986, at 3.

48. Office of Federal Housing Enterprise Oversight, *Report of the Special Examination of Fannie Mae* (May 2006), at 1, http://www.fanniemae.com/media/pdf/newsreleases/FNMSPECIALEXAM.pdf.

49. *Id.* at 260.

50. *Id.* at 10.

51. *Id.* at 201–2.

52. *Id.* at 262.

53. *Id.* at 263.

54. Paul, Weiss, Rifkind, Wharton & Garrison LLP, *A Report to the Special Review Committee of the Board of Directors of Fannie Mae: Executive Summary* (Feb. 23, 2006), at 28.

55. *Id.* at 269.

56. Press Release, US Securities and Exchange Commission, SEC and OFHEO Announce Resolution of Investigation and Special Examination of Fannie Mae: Fannie Mae Agrees to Pay $400 Million Penalty (May 23, 2006), http://www.sec.gov/news/press/2006/2006-80.htm.

57. Devine, *supra* note 1, at 44.

58. Press Release, Government Accountability Project, GAP Client Exposes Flawed Procedure in Procter & Gamble Drug Study (Feb. 22, 2006), http://www.whistleblower.org/press/press-release-archive/2006/882-gap-client-exposes-flawed-procedure-in-procter-a-gamble-drug-study.

59. *Id.*

60. Aubrey Blumsohn, *Authorship, Ghost-Science, Access to Data and Control of the Pharmaceutical Scientific Literature: Who Stands Behind the Word?* Professional Ethics Report (American Association for the Advancement of Science, Washington, DC), Volume XIX (Summer 2006), at 1–2, http://www.aaas.org/spp/sfrl/per/per46.pdf.

61. *See* http://www.thejabberwock.org/wiki/index.php?title=Image:20071012athes.gif; http://www.pharmalot.com/2007/10/boning-up-medical-journal-bolsters-disclosure-policy; and http://dcscience.net/?p=193.

62. Letter from Charles Grassley, US Senator, to Robert Essner, Chairman, President, and CEO of Wyeth Pharmaceuticals (Nov. 17, 2005), http://whistleblower.org/program-areas/public-health/proheart6/sen-grassleys-letter.

63. *Spotlight: A Conversation with GAP President Louis Clark—Victoria Hampshire,* BRIDGING THE GAP, Government Accountability Project (Washington, DC, Summer 2006), at 4, http://www.whistleblower.org/storage/documents/Newsletter Summer2006.pdf.

64. Letter from Charles Grassley, US Senator, to the Hon. Michael O. Leavitt, Secretary of Health and Human Services, and the Hon. Andrew C. von Eschenbach, Commissioner of the Food and Drug Administration (Feb. 6, 2008).

Chapter 3: What to Know Before You Blow

1. Associated Press, *Ex-WorldCom Accountant Was "Shocked" at False Entries*, NEW YORK TIMES, Feb. 4, 2005, http://www.nytimes.com/2005/02/04/business/04ebbers.html.

2. Kris Hundley, *She Audited and Told*, ST. PETERSBURG TIMES (Florida), March 1, 2006; http://www.sptimes.com/2006/03/01/Business/She_audited_and_told.shtml.

3. Michael Barrier, *One Right Path: Cynthia Cooper: MCI Vice President of Internal Audit Cynthia Cooper Believes That Where Ethics Are Concerned, You Have to Obey Your Conscience and Accept the Consequences*, ALL BUSINESS, Dec. 1, 2003, http://www.allbusiness.com/accounting-reporting/auditing/720646-1.html.

4. Associated Press, *Rattled Firm Outlines Trouble in SEC Filing*, CINCINNATI POST, July 2, 2002, http://www.highbeam.com/doc/1G1-88244021.html.

5. *Financial Collapse of Enron (Part 3): Hearing Before the H. Subcommittee on Oversight and Investigations of the Committee on Energy and Commerce*, 107th Congress (2002) (Statement of Sherron Watkins, Enron Employee), at 18.

6. *Financial Collapse of Enron (Part 4): Hearing Before the H. Subcommittee on Oversight and Investigations of the Committee on Energy and Commerce*, 107th Congress (2002).

7. Jennifer Frey, *The Woman Who Saw Red: Enron Whistle-Blower Sherron Watkins Warned of the Trouble to Come*, WASHINGTON POST, Jan. 25, 2002, http://www.washingtonpost.com/ac2/wp-dyn/A35005-2002Jan24.

8. *Financial Collapse of Enron (Part 3): Hearing Before the H. Subcommittee on Oversight and Investigations of the Committee on Energy and Commerce*, 107th Congress (2002) (Statement of Sherron Watkins, Enron Employee), at 22–24.

9. In a False Claims Act case JFM Glynn v. EDO Corporation et al., 2010 U.S. Dist. Lexis 86013 (D. Md.), a whistleblower supplied evidence to the FBI and Pentagon Office of Inspector General and filed a *qui tam* lawsuit alleging fraud by a defense contractor that compromised the reliability of devices used by troops in Iraq to jam terrorist IED (improvised explosive device) explosives. The contractor argued that by giving evidence of fraud to criminal investigators, he had stolen company property. Its basis? A confidentiality agreement signed as a prerequisite to employment states that anything an employee learns on the job is corporate property and may not be disclosed to anyone for any reason. The court

observed, "A review of district court opinions suggests that even where a party steals property or information, dismissal or default judgment is only warranted in extreme circumstances." While rejecting enforcement of a sweeping corporate gag order or liability for disclosures to the government, the court fined the whistleblower's lawyers $20,000 for their receipt of company records that were intellectual property or otherwise privileged. A key factor for a relatively low fine was a common criterion in these cases—the company was not significantly prejudiced.

10. Reporters Committee for Freedom of the Press, http://www.rcfp.org/taping/quick.html.

11. Niebur v. Town of Cicero, 212 F. Supp. 2d 790, 826 (N.D. Ill. 2002). *See also* Lachman v. Sperry-Sun Well Surveying Co., 457 F.2d 850, 851 (10th Cir. 1972), which upheld protection for disclosure of an employer's confidential records in the course of reporting allegedly criminal misconduct.

12. United States v. Northrop Corp., 59 F.3d 953, 962 (9th Cir. 1995) (quoting Town of Newton v. Rumery, 480 U.S. 386, 392 (1987)). "[A] Confidentiality Agreement would be void as against public policy if, when enforced, it would prevent 'disclosure of evidence of a fraud on the government.'" U.S. *ex rel.* Head v. Kane Co., 668 F. Supp. 2d 146, 152 (D.D.C. 2009) (quoting X Corp. v. Doe, 805 F. Supp. 1298, n.24 (E.D. Va. 1992) *aff'd sub nom*). Under Seal v. Under Seal, 17 F.3d 1435 (4th Cir. 1994); *see also In re* JDS Uniphase Corporate Sec. Lit., 238 F. Supp. 2d 1127 (N.D. Cal. 2002); United States *ex rel.* Grandeau v. Cancer Treatment Centers of America, 350 F. Supp. 2d 765, 773 (N.D. Ill. 2004); *see also* Saini v. Int'l Game Tech., 434 F. Supp. 2d 913, 923 (D. Nev. 2006); Maddox v. Williams, 855 F. Supp. 406, 415 (D.D.C. 1994) (citing *In re* Quarles 158 U.S. 532, 535-36 (1895)).

13. U.S. *ex rel.* Yesudian v. Howard Univ., 153 F.3d 731, 740 (D.C. Cir. 1998). "[Congress intended] to protect employees while they are collecting information about a possible fraud, *before* they have put all the pieces of the puzzle together." *See also* Childree v. UAP/GA AG CHEM, Inc., 92 F.3d 1140, 1146 (11th Cir. 1996).

14. Niswander v. Cincinnati Ins. Co., 529 F.3d 714, 725 (6th Cir. 2008). *See also* O'Day v. McDonnell Douglas Helicopter Co., 79 F.3d 756, 763 (9th Cir. 1996); Jefferies v. Harris County Cmty. Action Ass'n, 615 F.2d 1025, 1036 (5th Cir. 1980).

15. The court in *Niswander,* 529 F.3d at 725, listed six factors: "(1) how the documents were obtained, (2) to whom the documents were produced, (3) the content of the documents, both in terms of the need to keep the information confidential and its relevance to the employee's claim of unlawful conduct, (4) why the documents were produced, including whether the production was in direct response to a discovery request, (5) the scope of the employer's privacy policy,

and (6) the ability of the employee to preserve the evidence in a manner that does not violate the employer's privacy policy."

16. Ian Hoffman, *Whistleblower Pleads Guilty in Diebold Case: Man Gets Three Years' Probation for Publicizing Memos That Showed Firm Fielded Unapproved Software,* OAKLAND TRIBUNE, Nov. 22, 2006, http://www.insidebayarea.com/oaklandtribune/ci_4703875.

17. Alison Grant, *Jones Day Papers Focus of Theft Case: Diebold Information Leaked to Writer,* PLAIN DEALER (Cleveland, OH), April 24, 2006, http://www.heller legaldefensefund.com/cleveland.html.

18. Kevin Yamamura, *Diebold Voting Machines Ok'd: Secretary of State Certifies Firm After Delays and Glitches,* SACRAMENTO BEE, Feb. 18, 2006, http://digital.library .ucla.edu/websites/2006_997_099/index2.php%5Eoption=com_content&do_ pdf=1&id=92.pdf.

19. *Id.*

20. James Covert, *Unsafe at Home Depot: Whistleblower's Fraud Charge Led to His Suicide,* NEW YORK POST, July 27, 2009, http://www.nypost.com/p/news/business/item_nylrEIIvX86ONHEgnK9H8N.

21. Karen L. Soeken and Donald R. Soeken, *A Survey of Whistleblowers: Their Stressors and Coping Strategies* (unpublished manuscript 1987).

22. Philip H. Jos et al., *In Praise of Difficult People: A Portrait of the Committed Whistleblower,* 49 PUBLIC ADMINISTRATION REVIEW, 554 (Nov.–Dec. 1989).

23. Joyce Rothschild and Terance D. Miethe, *Whistle-Blower Disclosures and Management Retaliation: The Battle to Control Information About Organizational Corruption,* 26 WORK AND OCCUPATIONS, 107, 121 (Feb. 1999), http://wox.sagepub .com/content/26/1/107.short?rss=1&ssource=mfc.

24. William De Maria and C. Jan, *Eating Its Own: The Whistleblower's Organization in Vendetta Mode,* 32 AUSTRALIAN JOURNAL OF SOCIAL ISSUES, 45 (1997).

25. William Sanjour and Stephen M. Kohn, *Environmental Whistleblowers: An Endangered Species,* Environmental Research Foundation (Annapolis, MD, Feb. 1994), http://home.comcast.net/~jurason/main/Endangered.htm.

26. Transcript from Charles Hamel interview on *Democracy Now,* "Did BP Purposefully Allow Its Alaska Pipeline to Corrode in Order to Shut It Down and Boost Oil Prices?" Aug. 10, 2006, http://www.democracynow.org/article.pl?sid= 06/08/10/1339232.

27. David Whitney, *Alyeska, Hamel Fail to Settle Case,* ANCHORAGE DAILY NEWS, Dec. 11, 1993, at A1.

28. Sheila McNulty, BP *"Was Warned"* of *Corrosion*, THE AUSTRALIAN, Aug. 10, 2006, http://www.freerepublic.com/focus/f-news/1683411/posts.

29. Wesley Loy, *Total Shutdown Averted: Western Portion Will Be Vigilantly Monitored, Company Says*, ANCHORAGE DAILY NEWS, Aug. 12, 2006, http://www.alaskaforum.org/2006%20News%20Stories%20Sorted%20by%20Month/august_2006_news_stories.htm.

30. BP *Third-quarter Profit Declines*, SAN GABRIEL VALLEY TRIBUNE (West Covina, CA), Oct. 24, 2006.

31. Jim Carlton, *BP's Alaska Woes Are No Surprise for One Gadfly*, WALL STREET JOURNAL, Aug. 12, 2006, http://www.pogo.org/press-room/pogo-in-the-news/natural-resources/nr-pb-20060812.html.

32. *Important Information About EDGAR*, US Securities and Exchange Commission (2005), http://www.sec.gov/edgar/aboutedgar.htm.

33. *Form 10-K*, US Securities and Exchange Commission (2006), http://www.sec.gov/answers/form10k.htm.

34. *Id.*

35. *Form 8-K*, U.S. Securities and Exchange Commission (2005), http://www.sec.gov/answers/form8k.htm.

36. TCS Industries, Inc. v. Northway, 426 U.S. 438, 448–49.

37. US Department of Justice, *Guide to the Freedom of Information Act: Introduction* (March 2007), http://www.usdoj.gov/oip/foia_guide07/introduction.pdf (*"Guide to the FOIA"*).

38. 5 U.S.C. § 552(f)(2).

39. Juan Gonzalez, *A Toxic Nightmare at Disaster Site: Air, Water, Soil Contaminated*, NEW YORK DAILY NEWS, Oct. 26, 2001, http://www.nydailynews.com/archives/news/2001/10/26/2001-10-26_a_toxic_nightmare_at_disaste.html.

40. US House of Representatives Committee on Government Reform, *A Citizen's Guide on Using the Freedom of Information Act and the Privacy Act of 1974 to Request Government Records*, H.R. Doc. No. 109-226, 109th Congress, 1st Sess. (Sept. 20, 2005).

41. *Id.*

42. *Id.*

43. The other exemptions include internal agency rules, statutory exemptions, internal agency memoranda, bank reports, and oil and gas well data.

44. *Guide to the FOIA, supra* note 37.

45. Openness Promotes Effectiveness in Our National Government Act of 2007, Pub. L. 110-175 [S. 2488], 110th Congress (Dec. 31, 2007). For background on the amendment, see Harold C. Relyea, *Freedom of Information Act (FOIA) Amendments: 110th Congress,* Congressional Research Services (Jan. 7, 2008), http://www.fas.org/sgp/crs/secrecy/RL32780.pdf.

46. *White House Memorandum for the Heads of Executive Departments and Agencies* (Jan. 21, 2009), http://www.whitehouse.gov/the_press_office/FreedomofInforma tionAct.

47. *See* New York Times v. Sullivan, 376 U.S. 354 (1964); *see also* Curtis Pub. Co. v. Butts, 388 U.S. 130 (1967).

48. *See* Gertz v. Robert Welch, Inc., 418 U.S. 323 (1974).

49. *But see* Noonan v. Staples, Inc., 556 F.3d 20 (1st Cir. 2009), "under Massachusetts law, even a true statement can form the basis of a libel action if the plaintiff proves that the defendant acted with 'actual malice'" (citing Mass. Gen. Laws ch. 231 § 92).

50. *See generally* Eileen Finan, *The Fact-Opinion Determination in Defamation,* 88 Columbia Law Review, 809–40 (May 1988), http://www.jstor.org/pss/1122648.

51. *See* Restatement (Second) of Torts § 588 (1997).

Chapter 4: Where to Go When You Want to Blow

1. Press Release, Government Accountability Project, GAP Client Exposes Flawed Procedure in Proctor & Gamble Drug Study (Feb. 22, 2006), http://www.whistle blower.org/press/press-release-archive/2006/882-gap-client-exposes-flawed-procedure-in-procter-a-gamble-drug-study.

2. Press Release, Government Accountability Project, Proctor & Gamble Surrenders Data to GAP Client (June 16, 2006), http://www.whistleblower.org/press/press-release-archive/2006/885-procter-a-gamble-surrenders-data-to-gap-client.

3. Aubrey Blumsohn, *Authorship, Ghost-Science, Access to Data and Control of the Pharmaceutical Scientific Literature: Who Stands Behind the Word?* Professional Ethics Report (American Association for the Advancement of Science, Washington, DC), Volume XIX (Summer 2006), at 1–2, http://www.aaas.org/spp/sfrl/per/per46.pdf.

4. UNODC in partnership with PriceWaterhouseCoopers, *Anti-Corruption Policies and Measures of the Fortune Global 500,* http://www.unodc.org/unodc/en/corruption/anti-corruption-policies-and-measures-of-the-fortune-global-500.html.

5. Alec Koch, *Internal Corporate Investigations: The Waiver of Attorney-Client Privilege and Work-Product Protection Through Voluntary Disclosure to the Government,* 34 American Criminal Law Review (Jan. 1997), http://vlex.com/vid/investigations-voluntary-disclosures-53715861.

6. *Id.*

7. US Sentencing Commission, *2005 Federal Sentencing Guideline Manual,* ch. 8: Sentencing of Organizations (Nov. 2005), http://www.ussc.gov/2005guid/CHAP8.htm.

8. Sarbanes-Oxley Act of 2002, 107th Congress, HR 3763 ("SOX"), § 301.4.A.

9. *Id.,* § 301.4.B.

10. *Id.,* § 301.4.A.

11. *Id.,* § 301.A.

12. PricewaterhouseCoopers and Martin Luther University Economy and Crime Research Center, *Economic Crime, People, Culture and Controls: The 4th Biennial Global Economic Crime Survey* (2007), http://www.pwc.com/en_GX/gx/economic-crime-survey/pdf/pwc_2007gecs.pdf.

13. Voices of Scientists at FDA: Protecting Public Health Depends on Independent Science, Union of Concerned Scientists (2006) at 2, http://www.ucsusa.org/assets/documents/scientific_integrity/fda-survey-brochure.pdf ("Voices of Scientists").

14. Ken Stier, *Why Is the UBS Whistle-Blower Headed to Prison?,* Time, Oct. 6, 2009, http://www.time.com/time/business/article/0,8599,1928897,00.html.

15. Voices of Scientists, *supra* note 13.

16. Joyce Purnick, *A Whistle Still Ringing in Wall St. Ears,* New York Times, Dec. 11, 2003, http://www.nytimes.com/2003/12/11/nyregion/metro-matters-a-whistle-still-ringing-in-wall-st-ears.html.

17. Riva D. Atlas, *Fund Inquiry Informant Discloses Her Identity,* New York Times, Dec. 9, 2003, http://www.nytimes.com/2003/12/09/business/fund-inquiry-informant-discloses-her-identity.html?ref=edward_j_stern.

18. *Id.*

19. Brooke A. Masters, *Tipster Set Fund Scandal Snowballing,* Washington Post, July 23, 2006, http://www.washingtonpost.com/wp-dyn/content/article/2006/07/22/AR2006072200111.html.

20. Stephen M. Cutler, Director, Division of Enforcement, US Securities and Exchange Commission, Testimony Concerning Recent Commission Activity to Combat Misconduct Relating to Mutual Funds, Before the Senate Subcommittee

on Financial Management, the Budget, and International Security, Committee on Governmental Affairs (Nov. 3, 2003).

21. Reuters, *Key Events in Mutual Fund Trading Probe,* FORBES, Dec. 2, 2003.

22. Masters, *supra* note 19.

23. Testimony of Peter T. Scannell, Before Subcommittee on Financial Management, the Budget and International Security of the US Senate Committee on Governmental Affairs, Mutual Funds: Trading Practices and Abuses that Harm Investors (Jan. 27, 2004), at 15, 16.

24. Paul Tharp, *Big Fund Fallout: SEC Big, Putnam CEO Ousted Amid Probes,* NEW YORK POST, Nov. 4, 2003, at 35.

25. Order Making Findings and Imposing Supplemental Remedial Sanctions Pursuant to § 203(e) of the Investment Advisers Act of 1940 and § 9(b) of the Investment Company Act of 1940, US, Before the Securities and Exchange Commission, in the Matter of Putnam Investment Management, LLC (April 8, 2004) Admin. Proceeding #3-11317.

26. Christine Dugas, *Putnam Targets Its Cutthroat Culture,* USA TODAY, April 14, 2004, http://www.usatoday.com/money/perfi/funds/2004-04-14-putnam-culture_x.htm.

27. Testimony of Wendell Potter Before the U.S. Senate Committee on Commerce, Science, and Transportation, Consumer Choices and Transparency in the Health Insurance Industry (June 24, 2009), at 1.

28. 31 U.S.C. §§ 3729–33.

29. These include California, Delaware, Florida, Hawaii, Illinois, Louisiana, Massachusetts, Nevada, New Mexico, Tennessee, Texas, and Virginia. Taxpayers Against Fraud, http://www.taf.org.

30. § 3729(e).

31. Under a new federal law, the IRS also pays 15 to 30 percent for information on tax fraud (26 IRC § 7623). For information about the corresponding IRS Whistleblower Office, see http://www.irs.gov/compliance. This represents the modernization of a longstanding informant program rather than a whistleblower protection law.

32. HR 4173 § 748.

33. *Id.,* § 922.

34. Larry D. Lahman, *Bad Mules: A Primer on the Federal False Claims Act,* OKLAHOMA BAR JOURNAL, http://www.okbar.org/obj/articles_05/040905lahman.htm.

35. Taxpayers Against Fraud, http://www.taf.org/statistics.htm.

36. *Id.*

37. http://www.taf.org/whyfca.htm.

38. *See* http://www.taf.org/top20.htm.

39. Press Release, US Department of Justice, Gambro Healthcare Agrees to Pay Over $350 Million to Resolve Civil and Criminal Allegations in Medicare Fraud Case (Dec. 2, 2004), http://www.usdoj.gov/opa/pr/2004/December/04_civ_774.htm.

40. 5 U.S.C. § 3731(b)(1), United States *ex rel.* Sanders v. North American Bus Industries, Inc., 546 F.3d 288 (4th Cir. 2008).

41. 31 U.S.C. § 3729(b)(2).

42. 31 U.S.C. § 3729(a).

43. 31 U.S.C. § 3730(b)(2).

44. 31 U.S.C. § 3730(b)(1).

45. 31 U.S.C. § 3730(b)(2).

46. K. R. Sawyer, "The Test Called Whistleblowing," paper delivered to the National Conference of Whistleblowers Australia (Sept. 11, 2005), http://www.bmartin .cc/dissent/documents/Sawyer05.pdf.

47. Government Accountability Office, *DOD Procurement: Use and Administration of DOD's Voluntary Disclosure Program*, GAO/NSIAD-96-21 (Feb. 6, 1996), at 12–13, http://www.gao.gov/archive/1996/ns96021.pdf.

48. *Id.*

49. In ACLU v. Holder, Civil Action No.: 1-09-cv-042 (ED Va, Aug. 21, 2009), several public interest groups including GAP contended that the seal should not gag whistleblowers from disclosing imminent public health and safety threats. A district court disagreed and threw out the lawsuit, which currently is being reviewed by the Fourth Circuit Court of Appeals.

50. *ACLU v. Holder*, amicus curiae brief of Taxpayers Against Fraud (Dec. 30, 2009), http://www.cookkitts.com/resources/ACLUvHolderAmicusFiling.pdf.

51. Letter from Dr. Janet Chandler to Tom Devine (Oct. 15, 2010).

52. Cook County, Ill. v. U.S. *ex rel.* Chandler, 538 U.S. 119 (2003).

53. Josh White, *Worker Fired for Describing Conditions at Funeral Home*, WASHINGTON POST, July 7, 2009, http://www.washingtonpost.com/wp-dyn/content/article/2009/07/06/AR2009070602767.html.

54. http://www.proofpoint.com/news-and-events/press-releases/pressdetail.php ?PressReleaseID=273.

Chapter 5: Getting Help in Blowing the Whistle

1. Affidavit of Babak Pasdar (Feb. 28, 2008).

2. "Dear Colleague" letter from Representatives John Dingell, Edward Markey, and Bart Stupak, Re: New Whistleblower Allegations Warrant Further Investigation of Retroactive Immunity (March 6, 2008).

Chapter 6: Whistleblowing and the Law

1. The Public Company Accounting Reform and Investor Protection Act of 2002, Pub. L. No. 107-204, 116 Stat. 745 (July 30, 2002), also known as the Sarbanes-Oxley Act of 2002. The rights are codified at 18 U.S.C. § 1514A.

2. Richard E. Moberly, *Unfulfilled Expectations: An Empirical Analysis of Why Sarbanes-Oxley Whistleblowers Rarely Win*, 49 WILLIAM & MARY LAW REVIEW, 65–66 (Fall 2007), http://scholarship.law.wm.edu/cgi/viewcontent.cgi?article=1115&context=wmlr ("Moberly").

3. Energy Policy Act of 2005, Pub. L. 109-058 (Aug. 8, 2005), amending 42 U.S.C. § 5851.

4. 41 U.S.C. § 31105 (surface transportation employees); 49 U.S.C. § 20109 (public transportation and railroad employees); 10 U.S.C. § 2409 (defense contractor employees); 15 U.S.C. § 2087 (employees in retail manufacturing and commerce); Pub. L. 111-5 § 1553 (stimulus recipients); 29 § U.S.C. 218(c) and 42 U.S.C. § 300(gg-5) (health care employees); and Pub. L. 111-203 §§ 748 and 922 (bounty and associated retaliation, plus stronger anti-retaliation rights in § 1558 for noncommercial whistleblowing disclosures in the Dodd-Frank Wall Street Reform and Consumer Protection Act).

5. FDA Food Safety Modernization Act, Pub. L. 111-353 § 402 (January 4, 2011).

6. 31 U.S.C. § 3730(h).

7. The Labor Department system is highlighted because it offers the closest thing to consistent rights and remedies, evolved through several generations of laws. The other corporate whistleblower laws have broad ranges, including no due process in some asbestos laws; customized, solely administrative hearings and appeals for mine safety; Inspector General investigation followed by jury trials for stimulus recipients and defense contractors; and direct court access for False Claims Act whistleblowers challenging fraud in government contracts. *See* Tool E in the Whistleblower Toolkit for legal citations to text in the U.S. Code where you can pin down your specific rights.

8. Wood v. Department of Labor, 275 F.3d 107, 110 (D.C. Cir. 2001). The reason is Congress failed to provide any guidance in that early statute for how the secretary should exercise enforcement authority.

9. 29 C.F.R. § 24.107(b). Use or misuse of this discretionary power has been a source of deep frustration. If administrative law judges limit otherwise relevant discovery, complainants may be denied their due process right to study information necessary to assert their rights and may never get the opportunity to have their cases fully heard. A full and fair presentation of the case is critical to serving the Sarbanes-Oxley Act's purpose of protecting whistleblowers from retaliation. *See generally* English v. General Electric Co., 496 U.S. 72 (1990).

10. 29 C.F.R. §§ 1980.115, 24.115. The statutory basis for this provision is uncertain. Of particular concern is the suggestion that an administrative law judge may waive a rule even without good cause, in "special circumstances."

11. 29 C.F.R. §§ 1980.109(c) and 110(a), and 29 C.F.R. §§ 24.109(e) and 110(a).

12. 15 U.S.C. § 2622.

13. *See e.g.,* 49 U.S.C. § 20109(e)(3) (rail safety).

14. Most of the DOL-administered whistleblower statutes passed prior to 1989 do not specify the burdens of proof necessary to demonstrate unlawful retaliation. In these situations the burdens default to those specified by the Supreme Court in Mt. Healthy City Board of Ed. v. Doyle, 429 U.S. 274, 286–87 (1977), which require the employee to demonstrate that protected conduct was a primary or predominate motivating factor in the employer's decision to take an employment action. Once demonstrated, the burden then shifts to the employer to demonstrate by a preponderance of the evidence that it would have taken the action in the absence of the protected conduct. In 1989 the Whistleblower Protection Act lowered the employee's burden to demonstrate that protected conduct was a "contributing" factor, and the employer must then meet its burden by clear and convincing evidence. 5 U.S.C. § 1221(e). Corporate whistleblower laws passed since 1989 consistently reflect the WPA burdens. The only exception is with defense contractors. In a 2007 reform, Congress provided them with jury trials but did not address legal burdens of proof. 10 U.S.C. § 2409.

15. Fiscal 2009 runs from October 1, 2008, to September 30, 2009.

16. For case lists *see* Department of Labor, http://www.oalj.dol.gov/LIBWHIST.HTM.

17. US Government Accountability Office, *Whistleblower Protection: Sustained Management Attention Needed to Address Long-Standing Program Weaknesses* (GAO-10-722) (Aug. 17, 2010), http://www.gao.gov/products/GAO-10-722 ("2010 GAO Report").

18. US Government Accountability Office, *Whistleblower Protection Program: Better Data and Improved Oversight Would Help Ensure Program Quality and Consistency* (GAO-09-106) (Jan. 2009), http://www.gao.gov/new.items/d09106.pdf ("2009 GAO Report").

19. 18 U.S.C. § 1514A(b)(1)(B).

20. 18 U.S.C. § 1514A(a). Protection for subsidiaries was explicitly added by SOX amendments included in the Dodd-Frank bill, as well as protection for employees of any "nationally recognized statistical rating organization." The latter can be essential for any government program that replaces direct oversight with voluntary corporate sampling data gathered by private organizations.

21. Section 307 of the Sarbanes-Oxley Act of 2002 required the SEC to adopt rules requiring attorneys to report evidence of securities law violations or breaches of fiduciary duty by the company to the chief legal counsel or chief executive officer of the company. In the event such violations or breaches are not remedied, the attorney must report the evidence to the board of directors' audit committee or the full board. 15 U.S.C. § 7245. While the SEC rulemaking process predictably is bogged down in controversy, a 2009 decision permits SOX protection for lawyer whistleblowers despite the attorney-client privilege. Van Arsdale v. International Game Technology, 577 F.3d 989, 994–96 (9th Cir. 2009) ("*Van Arsdale*").

22. Robert Vaughn, *America's First Comprehensive Statute Protecting Corporate Whistleblowers,* 57 ADMINISTRATIVE LAW REVIEW, 1, 9–19 (2005).

23. Basic, Inc. v. Levinson, 485 U.S. 224, 231–32, 108 S. Ct. 978, 99 L. Ed. 2d 194 (1988) (quoting TSC Indus. [*58] Inc. v. Northway, Inc., 426 U.S. 438, 449, 96 S. Ct. 2126, 48 L. Ed. 2d 757 (1976)) (internal quotation marks omitted); Day v. Staples, 555 F.3d 57–58 (4th Cir. 2009) ("*Day*").

24. 18 U.S.C. § 1514A(a)(1).

25. *Van Arsdale, supra* note 21, at 1002.

26. *Day, supra* note 23, at 42, 54–56; Welch v. Chao, 536 F.3d 269, 275–77 (4th Cir. 2008) ("*Welch*"); Van Arsdale v. International Game Technology, 498 F. Supp. 2d 1321 (D. Nev. 2007); Kalkunte v. DVI Financial Services, ARB Nos. 05-139, 05-40 (Feb. 27, 2009) ("*Kalkunte*"); Allen v. Stewart Enterprises, Inc., ARB No. 06-081 at 10, 2004-SOX-60 (ARB July 27, 2006) ("*Allen*").

27. Johnson v. Econo Steel, LLC, ARB No. 07-111 (Feb. 23, 2009).

28. *Day, supra* note 23, at 58; *Allen, supra* note 26, at 481.

29. Wedderspoon v. Milligan, 80-WPCA-1, slip op. of ALJ, at 10-11 (July 11, 1980), adopted by SOL (July 28, 1980); Donovan v. R.D. Andersen Constr. Co., 552 F. Supp. 249 (D. Kan. 1982); Dobreuenaski v. Associated Universities, Inc., 96

ERA-44, D&O of ARB, at 9 (June 18, 1998); Simon v. Simmons Industries, Inc., 87-TSC-2, D&O of SOL, at 4 (April 4, 1994), citing Legutko v. Local 16, International Brotherhood of Teamsters, 606 F. Supp. 352, 358-59 (E.D.N.Y. 1985, *aff'd* (2d Cir. 1988); Nunn v. Duke Power Co., 84-ERA-27, D&O of Remand by Deputy SOL, at 13 (July 30, 1987).

30. Tides v. Boeing, 2010 U.S. Dist. LEXIS 11282 (Feb. 9, 2010) (slip op at 5–7).

31. Donovan v. R. D. Andersen Const. Co., 552 F. Supp. 249, 253 (D. Kan. 1982); Dobreuenbraski v. Associated Universities, Inc., 96-ERA-44, D&O of ARB, at 9 (June 18, 1998); Simon v. Simmons Industries, Inc., 87-TSC-2, D&O of SOL, at 6 (April 4, 1994), *aff'd* on other grounds 49 F.3d 86, 88 (8th Cir. 1995).

32. 18 U.S.C. § 1514A(a).

33. Burlington Northern and Santa Fe Railway Company v. White, 548 U.S. 53, 68 (2006).

34. *See* 49 U.S.C.A. § 42121(b)(2)(B)(iii) (2006).

35. Peck v. Safe Air International, Inc., ARB 02-028 at 6, 2001-AIR-3 (ARB Jan. 30, 2004) (citing BLACK's LAW DICTIONARY 1201 at 577 (7th ed. 1999).

36. *Welch, supra* note 26, at 8; Klopfenstein v. PCC Flow Techs Holdings Inc., ARB 04-149, 2004-SOX-00011 (ARB May 31, 2006).

37. 18 U.S.C. § 1514A(c).

38. Bohac v. Dept. of Agriculture, 239 F.3d 1334, 1341 (Fed. Cir. 2001) (citing Restatement [Second] of Torts §§ 905, 906) (1997); *cf.* Smith v. Atlas Off-Shore Boat Serv., Inc., 653 F.2d 1057, 1064 (5th Cir. 1981); Hanna v. WCI Communities, Inc., 348 F. Supp. 2d 1332, 1334 (S.D. Fla. 2004). One early decision, Murray v. TXU Corp., 2005 WL 1356444, slip op. at 1–3 (N.D. Tex. 2005) ("Murray"), held that compensatory damages (and therefore a jury trial) were not available because while the statute's title referenced "compensatory damages," the specific text did not repeat the term. Although that loophole has not caught on, it created initial ambiguity. In *Kalkunte, supra* note 26, the ARB resolved the issue by holding that "compensatory damages" are a subset of "special damages," which is explicitly included in statutory text.

39. 18 U.S.C. § 1513(e).

40. 18 U.S.C. § 1514A(e).

41. *See generally* 3 U. Pa. J. Lab. & Emp. L. 367, 368.

42. 49 U.S.C. § 42121.

43. Patient Protection and Affordable Care Act, Pub. L. 111-148 (March 23, 2010), § 1558 (March 23, 2010).

44. Immanuel, Henry W. v. The Railway Markey, ARB 04-062, 02-CAA-20 (ARB Dec. 20, 2005) ("Immanuel").

45. The burdens of proof are drawn from the 1977 Supreme Court decision Mt. Healthy v. Doyle, 429 U.S. 274 (1977).

46. 5 U.S.C. § 1221(e).

47. The employee prevailed in Parexel Int'l. Corp. v. Feliciano, 2008 WL 4847554 (E.D. Pa. 2008) ("Parexel"), but lost in Blagrave v. Nutrition Management Services Co., 2009 WL 440299 (E.D. Pa. 2009).

48. Schlicksup v. Caterpillar, Inc., 2010 WL 2774480 (C.D. Ill. 2010); Fraser v. Fiduciary Trust Co. Intern., 2009 WL 2601389 (S.D.N.Y. 2009); Malin v. Siemens Medical Solutions Health Services, 2009 WL 2500289 (Md. 2009); Smith v. Psychiatric Solutions, Inc., 2009 WL 903624 (N.D. Fla. 2009); Sequeira v. KB Home, 2009 WL 6567043 (S.D. Tex. 2009).

49. Murray, *supra* note 38; Skidmore v. ACI Worldwide, Inc., 2010 WL 2900113 (D. Neb. 2010); Van Arsdale v. International Game Technology, 2010 WL 1490349 (D. Nev. 2010); Jones v. Home Federal Bank, 2010 WL 255856 (D. Idaho 2010).

50. Moberly, *supra* note 2, at 90.

51. Letter from Dr. David Welch to Dr. David Michaels, Assistant Secretary of Labor, summarizing attached study (May 7, 2010), at 1 ("Welch letter").

52. *Kalkunte, supra* note 26.

53. *Parexel, supra* note 47.

54. *Van Arsdale, supra* note 21.

55. Testimony of Lynn Rhinehart, General Counsel, AFL-CIO, Hearings on HR 2067, US House Education and Labor Committee (April 28, 2010), at 5–6 ("Rhinehart testimony").

56. 2009 GAO Report, *supra* note 18, at 29–31.

57. Murray v. Alaska Airlines, 50 Cal 4th 860, 237 P.3d 565 (2010).

58. 2009 GAO Report, *supra* note 18. Even a 21 percent settlement rate is very low. To illustrate, in fiscal 2009 nearly 62 percent of cases filed by government employees to appeal employment decisions and not dismissed on timeliness or jurisdictional grounds were settled. US Merit Systems Protection Board, *Issues of Merit* (Sept. 2010), at 7, http://www.mspb.gov/netsearch/viewdocs.aspx?doc number=537724&version=539241&application=ACROBAT.

59. Moberly, *supra* note 2, at 96.

60. Anonymous e-mail and attached documents (Jan. 2010).

61. *Id.*

62. http://www.whistleblowers.gov/index.html. To illustrate the website's benefits, it contains both the official 2003 investigations manual and a draft update. This is a detailed guide for how investigators should act on your rights.

63. E-mail from confidential whistleblower (Oct. 13, 2010).

64. Public comments of Government Accountability Project, OSHA Docket No. 2010-0004 (March 30, 2010).

65. *Wood, supra* note 8, at 108.

66. *Id.*, at 110; Rhinehart testimony, *supra* note 55, at 7.

67. The full survey is on GAP's website, http://www.whistleblower.org.

68. 2010 GAO report, *supra* note 17, at 41.

69. *Id.*

70. *Id.,* Aug. 17, 2010, cover letter, at 2.

71. 2010 GAO Report, *supra* note 17, at 32.

72. *Id.,* at 31.

73. *Id.,* cover letter, at 2, report at 17–18.

74. *Id.,* at 10.

75. *Id.,* at 21–23.

76. *Id.,* at 27–28.

77. *Id.,* at 29.

78. *Id.,* cover letter, at 3.

79. US Department of Labor, Office of Inspector General, *Complainants Did Not Always Receive Appropriate Investigations Under the Whistleblower Protection Program,* Report 02-10-202-10-105 (Sept. 30, 2010), http://www.oig.dol.gov/public/reports/oa/2010/02-10-202-10-105.pdf.

80. *Id.*

81. Blackann v. Roadway Express, Inc., ARB 02-115, 2000-STA-38 (ARB June 30, 2004).

82. West v. Kasbar, Inc., ARB 04-155, 2004-STA-34 (ARB Nov. 30, 2005); Agee v. ABF Freight System, Inc., ARB 04-182, 2004-STA-40 (ARB Dec. 29, 2005).

83. Moberly, *supra* note 2, at 90, 103–5.

84. Moberly, *supra* note 2, at 121.

85. Bothwell v. American Income Life, 2005-SOX-57 (ALJ Sept. 19, 2005). *But see* 18 U.S.C. § 1514A(a); "Company" means a corporation, a partnership, an association, a joint-stock company, a trust, a fund, or any organized group of persons whether incorporated or not; or any receiver, trustee in a case under title 11 of the United States Code or similar official, or any liquidating agent for any of the foregoing, in his capacity as such. 15 U.S.C. § 78c(a)(19) and 15 U.S.C. § 80a-2(a)(8).

86. Welch v. Cardinal Bankshares Corp., 2003-SOX-15 (ARB May 31, 2007), slip op. at 12. In upholding the ARB decision, the Fourth Circuit Court of Appeals did not directly address that loophole.

87. Livingston v. Wyeth, 520 F.3d 344, 353 (4th Cir. 2008) (*"Livingston"*); Bishop v. PCS Admin. (USA), Inc., 2006 WL 1460032, *9 (N.D. Ill. May 23, 2006); Wengender v. Robert Half International, Inc., 2005-SOX-59 (ALJ March 30, 2006).

88. *Livingston, supra* note 87, at 352–53.

89. *Van Arsdale, supra* note 21, at 1002.

90. 29 C.F.R. § 24.102(a).

91. 69 C.F.R. § 52111 (Aug. 24, 2004).

92. 591 F.3d 239 (4th Cir. 2009).

93. Adam Geller, *The Whistleblower's Unending Story*, ASSOCIATED PRESS (April 26, 2008), http://www.allianceforpatientsafety.org/geller-bw.pdf. This summary also was supplemented with interviews of David Welch.

94. Paul M. Igasaki, chair, appointed in February 2010, previously served as chair, vice chair, and commissioner of the Equal Employment Opportunity Commission from 1994 to 2002. Vice Chair E. Cooper Brown, appointed in January, previously was an ARB associate board member for two years until 2001, afterward serving as chief appeals judge of the District of Columbia Compensation Appeals Board. Associate Judge Joanne Royce, appointed in July, served as counsel for several congressional committees, after representing whistleblowers for 15 years and serving as general counsel for the Government Accountability Project. Luis A. Corchado, also appointed in July, successively gained experience handling appeals of initial ALJ rulings as a member of the Colorado Real Estate Commission, before presiding over hundreds of hearings as an ALJ, and serving as director of litigation for the Denver City Attorney's Office, which is responsible for civil rights and employment cases. http://www.dol.gov/arb/members.htm.

95. Testimony of Jordan Barab, Deputy Assistant Secretary of Labor for Occupational Safety and Health, Before the US House Education and Labor Committee (April 28, 2010).

96. *UPS Pays $254,000 to Mechanic Following Whistleblower Investigation,* OH&S, March 20, 2008, http://ohsonline.com/articles/2008/03/ups-pays-254000-to-mechanic-following-whistleblower-investigation.aspx?sc_lang=en.

97. Letter from OSHA Boston Regional Administrator Marthe Kent to Gil Abramson, re: Southern Air, Inc. AIR21 Retaliation case (April 7, 2009).

98. Letter from Atlanta Regional Administrator Cindy Coe to Waverly Crenshaw, re: Tennessee Commerce Bancorp, Inc./Fort/4-1760-08-017 (March 17, 2010).

99. E-mail from Jason Zuckerman (April 16, 2010).

100. Welch letter, *supra* note 51, Appendix C.

101. Interim rules for 29 C.F.R. Parts 1982 and 1983, 75 C.F.R. 53533-44 (Aug. 31, 2010).

102. *See e.g.,* new 29 C.F.R. 1983.104(f).

103. Letter from Danielle Gibbs to Dr. David Michaels (Oct. 8, 2010).

104. Moberly, *supra* note 2, at 107; 29 C.F.R. § 1980.103(d).

105. Moberly, *supra* note 2, at 107–8; Szymonik v. TyMetrix, Inc., 2006-SOX-50 (ALJ March 8, 2006).

106. Hoff v. Mid-States Express, Inc., ARB 03-051, 2002-STA-6 (May 27, 2004); Immanuel, *supra* note 44.

107. Moberly, *supra* note 2, at 107.

108. Interviews with Nilgun Tolek, Director, Office of the Whistleblower Protection Program, US Department of Labor (October 2005); Speech by Jason Zuckerman, National Employment Lawyers Association Conference, *Representing Workers in Whistleblower and Retaliation Claims*, Chicago, Illinois (March 17, 2007).

109. 49 U.S.C. § 42121(b)(2)(B)(i); 18 U.S.C. § 1514A(b)(2)(A).

110. Bozeman v. Per-Se Technologies, Inc., 456 F. Supp. 2d 1282 (N.D. Ga. 2006); Hanna v. WCI Communities, Inc., 348 F. Supp. 2d 1322 (S.D. Fla. Dec. 2, 2004).

111. 29 C.F.R. § 1980.104(b)(1)(ii).

112. 29 C.F.R. § 1980.104(e); Moberly, *supra* note 2, at 126.

113. Tolek interview, *supra* note 108.

114. http://www.whistleblowers.gov/settlements_future_employment.html.

115. 29 C.F.R. § 1980.114(b).

116. Kalkunte v. DVI Financial Services, 2004-SOX-56 (ALJ July 18, 2005).

117. Neal v. Honeywell, Inc., 33 F.3d 860, 865 (7th Cir. 1994).

118. False Claims Amendment Act, Pub. L. 99-562, 100 Stat. 3157 (1986) (Amendment to 31 U.S.C. § 3729(h)).

119. *Id.*

120. § 1079B(c) of the Dodd-Frank Act, 31 U.S.C. § 3730(h)(3).

121. Taxpayers Against Fraud, http://www.taf.org/statistics.htm.

122. US *ex rel.* Scott v. Metropolitan Health Corp., 375 F. Supp. 2d 626 (W.D. Mich. 2005), affirmed 234 F. App'x. 341, 2007 WL 1028853, *cert. denied* 128 S. Ct. 1225; Robertson v. Bell Helicopter Textron, Inc., 32 F.3d 948 (5th Cir. 1994), *cert. denied,* 513 US 1154.

123. Devine, *Courage Without Martyrdom: The Whistleblower Survival Guide*, Government Accountability Project (1997), at 135. *See generally* Stephen Kohn, *Concepts and Procedures in Whistleblower Law*, SM027 ALI-ABA 1169 (Dec. 2006). Robert Vaughn, *State Whistleblower Statutes and the Future of Whistleblower Protection*, 51 ADMINISTRATIVE LAW REVIEW, 581 (1999).

124. DC Official Code 1-616.1.

125. Press Release, Government Accountability Project, GAP Hails New DC Whistleblower Protection Law (March 10, 2010), http://www.whistleblower.org/press/press-release-archive/447-gap-hails-new-dc-whistleblower-protection-law.

126. *E.g.* N.J. Stat. Ann. § 34:19-8, Cal. Lab. Code § 1102.5, Fla. Stat. § 448.102 (2006).

127. Cal. Lab. Code § 1102.5 (2006).

128. *Id.*

129. 2003 Cal. Legis. Serv. Ch. 484 (West).

130. Cal. Lab. Code § 1102.5(f).

131. *Id.* at § 1102.7 (2006).

132. Cal. Gov't. Code § 5847.

133. N.J. Stat. Ann. § 34:19-1 (2006).

134. Beasley v. Passaic County, 873 A.2d 673 (N.J. Super. Ct. App. Div. 2005).

135. Schlichtig v. Inacom Corp., 271 F. Supp. 2d 597 (D.N.J. 2003).

136. Abbamont v. Piscataway Township Bd. of Ed., 570 A.2d 479 (N.J. Super. Ct. App. Div. 1990).

137. Fla. Stat. § 448.102 (2006).

138. *Id.* at § 448.102(1).

139. *Id.*

140. *Id.* at § 448.102(2).

141. *Id.* at § 448.102(3).

142. Kohn, *supra* note 123.

143. 105 A.L.R. 5th 351 (2003).

144. Acuff v. IBP Inc., 65 F. Supp. 2d 866 (C.D. Ill. 1999).

145. 105 A.L.R. 5th 351 (2003).

146. Kohn, *supra* note 123.

147. Emerick v. Kuhn, No. CV 94-0460869S, 1995 WL 405678 (Conn. Super. Ct. June 14, 1995).

148. *See e.g.,* Darnall v. AN Homecare, Inc. No. 01-A-01-9807-CV-0034, 1999 WL 346225 (Tenn. Ct. App. 1999); Jie v. Liang Tai Knitwear Co., 107 Cal. Rptr. 2d 682 (Cal. Ct. App. 2001).

149. Altig v. GS Roofing Products Co. Inc. 182 F.3d 924 (9th Cir. 1999).

150. 14 Temp. Envtl. L. and Tech. J. 1 at 30–31.

151. English v. General Electric, 496 U.S. 72 (1990).

152. Congressional Record p. S7412; S. Rep. No. 107-146, 107th Cong., 2d Session 19 (2002).

Chapter 7: Corporate Whistleblower Reform

1. Ephraim Schwartz, *Support Your Local Whistle-Blower* (June 20, 2006), http://www.infoworld.com/d/security-central/support-your-local-whistle-blower-024.

2. US Sentencing Commission, http://www.ussc.gov/orgguide.htm.

3. Gerald D. Bloch, *Shaping Your Whistleblower System,* THE CORPORATE BOARD (May/June 2003), at 6, http://www.chugachelectric.com/pdfs/agenda/acagenda_100803_viii.pdf.

4. Marc I. Steinberg and Seth A. Kaufman, *Minimizing Corporate Liability Exposure When the Whistle Blows in the Post Sarbanes-Oxley Era,* 30 JOURNAL OF CORPORATION LAW, 445, 456 (Spring 2005).

5. Harry N. Mazadoorian, *Building an ADR Program: What Works, What Doesn't,* BUSINESS LAW TODAY, March/April 1999, http://www.abanet.org/buslaw/blt/8-4adrprogram.html.

6. University of Washington, Institute for Public Policy and Management, External Third Party Review of Significant Employee Concerns: The Joint Cooperative Council for Hanford Disputes 2 (1992) [1992 University of Washington study].

7. Jonathan Brock, *Symposium Whistleblower Protection: Full and Fair Resolution of Whistleblower Issues: The Hanford Joint Council for Resolving Employee Concerns,*

A Pilot ADR Approach, 51 ADMINISTRATIVE LAW REVIEW, Rev. 505, 506, 512, 513 (1999).

8. Hanford Concerns Council, Council Members, http://www.hanfordconcerns council.org/doc/members.htm.

9. Hanford Concerns Council Charter (June 1, 2008), http://www.hanfordconcerns council.org/download/council_charter.pdf.

10. Brock, *supra* note 7, at 515, 516.

11. Brock, *supra* note 7, at 510.

12. Press Release, Hanford Concerns Council, CH2M Hill Joins Hanford Concerns Council (March 22, 2010), http://www.hanfordconcernscouncil.org/download/ press_release_ch2mhill_20100322.pdf.

13. Hanford Concerns Council, Progress Report 2007, http://www.hanfordconcerns council.org/download/report_progressreport2007.pdf.

14. Annette Cary, *Parties Call Hanford Concerns Council a Success,* TriCityHerald .com, July 30, 2007, http://www.hanfordconcernscouncil.org/download/press_ tricityherald20070731.pdf.

15. Hanford Concerns Council, *supra* note 13, at 3.

16. Brock, *supra* note 7, at 509–25.

17. Brock, *supra* note 7, at 499, 500, 503, 504.

Tool A: Filing a Sarbanes-Oxley Whistleblower Complaint

1. 148 Cong. Rec. S 7350, 7355 (daily ed. July 25, 2002).

2. 148 Cong. Rec. S 7350, 7360 (daily ed. July 25, 2002).

3. 148 Cong. Rec. S 7350, 7351 (daily ed. July 25, 2002).

4. 148 Cong. Rec. S 7350, 7358 (daily ed. July 25, 2002).

5. 148 Cong. Rec. S 6524, 6528 (daily ed. July 10, 2002).

6. 148 Cong. Rec. S 6436, 6438 (daily ed. July 9, 2002).

7. 18 U.S.C. § 1514A(a) (2005).

8. 18 U.S.C. § 1514A(b).

9. 18 U.S.C. § 1514A(b).

10. 18 U.S.C. § 1514A(c).

11. *See* Filing of discrimination complaint, 29 C.F.R. § 1980.103 (2006).

12. *See* OSHA, Department of Labor, OSHA: Whistleblower Investigations Manual (2-3)-(2-4) (Aug. 22, 2003) ("OSHA Manual"). The manual describes the functions of OSHA personnel and the procedure for processing complaints under the various whistleblower statutes.

13. *See* Filing of discrimination complaint, 29 C.F.R. § 1980.103 (2006).

14. *Id.*

15. *Id.*

16. *See* OSHA Manual, *supra* note 12, at 2-1.

17. *Id.*, at (3-5)–(3-6).

18. *Id.*, at 2-1.

19. *Id.*

20. *See* Investigation, 29 C.F.R. § 1980.104 (2006).

21. 29 C.F.R. § 1980.104.

22. *See* Decision and orders of the administrative law judge, 29 C.F.R. § 1980.109 (2006).

23. OSHA Manual, *supra* note 12, at 2-2.

24. *Id.*

25. *Id.*, at 2-3.

26. *Id.*, at 2-2.

27. *See* Withdrawal of complaints, objections, and findings; settlement, 29 C.F.R. § 1980.111 (2006).

28. OSHA Manual, *supra* note 12, at 2-2.

29. *Id.*, at 1-8.

30. 29 C.F.R. § 1980.104 (2006).

31. OSHA Manual, *supra* note 12, at 2-3.

32. *Id.*, at 14-2.

33. 29 C.F.R. § 1980.104 (2006).

34. OSHA Manual, *supra* note 12, at 1-8.

35. *Id.*

36. *Id.*, at 2-3.

37. *Id.*, at 2-5.

38. *Id.*, at 14-4.

39. *Id.*, at (3-4)–(3-5).

40. *Id.*, at 3-2.

41. *Id.*, at 3-5.

42. *Id.*, at 3-7.

43. *Id.*, at 3-9.

44. 29 C.F.R. § 1980.104.

45. OSHA Manual, *supra* note 12, at 3-9.

46. 29 C.F.R. § 1980.104.

47. OSHA Manual, *supra* note 12, at (3-9)–(3-10).

48. *Id.*, at (5-3)–(5-4).

49. *Id.*, at (4-1)–(4-2).

50. *Id.*, at (4-2)–(4-3).

51. *See* Issuance of findings and preliminary orders, 29 C.F.R. § 1980.105 (2006).

52. OSHA Manual, *supra* note 12, at 14-3.

53. 29 C.F.R. § 1980.105.

54. 29 C.F.R. § 1980.111.

55. *Id.*

56. OSHA Manual, *supra* note 12, at 14-4.

57. *See* Objections to the findings and the preliminary order and request for hearing, 29 C.F.R. § 1980.106 (2006).

58. *Id.*

59. OSHA Manual, *supra* note 12, at 3-7.

60. *Id.*, at 6-1.

61. 29 C.F.R. § 1980.111 (2006).

62. OSHA Manual, *supra* note 12, at (6-3)–(6-4).

63. *Id.*, at 6-5.

64. *Id.*, at 6-4.

65. *Id.*, at 6-2.

66. 29 C.F.R. § 1983.1111(a).

67. OSHA Manual, *supra* note 12, at 6-5.

68. *See* Representation, 29 C.F.R. § 18.34 (2006).

69. *See* Legal Assistance, 29 C.F.R. § 18.35 (2006).

70. *See* Representation, 29 C.F.R. § 18.34 (2006).

71. *See* Waiver of right to appear and failure to participate or to appear, 29 C.F.R. § 18.39 (2006).

72. OSHA MANUAL, *supra* note 12, at 14-4.

73. *See* Expedited proceedings, 29 C.F.R. § 18.42 (2006).

74. *See* Authority of administrative law judge, 29 C.F.R. § 18.29 (2006).

75. 29 C.F.R. § 18.39.

76. 29 C.F.R. § 18.29.

77. OSHA MANUAL, *supra* note 12, at 14-4.

78. *See* Parties, how designated, 29 C.F.R. § 18.10 (2006).

79. *See* Amicus curiae, 29 C.F.R. § 18.12 (2006).

80. *See* Time computations, 29 C.F.R. § 18.4 (2006).

81. *See* Motions and requests, 29 C.F.R. § 18.6 (2006).

82. *See* Time computations, 29 C.F.R. § 18.4 (2006).

83. *See* Prehearing statements, 29 C.F.R. § 18.7 (2006).

84. *See* Prehearing conferences, 29 C.F.R. § 18.8 (2006).

85. *See* Closing the record, 29 C.F.R. § 18.54 (2006).

86. *See* Decision of the administrative law judge, 29 C.F.R. § 18.57 (2006).

87. 29 C.F.R. § 1980.109.

88. *Id.*

89. 18 U.S.C. § 1514A(c).

90. *See* Decisions and orders of the Administrative Review Board, 29 C.F.R. § 1980.110 (2006).

91. *Id.*

92. *See* Judicial enforcement, 29 C.F.R. § 1980.113 (2006).

93. *See* Judicial review, 29 C.F.R. § 1980.112 (2006).

94. *See* Motion for summary decision, 29 C.F.R. § 18.40 (2006).

95. *See* Consent order or settlement; settlement judge procedure, 29 C.F.R. § 18.9 (2006).

96. *See* US Department of Labor Office of Administrative Law Judges, *Alternative Dispute Resolution—Settlement Judges, at* http://www.oalj.dol.gov/SETTLE MENT_JUDGE.HTM.

97. 29 C.F.R. § 18.9 (2006).

98. *Id.*

99. 29 C.F.R. § 1980.111.

100. 29 C.F.R. § 1980.110 (2006).

101. 29 C.F.R. § 1980.111.

102. *Id.*

103. 29 C.F.R. § 1980.112 (2006).

104. 18 U.S.C. § 1514A(b).

105. *See* District Court jurisdiction of discrimination complaints, 29 C.F.R. § 1980.114 (2006).

106. OSHA Manual, *supra* note 12, at (1-7)–(1-8).

107. *Id.,* at 1-7.

108. *Id.,* at 1-8.

109. *Id.*

Glossary

Some of the definitions in this glossary have been adapted from OSHA publications and Black's Law Dictionary.

adjudicatory proceeding Due process litigation, generally before a court of administrative board, leading to the formulation of a final order.

administrative law judge (ALJ) An official who presides at an administrative trial–type hearing to resolve a legal complaint. The ALJ is usually the initial trier of fact and the decision-maker. ALJs can administer oaths, take testimony, rule on questions of evidence, and make factual and legal determinations. ALJ-controlled proceedings are comparable to a bench trial, and, depending on the agency's jurisdiction, may have complex multiparty adjudication.

administrative review board (ARB) The Department of Labor's appellate forum, which is delegated to issue final agency decisions on behalf of the secretary of labor.

advocacy partner Public interest groups, employee organizations, and other whistleblower allies who provide advice and support as well as resources and connections. They are an essential link in the chain of accountability that can turn whistleblowing information into power.

alternative dispute resolution (ADR) A counterweight to more-traditional adversarial methods that provides an effective win-win resource for resolving whistleblower complaints. ADR includes mediation and binding arbitration.

American Civil Liberties Union (ACLU) The nation's oldest nonpartisan, transideological advocate for civil liberties, whether the context is litigation, legislation, or public dialogue.

amicus curiae A party who is not involved in a particular litigation but who is allowed by the court to advise it on a matter of law directly affecting the litigation.

area director (AD) The OSHA representative who receives whistleblower complaints and transmits them to the supervisor.

attorney-client privilege The fundamental legal doctrine that protects the confidentiality of communications between an attorney and a client or prospective client.

attorney general (AG) The cabinet member who heads the Department of Justice as the nation's chief prosecutor and counsel for the United States.

at-will employees All employees who do not work under contract for a definite term without employment rights under common law other than the public policy or analogous exceptions, depending on the state.

bench trial A trial in court presided over by a judge but without a jury's participation.

binding arbitration A hybrid form of alternative dispute resolution that combines traits of both mediation and traditional litigation. Parties refer their dispute to one or more arbitrators and agree to be bound by their decision. The arbitrators may conduct a formal hearing with witnesses, testimony, evidence, and legal arguments but have the discretion to simplify the process. Arbitrators may base their decision-making on actual statutory and case law or on personal judgments. Arbitration is legitimate only when two factors are present: mutual strike selection to ensure a consensus on who will be the arbitrator; and sharing in the cost of compensating the arbitrator so that there is no conflict of interest. Arbitration can be a low-cost, streamlined alternative to conventional litigation.

Clean Air Act of 1977 (CAA) The foundation environmental statute with pioneering whistleblower protection rights that reflect the earliest, crudest form of free-speech shield.

clear and convincing evidence Evidence that a thing to be proved is highly probable or reasonably certain. Clear and convincing evidence requires a greater burden than preponderance of the evidence.

common law The system of laws originating and developed in England and based on court decisions, on the doctrines implicit in those decisions, and on customs and usages rather than on codified written laws.

complainant A person who is seeking relief as a result of an act or omission that is a violation of a statute, executive order, or regulation.

complaint Any document that initiates a legal proceeding.

Comprehensive Environmental Response, Compensation, and Liability Act (CERCLA) Another core environmental statute with the earliest, crudest whistleblower protection rights.

de novo Starting fresh; anew.

Department of Energy (DOE) The cabinet department that oversees nuclear weapons activity and the development of new energy sources.

Department of Justice (DOJ) The cabinet department that legally represents the United States and is responsible for the enforcement of criminal law.

Department of Labor (DOL) The cabinet department charged with implementation and oversight of private-sector employment rights, including nearly all the nation's corporate whistleblower laws.

discovery Data or documents that a party to a legal action is compelled to disclose to another party either before or during a proceeding.

due process An established course for judicial proceedings or other governmental activities designed to safeguard the legal rights of the individual.

Electronic Data Gathering, Analysis, and Retrieval system (EDGAR) A computer software system for retrieval of documents at the Securities and Exchange Commission.

Energy Reorganization Act (ERA) The first, crude corporate whistleblower statute; subsequently the first law amended to modernize legal burdens of proof and amended again as the first law after the Sarbanes-Oxley Act to provide jury trials for whistleblowers.

Environmental Protection Agency (EPA) The nation's civil law enforcement for environmental laws. Most corporate whistleblower laws protect witnesses seeking to help EPA environmental enforcement.

fait accompli An accomplished, presumably irreversible deed or fact.

Federal Bureau of Investigation (FBI) The nation's chief law enforcement investigative agency, which is an autonomous subdivision of the Department of Justice.

Federal False Claims Act The nation's most effective law against corporate fraud in government contracts, first enacted during the Civil War at President Abraham Lincoln's urging.

Federal Trade Commission (FTC) The nation's chief regulatory authority for commerce.

Federal Water Pollution Control Act (WPCA) Another early environmental protection law with the crude model for whistleblower protection.

Food and Drug Administration (FDA) The nation's top regulatory agency for public health and safety issues connected with food and drugs.

Freedom of Information Act (FOIA) The nation's primary transparency law, which provides a public right to know for government records.

front pay An award for future earnings; monetary relief for any future loss of earnings resulting from past discrimination. Generally front pay is awarded when reinstatement is not possible.

good faith Compliance with standards of decency and honesty.

Government Accountability Office (GAO) The investigative arm of Congress.

hearing The part of a proceeding that involves the submission of evidence by oral presentation.

inspector general (IG) The law enforcement investigative unit that acts as a watchdog against fraud, waste, and abuse within a corresponding government agency.

intergovernmental organization An organization whose members are governments, such as the United Nations.

investigator For purposes of this handbook, the OSHA representative who screens incoming complaints to determine if they warrant field investigation. An investigator interviews parties and witnesses, reviews pertinent records, and obtains written statements and supporting documentary evidence where appropriate. After applying legal elements and evaluating the evidence, the investigator writes an investigation report discussing the facts, analyzing the evidence, and providing recommendations for appropriate action. In addition, the investigator may negotiate with the parties to facilitate a settlement agreement; monitor the implementation of agreements or court orders; and, where necessary, recommend further legal proceedings to obtain compliance. When assigned by the regional administrator or supervisor, the investigator will interact with other agencies and OSHA area offices. The investigator assists in the litigation process and may testify in trial proceedings.

mediation A type of alternative dispute resolution in which an impartial third-party facilitator assists the disputing parties in reaching a consensual agreement. Being voluntary, it tends to have greater buy-in and compliance than something imposed from the outside. Despite strong results among parties who are open to dialogue, mediation is less effective where there is a lack of good faith or an imbalance of power.

National Employment Lawyers Association (NELA) The professional society for trial lawyers who specialize in advocacy of employee rights.

national solicitor of labor (NSOL) OSHA representative who provides assistance to the regional solicitors, gives advice to the Office of Investigative Assistance, and litigates on OSHA's behalf before the Administrative Review Board and the courts of appeals. The Division of Fair Labor Standards within NSOL office provides legal services for Sarbanes-Oxley cases.

nongovernmental organization (NGO) A citizen organization that acts independently of government authority.

Nuclear Regulatory Commission (NRC) The nation's chief regulatory agency for commercial nuclear power.

Occupational Safety and Health Administration (OSHA) The Department of Labor agency responsible for worker health and safety.

Office of Investigative Assistance (OIA) The OSHA body responsible for developing policies and procedures for the Whistleblower Protection Program. The office also provides technical assistance and legal interpretations and distributes significant legal developments to the field investigative staff. OIA assists in developing legislation on whistleblower matters and is often involved in the investigation of complex cases or provides assistance as requested. In addition to conducting regional audits of case files to ensure national consistency, the OIA maintains a statistical database on whistleblower investigations.

Office of the Solicitor (SOL) Governmental body that meets the legal service demands of the entire Department of Labor and provides legal advice regarding how to achieve those goals. It represents the secretary of labor and the client agencies in all necessary litigation—including both enforcement actions and defensive litigation—and in alternative dispute resolution activities, by assisting in the development of regulations, standards, and legislative proposals and by providing legal opinions and advice concerning all DOL activities.

order The whole or any part of a final procedural or substantive disposition of a matter by a court or administrative law judge.

petition A written request to a court.

pleading A formal document in which a party to a legal proceeding sets forth or responds to allegations, claims, denials, or defenses.

prejudice Damage or detriment to one's legal rights or claims.

prima facie case A party's production of enough evidence to allow the fact-trier to infer the fact at issue and rule in the party's favor. A prima facie whistleblower case is had when the employee can show that: the employee engaged in protected activity or conduct; the employer knew or suspected that the employee engaged in the protected activity; the employee suffered an unfavorable personnel action; and the circumstances are sufficient to conclude that the protected activity was a contributing factor to the unfavorable action.

Project on Government Oversight (POGO) An organization that provides a wide range of support for whistleblowers independently of litigation; it specializes in oversight of government contracts.

pro se A party to a lawsuit who is proceeding without an attorney.

Public Employees for Environmental Responsibility (PEER) A whistleblower support organization for employees of federal, state, and local government environmental agencies.

Public Information Disclosure Act (PIDA) Great Britain's whistleblower protection law.

qui tam A lawsuit by a private citizen on behalf of the "king" or government, first created as part of the Magna Carta, and the structure for whistleblower lawsuits under the False Claims Act.

regional administrator (RA) The OSHA representative with overall responsibility for all whistleblower investigation and outreach activities. The RA may issue determinations and approve settlement of complaints filed under various whistleblower statutes. SOX complaints, however, have an added procedure before settlement.

regional attorney OSHA representative who recommends action on whistleblower cases as assigned by the regional solicitor of labor. Regional attorneys represent the secretary of labor in federal district court proceedings under the various whistleblower statues and the assistant secretary for OSHA in proceedings before the Office of Administrative Law Judges.

regional solicitor of labor (RSOL) OSHA representative who reviews for legal merit all cases submitted by the regional attorney. The RSOL will make decisions regarding the merits and litigates those cases deemed meritorious as appropriate. Generally, the RSOL will not participate in a Sarbanes-Oxley case, but he may participate as amicus curiae before the administrative law judge or Administrative Review Board when it is believed that the public has an interest in the complaint.

regulatory capture Regulatory agency practice of hiring industry loyalists, a policy shift from agency oversight to cooperation with the regulated industry, or even bribery.

respondent A party to an adjudicatory proceeding against whom findings may be made or who may be required to provide relief or take remedial action.

retaliatory action The discharge, suspension, or demotion of an employee, or other adverse employment action taken against an employee in the terms and conditions of employment initiated as punishment for protected activity.

Safe Drinking Water Act (SDWA) Another pioneer environmental law with crude whistleblower protection for witnesses helping in its enforcement.

Sarbanes-Oxley Act of 2002 (SOX) The landmark financial industry reform law that included whistleblower protection with the paradigm shift to jury trials.

Securities and Exchange Commission (SEC) The federal agency responsible for the regulation of investments, such as publicly traded stock, and the protection of shareholder rights.

settlement judge An active or retired administrative law judge who convenes and presides over settlement conferences and negotiations. The judge may confer with the parties individually or jointly. The settlement judge does not make a formal judgment or decision on the matter. The judge facilitates resolution and may provide an assessment of the relative merits of the parties' positions.

stipulation A voluntary agreement between opposing parties concerning some relevant point.

strategic lawsuit against public participation (SLAPP) A lawsuit that is intended to censor, intimidate, and silence critics by burdening them with the cost of a legal defense until they abandon their criticism or opposition.

stay A suspension or postponement of a legal action.

substantial evidence The minimum degree of evidence a reasonable mind would accept as adequate to support a conclusion, generally considered more than a scintilla but less than a preponderance.

supervisor The OSHA representative who serves under the direction of the regional administrator and is responsible for supervising field whistleblower investigations. The supervisor receives whistleblower complaints and assigns investigative cases to individual investigators. In cases that are unusual or complex, the supervisor may conduct investigations or settlement negotiations himself. The supervisor reviews investigation reports for comprehensiveness and technical accuracy. At the direction of the RA, the supervisor is also responsible for coordinating and acting as a liaison with the Office of the Solicitor and other government agencies regarding matters within their geographical area.

Taxpayers Against Fraud (TAF) The NGO support group for lawyers and employees who participate in False Claims lawsuits.

Toxic Substances Control Act (TSCA) Another foundation environmental law that includes crude, pioneering whistleblower rights.

Wage and Hour Division (WHD) The Department of Labor division responsible for enforcing employees' salary rights; it conducted initial investigations of whistleblower lawsuits prior to OSHA's assuming that responsibility.

whistleblower A person of conscience who uses free-speech rights to challenge abuses of power that betray the public trust and who acts for the good of the public at great personal risk.

Whistleblower Protection Act (WPA) The free-speech law that protects federal government employees.

Bibliography

Alford, C. Fred. 2001. *Whistleblowers: Broken Lives and Organizational Power.* Ithaca, NY: Cornell University Press.

Badaracco, Joseph. 1997. *Defining Moments: When Managers Must Choose between Right and Right.* Boston: Harvard Business School Press.

Bernabei, Lynne, and Alan R. Kabat. 2003. *Whistleblower Litigation: Limitations on the Employment-at-Will Doctrine.* Georgetown University Law Center Employment Law and Litigation Institute. http://www.bernabeipllc.com/pdfs/2003%20whistleblower%20update.pdf.

Bloch, Gerald D. 2003. "Shaping Your Whistleblower System." *The Corporate Board* (May/June). http://www.chugachelectric.com/pdfs/agenda/acagenda_100803_viii.pdf.

Bok, Sissela. 1978. *Lying: Moral Choice in Public and Private Life.* New York: Pantheon Books.

Delikat, Michael. 2004. *Whistleblowing in the Sarbanes-Oxley Era.* New York: Practicing Law Institute.

Devine, Tom. 1997. *The Whistleblower's Survival Guide: Courage without Martyrdom.* Washington, DC: Fund for Constitutional Government.

Glazer, Myron, and Penina Glazer. 1989. *The Whistleblowers: Exposing Corruption in Government and Industry.* New York: Basic Books.

Government Accountability Project, Project on Government Oversight, and Public Employees for Environmental Responsibility. 2001. *The Art of Anonymous Activism: Serving the Public while Surviving Public Service.* Washington, DC.

Guyer, Thad M., and Stephani L. Ayers. 2006. "Litigating Sarbanes-Oxley Cases in Federal District Courts: The Dimensions, Issues and Pitfalls of Federal Question Jurisdiction Over Corporate Accountability Whistleblower Cases." New York: Practicing Law Institute Litigation and Administrative Practice Course Handbook Series 735: 365–85.

Kohn, Stephen M., Michael D. Kohn, and David K. Colapinto. 2004. *Whistleblower Law: A Guide to Legal Protections for Corporate Employees.* Santa Barbara, CA: Praeger.

Miceli, Marcia P., and Janet P. Near. 1992. *Blowing the Whistle: The Organizational and Legal Implications for Companies and Employees.* New York: Lexington Books.

Putnam, Robert D. 2000. *Bowling Alone: The Collapse and Revival of American Community.* New York: Simon & Schuster.

Safon, David M., et al. "2006 Annual Update on the Whistleblower Provisions of the Sarbanes-Oxley Act of 2002." American Bar Association Section of Labor and Employment Law Subcommittee on the Sarbanes-Oxley Act of 2002 (February). http://www.employmentlawgroup.net/Articles/JZuckerman/SarbanesOxley-2006-2008.html.

Vaughn, Robert G. 2005. "America's First Comprehensive Statute Protecting Corporate Whistleblowers." *Administrative Law Review* 57: 1–105 (Winter).

Watchman, Gregory, R. 2005. *Sarbanes-Oxley Whistleblowers: A New Corporate Early Warning System.* Washington, DC: Government Accountability Project.

Westin, Alan F. 1981. *Whistleblowing: Loyalty and Dissent in the Corporation.* New York: McGraw-Hill.

Zuckerman, Jason M., and Billie P. Garde. 2004. "Litigating Whistleblower Claims before the DOL from the Plaintiff's Perspective." http://zuckermanlaw.com/docs/dec2004.pdf.

Index

About the Government Accountability Project

The mission of the Government Accountability Project (GAP) is to protect the public interest by advancing the rights of employees to speak out about serious problems they learn about at work. To achieve this mission, GAP assists persons of conscience in making ethical disclosures to institutional policymakers, the public, and the media. Over the decades, GAP's staff has developed in-house expertise in several broad program areas, including strengthening the legal rights of whistleblowers, increasing food and drug safety, ensuring safe and cost-effective cleanup at nuclear weapons facilities, enforcing environmental and worker protections, pursuing national security, promoting corporate accountability, and increasing accountability mechanisms in international institutions.

Since GAP's founding in 1977, we have helped more than 5,000 whistleblowers and have expanded to a 20-member staff in our Washington, DC, office. We also conduct an accredited legal clinic for law students and operate a highly popular internship program. GAP's strategy involves four key day-to-day activities:

- First, we represent government and corporate whistleblowers against retaliation, generally to advocate a significant point of law or to help monitor how laws are working in practice. For those whistleblowers we do not represent, we offer legal referrals and self-help materials, such as those found on our website and in books like this one.

- Second, we represent whistleblowers to make a difference. We do this by conducting broader investigations of their charges and connecting them with the societal institutions that can turn their information into power. We collaborate with the news media, grassroots citizens' organizations, private attorneys, and the broader public interest community to reveal, publicize, and galvanize a public response to misconduct that would otherwise be sustained by secrecy. We also assist whistleblowers in taking their evidence of wrongdoing to select government agencies, congressional committees, and others on Capitol Hill to investigate, expose, and rectify the problem. GAP cases are regularly featured in major news outlets.

■ Third, we work steadily to strengthen the laws protecting freedom of dissent and to monitor how they work in practice. We help draft both model and actual legislation for federal, state, and local governments as well as for international NGOs and foreign governments. For example, we helped draft or spearheaded the movement to adopt the whistleblower provisions of the 2006 United Nations Anti-Retaliation policy, the 2002 Sarbanes-Oxley Act, the Energy Policy Act of 2005, all federal corporate whistleblower laws passed since 2006 except the False Claims Act amendments, the 2000 model law adopted by the Organization of American States, and the Whistleblower Protection Act of 1989 for federal employees. Our campaigns have earned corporate whistleblower rights for airlines safety workers, defense contractors, ground transportation crews, and nuclear and pipeline whistleblowers. Legislators and other policymakers often formally request our assistance. We also scrutinize the implementation of whistleblower laws at the relevant agencies, seeking to identify good and bad practices as well as new legislative opportunities.

■ Fourth, we act as experts on occupational free-speech and scientific dissent issues. We regularly share our views in academic and nonacademic publications, tutor journalists, advise agencies and companies on internal policies, and engage in public speaking to promote whistleblowing as a fundamental and quintessential freedom of speech.

Hundreds of whistleblowers contact GAP each year. Unfortunately, due to budget constraints, we are able to take less than 5 percent of relevant cases that come to us, no matter how worthy they may be. Our goal is that regardless of whether we can provide representation, you will be better off as a whistleblower for having contacted us. If nothing else, we will diagnose your options and provide attorney referrals.

To learn more about GAP, please visit our website. To request GAP assistance in blowing the whistle or challenging whistleblower retaliation, please fill out our Intake Application via the "Blow the Whistle!" link on our home page.

Government Accountability Project
1612 K St. NW, Suite 1100
Washington, DC 20006
http://www.whistleblower.org
info@whistleblower.org
Tel: (202) 457-0034
Fax: (202) 457-0059

Berrett–Koehler
Publishers

Berrett-Koehler is an independent publisher dedicated to an ambitious mission: *Creating a World That Works for All.*

We believe that to truly create a better world, action is needed at all levels—individual, organizational, and societal. At the individual level, our publications help people align their lives with their values and with their aspirations for a better world. At the organizational level, our publications promote progressive leadership and management practices, socially responsible approaches to business, and humane and effective organizations. At the societal level, our publications advance social and economic justice, shared prosperity, sustainability, and new solutions to national and global issues.

A major theme of our publications is "Opening Up New Space." Berrett-Koehler titles challenge conventional thinking, introduce new ideas, and foster positive change. Their common quest is changing the underlying beliefs, mindsets, institutions, and structures that keep generating the same cycles of problems, no matter who our leaders are or what improvement programs we adopt.

We strive to practice what we preach—to operate our publishing company in line with the ideas in our books. At the core of our approach is stewardship, which we define as a deep sense of responsibility to administer the company for the benefit of all of our "stakeholder" groups: authors, customers, employees, investors, service providers, and the communities and environment around us.

We are grateful to the thousands of readers, authors, and other friends of the company who consider themselves to be part of the "BK Community." We hope that you, too, will join us in our mission.

A BK Currents Book

This book is part of our BK Currents series. BK Currents books advance social and economic justice by exploring the critical intersections between business and society. Offering a unique combination of thoughtful analysis and progressive alternatives, BK Currents books promote positive change at the national and global levels. To find out more, visit **www.bkconnection.com**.

Berrett–Koehler
Publishers

A community dedicated to creating
a world that works for all

Visit Our Website: www.bkconnection.com

Read book excerpts, see author videos and Internet movies, read
our authors' blogs, join discussion groups, download book apps, find
out about the BK Affiliate Network, browse subject-area libraries of
books, get special discounts, and more!

Subscribe to Our Free E-Newsletter, the *BK Communiqué*

Be the first to hear about new publications, special discount offers,
exclusive articles, news about bestsellers, and more! Get on the list
for our free e-newsletter by going to **www.bkconnection.com**.

Get Quantity Discounts

Berrett-Koehler books are available at quantity discounts for orders
of ten or more copies. Please call us toll-free at (800) 929-2929 or
email us at **bkp.orders@aidcvt.com**.

Join the BK Community

BKcommunity.com is a virtual meeting place where people from
around the world can engage with kindred spirits to create a world
that works for all. **BKcommunity.com** members may create their own
profiles, blog, start and participate in forums and discussion groups,
post photos and videos, answer surveys, announce and register for
upcoming events, and chat with others online in real time. Please join
the conversation!

Mixed Sources
Product group from well-managed
forests and recycled wood or fiber
www.fsc.org Cert no. SW-COC-003925
© 1996 Forest Stewardship Council

T